Table of

PART 1
TEMPTATIONS

PART 2
DISILLUSIONS

PART 3
BREAKTHROUGHS

If She Only Had a Brain

C ancer is not pretty. I can't make cancer pretty. Cancer doesn't care if you're pretty or not or how much people love you. Cancer just takes and takes and takes, and leaves nothing pretty behind.

My destiny was shaped by my family and friends, and even strangers who repeatedly uttered one simple phase that I heard throughout my entire childhood: Isn't she pretty!

My face, my womanly and curvaceous body, my remarkable red hair: these were the assets I was given. People seemed to just love looking at me. So why wouldn't I think that modeling would be a viable and lucrative profession? Photographers couldn't get enough of taking my picture. I knew how to dress, how to move, how to use makeup correctly to enhance my natural assets to maximum wattage. Inherently shy, I taught myself to stand in the spotlight.

So why wouldn't I accept the challenge to become one of the most recognized women in the United States, appearing in the top-selling monthly magazine on America's newsstands? In 1976, *Penthouse* publisher Bob Guccione selected me as centerfold, then Pet of the Year, gracing more publications that any other *Penthouse* model. It brought me fame and took me to Hollywood, giving me a niche in movies and television.

People's reactions to my life's choices were varied. Some turned up their noses. Others gave me applause, a high five, and a "Way to go, girl." And then the final group felt obligated to express their disdain for my career at every opportunity. This group I imagined were filled with glee when news of my cancer became public. "I guess she got what she deserved," they could finally say.

One after another, my natural assets began to betray me. My thick and famous red hair was gone, lost to chemo. My breasts, which Bob Guccione once described as the most beautiful he'd ever seen, were not only no longer attractive, but battered and disfigured. Photography was no longer a tool to highlight my allure, but a way to examine clearly every organ and tissue on my body. My naked self was more exposed that it was ever in the pages of *Penthouse*. My body was betraying me.

As I wrote in my journal, "I am totally exposed. My left breast has been squeezed and imaged and aspirated so many times it no longer holds any sense of pleasure it once had. I've been turned inside out, like a piece of laundry tossed in a dryer too long. My intestines, my bowels, my guts are exposed and open. Every fiber of my breast, every tissue of my brain is existing only to be examined and prodded. What once appeared beautiful to so many, is now being eaten away by horrid spots of this cancer. I feel so naked, so very naked."

The primary difference between my cancer story and others is that I have been in continual treatment for thirteen years since diagnosis. I still receive gene therapy treatment in the hospital every three weeks, and for as long as I continue to fight this battle, I will always be in treatment if I so choose. Remaining "stable" requires it.

Another way that my story differs is that I refuse to be considered a cancer "victim." I took responsibility for attacking the monster that seeks to destroy me.

When I was diagnosed in July 1998, the doctor's words slashed at me like the Grim Reaper's blade: *Breast cancer. Stage 4, no cure. Metastasized to all major organs. No need for a mastectomy, since the cancer has already left the primary site.* In other words, it was too late. My entire life was predicated on beauty, and no one thought I would be strong enough to survive the devastation.

Too much of a realist to think I would actually beat Stage 4 cancer, I was determined to live as well as possible in the time remaining. When I learned of a treatment therapy called Herceptin, which at that time had recently been FDA approved and was still unproven in the real world, I chose Herceptin over my doctors' "last resort" decision, an allogeneic bone marrow transplant, and Herceptin worked. After thirteen years, five breast surgeries, and removal of seven brain tumors, I'm still living as well as possible — eleven and a half years longer than predicted.

Throughout the battle, I repeatedly have overcome "insurmountable" odds and defied time and again even the most optimistic predictions of the most experienced cancer physicians in the world. When asked how, these physicians all reply with the same basic answers: "She has an indomitable spirit." "She never gives in." "She keeps her sense of humor." Most of all: "She educated herself about her disease and participated in her own treatment."

In other words, the woman no one suspected of having a brain, because they couldn't see past "pretty," past the red hair and sexy curves, used her most underrated, ignored, and seemingly insignificant organ to — if not beat the monster, at least keep it growling inside its cage.

Ultimately, my survival has come from the same source that brought me success in my modeling career: tenacity, determination, and a desire to experience all that life has to offer. These were traits no picture could ever convey, and no matter how much of my hair, my breasts, my brain, or other body parts were lost to my disease, these inner traits I refused to let cancer rip away. I once admired a young patient at MD Anderson wearing a T-shirt that said, "If you're not living life on the edge, you're taking up too much space." Living with Stage 4 Cancer, constantly kicking death to the curb, is living life on the edge.

Cancer is still a part of me. I'm still in treatment, but no matter what happens next, I've already won my greatest battle. If my story can be a source of hope and inspiration, not only to cancer patients but to anyone wrestling with life-altering challenges, then I've struck the beast another debilitating blow. There are many people fighting to see cancer eliminated. Every year I survive is a step closer to that reality.

Sitting at the hospital undergoing yet another treatment, I remind myself, there's no time like now to enjoy life. Or as my Southern grandmother used to say when things got tough, "It's time to use the good china."

PART 1

TEMPTATIONS

Christmastime in Georgia. Family and friend.

CHAPTER 1

The Hottest Ticket in Town

Mableton, Georgia, 1968

The man standing in front of me, smelling of coffee breath and Aramis cologne, couldn't keep his groping eyes above my neck. At the back of the dress shop, metal hangers clinked loudly as his wary wife marked down sweaters and shoved them along a chrome rod, occasionally tossing suspicious looks our way.

The man clasped his hands together, as if to keep them from being ineluctably drawn toward the objects of his interest.

"Victoria," he mumbled, tugging his eyes up to meet mine, "I see an exciting role for you here."

Shortly after turning sixteen, I'd set about the task of landing my first summer job with the same resolve and intuition that would influence decisions continually throughout my life. One of my friends was applying at the local Dairy Queen in our rural town near Atlanta, but squishing soft sugary goop into ice cream cones and serving it to boys from school cruising around in their souped-up Mustangs was not my idea of a promising career start. I wanted an exhilarating and unique job my friends would never even imagine. I wanted to be different.

My first choice was the recently opened Six Flags Over Georgia, with its roller coasters and excitement, which attracted fascinating people from all over the state. After Six Flags turned me down, this dress shop in Mableton's new Hawthorne Plaza was my second choice.

"I think this would be a lovely place to work," I said. "What would I do exactly?"

"How would you feel about being our in-store model?" the man asked.

Those words were like magic. Only the most exclusive New York designer stores invited their customers to sit and sip tea or coffee while a model strolled by in a private showing. This shop owner was obviously ahead of his time for Georgia. I delighted in the possibility of helping him bring sophistication and refinement to our small-town environment.

But glamorous though it sounded, the job had drawbacks.

"What we need to do first," my new boss informed me on the day I reported to work, "is to draw more shoppers into the store."

"That's a great idea," I said truthfully. "How will we do that?"

He pointed a neatly manicured finger toward the wide store window that faced the street and walkway.

"You will be our live window mannequin! What do you think?" He obviously thought it a brilliant idea.

"You want me to put on outfits and stand in the window?"

"Exactly!"

My secret self-consciousness churned inside as I considered what he proposed. Truthfully, it made sense. If there were no shoppers *inside* the store as I modeled the latest fashions — perhaps a midriff blouse with bellbottom hip-huggers in an exotic flower design, a matching scarf tied in my long red hair, and my white Beth Levine Go-Go boots — the job would not only be pointless but boring. On the other hand, if I modeled the same outfit in the store window, everyone walking by outside would see it.

"Okay," I said.

Going along was a policy I'd adopted because I didn't like making waves. Not that I didn't make my own decisions or have my own opinions — often quite the opposite from everyone else's — but when one choice seemed as good as another, why not make people happy? On the occasions I did choose to assert my own judgment against popular opinion, the upheaval usually left everyone gasping, *"Wow, she really did that."*

Sizzling Summer Style

"Wait till you see the summer rage," my boss said, waggling his fingers for me to follow him to the back room.

His watchful wife came in right behind us, thank God.

A fat cardboard box sat on a table against the wall. As I imagined what might be inside the box, my brain quickly filled with fashion photos from all the magazines tucked away in my bedroom. Ever since Jacqueline Kennedy became First Lady, in her Oleg Cassini suits and pill box hats, her notched-lapel jackets had become mature ladies' daywear of choice for special occasions, with A-line dresses or even white jeans for more casual wear. Girls my age were into miniskirts in bold plaids worn with wide shiny belts.

My new boss reached into the box and, with a flourish, brought out a thing that was blue with white polka dots. I hated polka dots.

It wasn't quite as big as a man's handkerchief, and only after he held up the matching piece did I realize it was a bikini. The tiny top tied provocatively in front; the miniscule bottom tied at each side.

"That's what you want me to model in the store window?" I said.

"It's summer. This is what people want."

"Mmmm," his wife murmured, reaching into the box and lifting out a turquoise maillot. "Some of our customers might prefer less fad and more fabric."

Backless, with high-cut legs and plunging neckline, it would still cover more skin than the polka-dot number.

"Okay," I said again. These *were* the hottest summer fashions, and they *would* make people happy.

Creative Career Moves

My boss was right about one thing. A live sixteen-year-old mannequin with generous grownup curves and a shocking mane of red hair modeling swimwear in a store window certainly brought shoppers to a halt. Small crowds would gather on the sidewalk. Cars moving along the street slowed to a crawl. A sense of humor was essential, so I had fun with it. I complemented every suit with a matching or boldly contrasting cover-up and practiced the fashion moves I'd learned, casually removing the cover as I strolled with nonchalant poise along my side of the glass divider.

Other times I'd stand motionless, not blinking, scarcely breathing, as much like a plastic mannequin as possible, until a passerby came close to the window. Then I'd blink or move a finger, causing the person to do a double take. I'd quickly follow up with a smile. The startled spectator would wave good-naturedly before moving on.

Despite the occasional prank, I took my modeling job seriously. I showed off every outfit for the matronly women of Mableton as if it were the latest Paris *couture*. People began crowding into the store and plunking down money for swimsuits and summer frocks they'd watched me model. My first job at barely sixteen, and Vicki Lynn Johnson was the hottest ticket in town. Secretly, I couldn't help feeling vindicated that Six Flags Over Georgia had been too short-sighted to recognize my talent.

Perhaps being doted on as an only child for the first ten years, until my sister was born, had led me to expect doors to open wherever I chose to go. When my sister, Carla, was born, I was happy Mom had a new little girl to cherish, as I was clearly growing up fast, approaching middle school, and beginning to establish my independence. My parents listened to me and encouraged me to participate in family decisions. I learned quickly that planning situations in advance and working hard would help me achieve the goals I set for myself. I became president of Drama Club and co-captain of drill team. Seldom content to be a follower, in any project that interested me, I expected to lead.

Out of the Window, into the World

Eventually, bikini weather gave way to fall fashions, which in many respects were more fun to model. There's only so much you can do with swimwear. When summer ended, I continued to work at the dress shop on weekends. Amazingly, my boss managed to get an early shipment of bathing suits, so I found myself shivering in the window wearing a bikini again during a March ice storm.

Believing the job would be different once I began modeling professionally, I taught myself to ignore any unwanted attention, from the morally offended prudes of Mableton as well as from my voyeuristic boss. This turned out to be a valuable skill for my future, because even though things were different when I started modeling professionally, they weren't *that* different.

Spray Glue and the Georgia Mountains
Atlanta, 1971

Five imposing advertising executives of various ages sat behind the mahogany table, stern-faced and smartly fashionable in their business leisure suits, brightly patterned ties and salon-styled hair, busily studying my photos and résumé while sneaking peeks at me from the corners of their eyes. These men controlled a significant portion of Atlanta advertising, and at the moment they controlled my immediate career advancement.

At nineteen, I was vigorously independent. A recent graduate of the Bauder College of Fashion and Modeling in Miami, Florida, I not only had lived totally on my own there but also had organized my roommates' social lives. While still in high school, I often was featured in local newspaper articles and was calculating enough to figure out how to avoid classes on Thursdays, my modeling days, yet still graduate. Now, after three years of amateur experience, I was on the brink of becoming established in print ads for many of Atlanta's major advertisers.

But the more serious work — and serious money — lay in television. Today I was auditioning for my first major TV commercial. Why did it take five men to select one bikini-clad model for a television commercial? On the other hand, this was my first professional TV audition, so what did I know?

Upon arriving back in Atlanta from college, I'd bolstered my nerve, knowing I had to sign with an agency. Being bold and assertive was against my nature, but I couldn't let them see that I was scared to death, so I armored myself in my most glamorous fashions, applied my makeup with meticulous attention to detail, and fluffed my hair into a feathery swirl. The first agency I visited, Peachtree Models, handled primarily fashion models, including the top ten most successful in Atlanta, and their girls got the choicest fashion shoots. At barely five-foot-five-inches tall, I received lukewarm acceptance there, at best. The second agency, Atlanta Models and Talent, provided clients of every description and of all ages — men, women, children, actors, dancers, comedians — you name it, they could cast it.

Kathy, the woman who interviewed me, cocked a dubious eyebrow. I tried not to focus on the fear gnawing at my stomach, or on the word "Talent" in their company name. I didn't have a stage talent. I was a too-short fashion model. All I had was my hair. The cold breath of rejection wafted toward me as Kathy studied my carefully structured four-page composite of glamorous fashion shots — bathing suits on the beach, elegant evening gowns — all taken by a brilliant student photographer while I was at Bauder College.

"This won't quite work, Vicki. What we need is a single

eight-by-ten head shot, with your statistics. Height, weight, dress size. And a résumé that includes a list of every talent job you've done." A substantial, hard-edged, and imposing woman, Kathy devoted her busy days to coping with clients and sizing up talent. I was only one of many hopeful, wide-eyed girls who'd walked through her door that day. "Are you a member of AFTRA? SAG?"

"I can get the photograph and résumé right away," I assured the agent, even though I'd have to be slightly inventive in describing my job history.

At home, I looked up the acronyms. AFTRA: the American Federation of Television and Radio Artists. SAG: the Screen Actors Guild. Why would I need to be a member of either, since what I wanted was to model fashions for runway or print?

Although I supplied the requisite 8x10 photograph, as promised, along with a creative description of every pageant and local TV appearance I'd participated in during and after high school, I wrote off the interview with Kathy as "not very promising" for either of us.

I drove home that day with disappointment weighing upon my shoulders as it never had before in my young career. For as long as I could remember, fashion had been my passionate focus. As a child, even before I discovered my paper-doll world, my most treasured gift was the dressing table and pretend makeup I received for my fifth birthday. As a high school junior, I'd won an award from the McCall's Magazine's Teen Fashion Board for "Outstanding Achievement in Sewing and Clothing Classwork." At Bauder College, I'd studied not only modeling but also the design and creation of women's fashions, which was the part I truly loved. But Atlanta didn't offer many opportunities for fashion designers. And modeling had come to me so easily that it seemed the natural first step toward the creative vocation I craved.

Now, that first step appeared impossible to climb.

Incredibly, Kathy phoned a few days later.

"You have an audition. Take a bikini and a glossy, and look as much like Eve as possible." She rattled off the address of an advertising agency in downtown Atlanta.

"Eve? As in —"

"Yes, as in the Biblical co-star of Adam." The agent paused a moment before adding, "I'm sending you because of your hair."

Entering the ad agency lobby, I caught my breath and took a step back. The room was crowded with models sitting or standing against the wall, all gorgeous to varying degrees, all wearing the latest platform shoes with their bikinis. Besides the receptionist, I was the only person in the room fully clothed — not for long, I suspected — and I was inches shorter than everyone.

I squared my shoulders and, through a vapor of perfume from Yardley English Lavender to Chanel Number 5, headed to the receptionist. My coordinated pantsuit, blouse, and shoes, the "business look of the moment," had armed me with confidence when I left home that morning. I knew the suit accentuated the natural poise and grace my teachers at Bauder College had deemed an asset, as well as an intuitive sense of style which I continuously refined through diligent research. Young photographers had often selected me among the other models as a subject for their portfolios. It was the red hair, of course, that attracted them, but one young photographer had remarked that I had "fresh, unspoiled charm without the boring allusion of girl-next-door perkiness." Now, feeling noticeably overdressed with all the bare flesh flashing around me, I summoned those esteem-boosting comments as I placed one foot fluidly in front of the other, chin up, eyes forward, exactly as I'd practiced for the runway, and made the long walk to the reception desk.

The room seemed to stretch forever. Many of the faces I recognized from the Peachtree book picturing all of their models, a book I'd pored over for hours. Only a few of the girls were from Atlanta Models and Talent. I spied the city's "Top Ten" clustered in an intimate clique, chatting as if they were actually friends and not fierce competitors for every juicy modeling gig in Atlanta. Was it my imagination or were they studying me, the freshest meat in the room, and calculating where to plunge the dagger?

I wished I'd known how to better prepare for this audition. Instead, I was winging it, doing the best I could with what I knew, precisely as I had since my very first modeling experience, showing off Winnie-the-Pooh fashions in a children's style show at Sears.

Finally, I arrived at the desk.

"Change into your swimsuit, please." The receptionist pointed toward a changing room. "Then join the others out here."

Five minutes later I quietly took my place in the crowd, wearing a crocheted two-piece in a rosy shade of beige, as close as possible to the "nude" look that Eve wore before taking a bite out of that shiny red apple. Listening to the other models' conversations, I felt upstaged by their vast experience and thirsty for every word as they compared stories from various shoots. When one of the Peachtree girls emerged from the dressing area after completing her audition, she whispered something to another model. The second model gasped.

"Run? In a bathing suit?" She giggled in mock indignity. "I'll have to suck it in, not breathe, run on my tiptoes to make sure my tummy doesn't jiggle."

Mystified, I glanced at the closed door, where each girl in turn had disappeared for an audition and wondered what could be happening back there. *Running? Jiggling? How did that fit with a TV commercial?*

Now that I was behind that closed door, I wondered why no one had mentioned the five stern-faced executives. I also wondered why the agency was still auditioning. They'd already seen the crème de la crème among experienced Atlanta models. What could I offer that these men hadn't already seen?

"Would you walk across the room, please?" one of them instructed.

Feeling panicky and self-conscious, I hesitated. I'd done this a million times at modeling school, and even before that in beauty pageants and local fashion shows, but this time was different. This was the determining test of a possible career in TV commercials. True, I didn't expect to be a model forever and wasn't sure I could even make a living at it. I was savvy enough to know it was a profession where even the most popular reach their pinnacle early and age out by thirty, but until I got a real job, I needed a paycheck.

Eyes forward, tummy tightened to prevent any jiggling, I applied myself to the task of strolling the length of the room while five pairs of critical eyes scrutinized my every step.

"That's nice, but what we really need you to do is more like … float." A different voice this time.

"No, Don, not float, frolic. Can you frolic, sweetheart?"

Frolic? What did that mean exactly? I picked up the pace and sort of skipped.

"Much better. You're a nymph in the Garden of Eden. Now glide back the other way and swing your hair around as you turn."

Kathy's words echoed in my head: *I'm sending you because of your hair, Victoria.* When Hilda and Carroll Johnson, my beautiful brown-haired mother and my handsome black-haired father, brought me home from the hospital, I already had a thick crop of red hair. Visitors who couldn't help touching it must have wondered. "What a darling baby, Hilda, with such pretty *red* hair!"

"Do that once more," the first agency man said, teeth gleaming like piano keys. "Swirl your hair around as you turn and look this way."

I turned and swirled and frolicked, the crocheted scraps of my swimsuit useless against the chilly air in the air-conditioned room. Finally, one of the men asked the others, "Hmmm, what do you think?"

Their collective murmurs were too low for me to distinguish words. Then their whispered conversation suddenly hushed.

"Sweetheart, will you have a problem working topless?"

Taking the Good with the Naked

At home, my mother asked how the audition went.

"All right, I suppose, but there must have been thirty models and I was the least qualified." I didn't mention the topless question. Why bring it up and alarm my mother when I wasn't likely to get the job? Anyway, I'd been so flustered I couldn't actually remember what I answered.

It must have been affirmative, because a few days later, Kathy phoned with the good news — exciting but also a little disquieting.

"It's a two-day shoot at a resort in the Georgia Mountains. You'll stay on the property overnight, so bring a bag with everything you'll need."

Two days, frolicking? "Kathy, I know we talked about it, but what exactly will I be doing?"

"Whatever they tell you to do. Walnut Mountain is an elite new resort that's being built in the area where you'll be shooting. This commercial will entice the rich and influential to invest in a distinctive home with the most extraordinary mountain view in Northern Georgia."

"Where will the commercial be shown?"

"Throughout the state, I'm sure, and perhaps the Southeast. It's an exceptional job, Victoria. Be happy."

Maybe my parents wouldn't be home when it ran. Or maybe I could break the TV for a month.

"So, as Eve, I'm supposed to frolic with Adam, through the trees around this resort. Topless."

Kathy laughed. "Really, Victoria, this is television. You won't *actually* be shown topless."

All the tension whooshed out of me like air from a balloon as I thanked the censor gods for the restrictions of television.

"But you probably will have to *work* topless," Kathy added.

Reality Bites

The Georgia mountains sneak up on you. They don't jut sharply upward like the Rockies; they roll along gently until you look around and realize you're traveling through gorgeous cliffs flanked by white pine, rhododendron, and hemlock, chock-full of secluded waterfalls, inviting pools, and shimmering streams. As you drive on, you begin to sense that your surroundings are rather mystical, as if time is holding its breath. The resort developers had taken full advantage of this magical quality to initiate a whole new level of lavish mountain living.

I spent the first day focused emotionally on playing the role of Eve, guileless, innocent, unworldly, and unaware of society's clothing taboos. My instructions were to swing my long hair in such a way that it continuously covered my breasts, no matter how wildly I frolicked.

"Stop!" the director called more than once. "We need to try something different with your left breast. I can see your nipple."

If it wasn't the left breast misbehaving, it was the right one. Or both.

Actors have to sacrifice for the roles they play — I'd learned that in Drama Club — and I was willing to do whatever needed to be done for this commercial. But this was the first movie camera I'd encountered in real life, right in my face and capturing my every jiggle. For an Atlanta upstart, this commercial was a major career opportunity, my first significant appearance on television — so I struggled valiantly to keep my pink nipples from peeking through my red locks.

"This isn't working, Victoria!" The director sounded frustrated and ready to quit. "You've got to control that hair."

I tried moving my head with less energy, but that wasn't the mood they wanted. The stylist tied my hair in two big clumps that fell in front of my shoulders, but that was too restricted, not "free" the way Eve would be free, or the way Walnut Mountain wanted to showcase the blissful freedom of their wilderness paradise.

"What if we glue it in place?" suggested the hairdresser. "It's so thick we could spray-glue just the front under layer, to her breasts, leaving the top layer to swing with her movements."

Spray glue? What would that do to my hair, not to mention my skin? My breasts? But I didn't want to lose the job.

And it worked.

Looking back now, I realize that despite my initial concerns, the production crew acted professionally during the shoot, and I was treated as a professional. Only when the camera was rolling was I ever nude. Whenever the director called, "cut," wardrobe immediately brought my robe. Nobody stood around leering, at least not obviously.

In the end, the commercial turned out to be stunning and tasteful, a make-you-stop-in-front-of-the-TV moment. People all over Georgia recall the final scene: A white dove, trained to come to my hand, flies away and returns. Drama builds as the camera closes in. I'm holding a brilliant red apple about to take a seductive bite — the camera closes in tighter — a voice-over says, "If I had it to do over again, I'd do it at Walnut Mountain."

The perceived nudity pushed the boundaries of what could be shown on television in 1971, and while it was a shocker for our rural community, for my parents, for my future husband and his parents, for all our neighbors and friends, the commercial was so elegant and visually appealing that it was impossible not to be caught up in its charm. It played throughout the Southeast, around the clock, for months. Practically everyone who lived there during those years remembers the closing line. For my part, I received only positive response.

Carving My Niche

It was never my goal to be a nude model, and God knows I spent a great deal of time and effort trying to get jobs with my clothes on. I was and am, however, determined not to settle for ordinary when I can choose exceptional. Long before Walnut Mountain, I'd learned that I enjoy pushing the envelope, whether challenging the drill team to dress their best or drawing a crowd of Mableton shoppers as I paraded half-naked in a dress store window.

I was too short for Peachtree Models, too glamorous for Atlanta Models and Talent, with no singing, dancing, or acting ability to fall back on. My mom was supportive, but she wasn't a stage mom, clearing the way for me, knocking aside any obstacles. I had to create my own niche.Most of the jobs I landed were ordinary photo shoots, and thanks to playing the challenging role of Eve, I learned to mold myself into the type of woman each situation required. Wearing a pretty dress or casual sports attire, I gracefully displayed products such as Lip Quencher by ChapStick. Appearing perky and youthful, I modeled for a regional print campaign for Six Flags Over Georgia, the same amusement park where at sixteen I'd applied for a job and was turned down. Looking cool and professional, I frequently posed for business brochures, including one for Delta Airlines.

Yet throughout my career, many of my high-profile jobs, such as a tastefully striking ad for *Charles of the Ritz* body lotion, required me to be either nude or partially nude, even when the message was not at all sexual. The modeling business is all about your "look." My look worked well with clothes, but it worked *really* well in the nude.

At barely sixteen, I'd won the Miss Perfect Figure state contest at Lake Spivey, a popular manmade beach south of Atlanta. While I didn't recognize it at the time, that crowning moment forecasted the niche I would eventually carve for myself in modeling. Whenever an assignment required unequivocal sensuality, whether a catalog of diaphanous lingerie, an ad for sexy European jeans — the denim jacket unbuttoned to expose my bare torso — or numerous calendars featuring industrial or automotive equipment and a different bikini shot for each month, I topped every photographer's list of preferred models.

In time, I accepted the reality: If I wanted to work at glamorous, high-income jobs, I had to get used to taking off my clothes.

CHAPTER 2

A Call to the Wild Side

Atlanta, 1976

When the sexual revolution finally hit prim and proper Georgia, it was already significant in most of the Western World. The "pill" changed forever the way women thought about sex. No longer willing to be the sexually responsible gender, or to save themselves for marriage, women everywhere were flexing their new wings. Premarital sex was widespread, and most couples considered living-together-before-vows to be a sensible way to avoid divorce.

Mainstream magazines and motion pictures frequently contained material once branded pornographic. Feminism knocked down corporate doors, and "Gay Pride" was quietly gaining ground in political circles as marchers boldly turned out with banners at bicentennial celebrations.

Having come of age during the heart of the revolution, I harbored mixed emotions about these new codes of sexual behavior. In my opinion, the "liberated" people were trying to impose their no-limits lifestyle on everyone, as if what was good for them was good for all of us. Instead of "free love," I believed in "free thinking." People should have the option of making their own choices in every part of their lives, without anyone dictating their behavior or passing moral judgment. Personally, I felt as comfortable with my parents' conservative values as I did with the sexual liberation being embraced by the nation's youth.

In the real estate industry, a contemporary, unconventional lifestyle took hold in the form of "swinging singles" apartment complexes, and I was hired to model for a brochure promoting one of the most glamorous complexes in Atlanta. Although the modern apartments were adjacent to a city expressway for convenience, the developer had tucked them cleverly into a wooded setting, where buildings of natural cedar nestled among well-tended trees and shrubs, promoting an impression of sensuous seclusion.

Inside the apartments, thick shag carpet, shiny Mylar wall coverings, and black bathroom fixtures continued the theme of trendy mid-1970s designer living. Balconies overlooking the pool invited neighbors to socialize after work. A fresh, woodsy smell completed the ambiance.

Two couples had been selected to depict the energy and excitement that independent young singles could enjoy at this exclusive residence. Wearing a white Lycra swimsuit, I lounged by the pool with my "friends," engulfed in the fragrant aroma of baby oil applied to my skin to create a warm glow for the camera. At the bar, wearing a jet-black chiffon cocktail dress, I sat laughing and drinking with my male model "date." On the woodland trails, I biked alongside my "friend," red curls trailing theatrically in the breeze. The hot-tub scenes, where we appeared to be nude, were suggestive of the sensual pleasures to be enjoyed by combining good friends, champagne, laughter, and steamy jasmine-scented water with the soulful sounds of Barry White playing in the background.

The photographer was exceptional, the shots came out great, and somehow the brochure landed on the desk of Bob Guccione, a man soon to become very important in my life, although I had no idea at the time. Shortly after the brochure was printed, I received a call from Kathy's soft-spoken assistant at Atlanta Models and Talent.

"Victoria, someone inquired about you today from *Penthouse* magazine."

"Really? I didn't get a call from the agency."

"Kathy felt sure you wouldn't be interested."

"What kind of inquiry?" And why wouldn't I be interested? It frustrated me for anyone, even my agent, to make decisions about my career without asking me. "What did they want?"

"An East Coast fashion photographer wanted to talk to you about a photo shoot for *Penthouse*, but Kathy told them you wouldn't want to model for that magazine. That's not the kind of thing you do."

"Really?" I said again, striving to keep the irritation out of my voice.

"I've got his number, if you want it."

Stan Malinowski was an up-and-coming fashion photographer whose unique, dramatic style often graced the pages of *Playboy* and *Penthouse* magazines, among others, and would soon be featured frequently in *Vogue* and *Harper's Bazaar*, nationally and internationally. Intrigued that such an accomplished photographer had sought me out, and curious about how he'd come across my name, I took down his number. If I didn't call him, what might I be passing up? And wasn't it merely good business to find out specifically what he wanted?

Stan offered a list of credentials before telling me that he would like to set up some test shots for the *Penthouse* centerfold. Would I be interested?

Knowing that *Penthouse* was more explicit than *Playboy,* and far more explicit than anything I'd done in the past, I was surprised even to be considered.

"I'm not sure I'd be comfortable doing those kinds of photographs," I admitted. "Since you've worked for this magazine before, what can you tell me about it?"

"It's a good company. The magazine is growing fast, expected by the experts to overtake the industry before long." He mentioned a number of photo spreads he'd done. "If you're selected as a *Penthouse* model, Victoria, you'll be well taken care of."

Well taken care of — what did that mean exactly? I couldn't help being fascinated with the offer and inquisitive about the specifics. "How much does it pay?"

"They don't pay for test shots." He seemed mildly surprised by the question. "But if you're chosen to be the centerfold, you'll receive a check immediately for five thousand dollars."

I was making scale, about $500 a day, so the fee sounded fine, generous even, except for the fact that I'd be working unclothed again, and this time the nude photographs would be available to every voyeur willing to pay the magazine's cover price. Typical of my nonconformist nature, I was intrigued by the prospect of going against imposed judgments and boundaries set by society. And I'd modeled on "spec" assignments before, though I wasn't sure I was willing to accept those conditions now.

"How many models are tested?" I asked.

"Hundreds submit photographs unsolicited, and a number of those women appear in secondary features each month. But only one model, usually from dozens of professional submissions, is selected for the cover or the coveted centerfold and Pet of the Month."

For my business mind, the money was actually secondary to the opportunity to appear as a featured model in a national magazine. Yes, I'd rather it was *Cosmopolitan* or *Harper's Bazaar*, but this break had fallen into my lap. How could I not at least consider it? The substance of a model's income was *not* just her looks and her time. She had to know how to work in front of a camera and how to best represent a product. She was expected to always be prepared, professional, and on time. She needed an impressive portfolio just to get a job, and if she didn't know how to manage her career, she could end up running sixteen hours a day to barely make a living.

I was now a full-time working model in Atlanta, constantly in demand to represent such products as Strauss Jeans, Faded Glory, ChapStick, Head Start Hair Products, or Coca-Cola's Fanta. I also modeled for major department stores, industrial videos, company brochures, catalogs, and stock photos. To make a good living in this highly competitive career choice, I occasionally did some showroom modeling, strolling around like Vanna White at boat or car shows, pointing prettily if vacuously at the product's outstanding features.

Despite having a reasonable understanding of the modeling business, I knew practically nothing about the world Stan Malinowski presented. I took notes as I listened to his answers.

"Where would we do the test shoot?" I asked.

"*Penthouse* prefers exotic locations. The natural light and color in Puerto Rico this time of year are ideal. We'd stay in the best hotel, of course, on the beach, all expenses paid."

The travel sounded glamorous and appealing but could also be time wasted for no return. I had an excellent portfolio. Why spend days modeling for test shots on spec, as I had when first starting out, especially since they stood little chance of being published?

My career was moving along, so money wasn't my driving force. Working nude didn't bother me anymore—I'd grown past that long ago—but *Penthouse's* popularity came from its over-the-edge explicitness. Once I moved in that direction, there'd be no going back.

What would my very conservative parents, who usually supported my decisions, think about this proposition? I also had a husband now to consider. Jim and I had been married almost two years, and he was supportive, too, but how would he feel about his wife appearing in *Penthouse*? Perhaps I was looking for a good excuse to pass on Stan's offer.

"I promise you won't have to do anything on the test shots you find uncomfortable," he said. "Also, you can change your mind at any time."

Those two statements were important to me, and I found myself leaning toward acceptance. A part of me secretly hoped that this prominent, world-traveled photographer would, after seeing me in person, say, "Forget *Penthouse,* Victoria. You'll be perfect in the fashion spread I'm doing for *Vogue.*"

Still, I had a busy working schedule already, and I'd come a long way since the days when every opportunity looked like a shiny gold ring I should jump through hoops to capture.

"Stan, I appreciate talking to you, and I appreciate the magazine's consideration, but I'm not interested in doing a test shoot without being compensated."

Jump Right In

After hanging up, I had plenty of time to think about his offer while on other assignments. *Penthouse* magazine was a chance to step outside the ordinary boundaries of modeling and do something audacious—a slap in the face to those lascivious old goats in the industry who wanted my clothes off in a shoot even when it wasn't necessary. "Instead of doing it behind closed doors," I wanted to tell them, "I'll do it where everyone can see."

In my eight years of modeling, I'd often encountered the seedier side of the industry. Models sleeping with photographers or executives for jobs and pretending they were oh-so-demure as they smiled for a Revlon lipstick ad. Doing drugs and pretending they were oh-so-respectable as they posed for ads in *Good Housekeeping.* I was never a rebellious person, but it irked me that the career I'd chosen, a business I loved and worked so hard at, had such dirty laundry under its posh and polished façade.

So when Stan Malinowski, in talking about *Penthouse* magazine, had said, "You'll be well taken care of," his words struck a major chord with me.

One reason I'd turned down Stan's offer had nothing to do

with money and lay much deeper in my heart and soul than I like to think about. The same caution haunted me all of my life: a feeling that I might not measure up. What if I went on the shoot and later wasn't accepted? What if I was accepted and then realized I didn't want to be in such an explicit magazine? What if the magazine came out and my photos didn't have the same success as others had?

Even people who knew me well never imagined I had an ounce of insecurity. I tried to come across always as confident and decisive. Wanting more out of life than mediocrity, I persistently aimed at achieving excellence, despite my insecurities. The desire to accomplish beyond what most people consider satisfactory often pushed me to jump right into the very situations that frightened me.

CHAPTER 3

You're Just Going to Marry and Have Babies

I've heard women discuss modeling in a wistful "what if" voice that tells you they've dreamed of being the girl in the beauty ads, the high-fashion figure on the runway, the beauty queen wearing a diamond tiara and a dazzling smile for an audience of admirers. Although I took my career seriously, I always craved more from life. For me, modeling was simply the smart thing—and in many ways, the easy thing—to do in the meantime.

Mom and Dad encouraged me to do whatever would make me happy, never pushing in any direction. The expectation that I should enter beauty pageants came from friends at school, teachers, or neighbors. In local contests I usually won or at least placed. In addition to Miss Perfect Figure, I won the state title for Miss Georgia Queen of Posture and placed in the finals for Miss Georgia World.

That single phrase, *"Oh, my, she's so pretty,"* repeated since my earliest years by family, friends, and strangers, worked on my brain like subliminal marketing. Subconsciously, I was conditioned to be pretty. As I began modeling, I was doing what my social environment had conditioned me to do.

Being pretty, I wasn't expected also to be smart, although I usually made good grades in subjects I found interesting. School wasn't taught in a way that made children want to learn, and the subject matter was uninspiring. Most conventional classes bored me. While I had no desire to become a teacher, nurse, or accountant, I was intensely interested in literature, design, fashion, and drama.

I also loved nature and learning about faraway lands. I

imagined visiting Paris, Rome, Madrid, always in high style. I once mentioned to a counselor that I would like to take a Spanish class, if I could squeeze it into my schedule.

She looked me over and said, "Why in the world would *you* be interested in taking Spanish? You're just going to grow up, get married, and have babies."

Whether the woman meant what she said or was merely having a bad day, for me the remark was crushing. Recalling it now, I'm certain that was the moment my high school studies became secondary and everything interesting I could cram into my life became primary. I kept up my grades, but I poured my energy and enthusiasm into drill team, Drama Club, my "live mannequin" job at the dress shop, and the Len Chris Ann School of Charm and Modeling.

When I found Len Chris Ann, I knew I'd found my world.

"Ladies sit with style, they don't plop, plunk, or spraddle." For me, the teacher's words were like nectar to a starving bird. "Cross your legs at the ankles then draw them gracefully to one side."

A lovely woman, probably in her thirties, Marion Smith was the perfect example of what a woman of any age should be. She became an inspiration that would affect every part of my future. In addition to learning the proper way to use a knife and fork, to sit down and stand up properly from a chair, to sit with hands to the side in a fashion that was comfortable but appropriate, to walk and speak with elegance, there was an underlying message at Len Chris Ann. It was about self-confidence and image, being the best you can be.

Marion Smith brought out my true talent for fashion: dressing with style, knowing how to do the makeup and hair as well as the clothes. She brought out my undeveloped flair for presentation, for interacting with the world in a dignified, poised, appropriate, and confident manner. I took to all of it like a baby duck to water.

Danger Beckons

Boys were on my "okay" list, but not a significant part of my life. I'd moved past my schoolgirl crushes and I dated casually, a new guy every couple of months. Nothing special.

I wonder now if my nonchalance about my career in the early 1980s was because I was so serious about it as a teenager. People tell me I was a serious child, as well, spending hours with my paper dolls, "playing" with grave intensity. Every piece of clothing had to be exactly right, every tab neatly folded to keep the dresses in place, every purse and pair of shoes perfect for the outfit. A fashion model in training. Then in the summer of 1969, just before my senior year, I met a dangerously handsome young man two and a half years older than me and just different enough from other boys to capture my attention.

Marion Smith frequently received requests from clothing stores throughout Cobb County. Although I'd officially completed her classes, she kept me at the top of her list, and one assignment turned into a regular job throughout the summer. The location was the newest hotel in town, the Holiday Inn, and its restaurant was a popular place for "ladies who lunch." When a group called the Eastside Mariettans dined there, a local women's clothing store held a fashion show for them.

Every Thursday I modeled four or five outfits between twelve and two p.m. One day Marion Smith wanted me to meet the mother of a young student, Carol Ann Arnold, whom I'd recently introduced to store-window modeling.

Mrs. Arnold took my hand, squeezed it gently, and spoke in a warm, crisp voice.

"My daughter has told me so much about you," she said. "I think you're something of a role model for her. Carol Ann and I would like you to meet my son, Jim."

I smiled and thanked her but wasn't keen on being set up with someone's son, a boy who was probably bucktoothed and bow-legged if he couldn't meet girls on his own.

"Maybe we'll meet one day," I said, attempting to brush the lady off firmly but kindly.

"He works here, at the front desk. So you can meet him today."

Uh-oh. Maybe she'd forget by the time the fashion show was over.

"We moved here from Baltimore a few years ago," she added, "Jim goes to college and works at the hotel in his free time."

I'd never known anyone who'd lived in Baltimore. Although I'd traveled a bit with pageants, any city outside Georgia still seemed like a foreign country to me, so Jim Arnold sounded instantly more fascinating.

"Maybe you saw his new Corvette when you drove in?" Carol Ann told me later, when we met up in the changing room.

He drove a Corvette? How dangerous. Jim might be worth meeting, after all.

"He's nineteen," his mother said. "How old are you, dear?"

"Seventeen." But I was attracted to older men.

Charming, Witty, and We Matched

Jim's legs, as it turned out, *were* slightly bowed, but his teeth were perfectly straight and sparkling white. Everything I liked about Jim Arnold was exactly what I knew my mother wouldn't like. He was too old for me, and too different. He was a Yankee. He didn't talk like us, didn't act like us. He was a little arrogant and cocky. For Mom, Jim's Corvette was a sign of peril.

Jim called me the same evening we met. The following Saturday night we went to a movie, and after that he was "my guy," showing up to watch me on the drill team, taking me to the after-game events. At parties, we danced to music by the Fifth Dimension, Three Dog Night, or The Beatles. We liked being

How does someone summarize a relation- ship that could simply never be destroyed? I don't think neither Jim, nor I, ever lost our deep love and affection for each other. We endured.

together. Often we just drove around, showing off: the cool couple in the cool car.

Jim matched my life. His car complemented my hair. His clothes matched my clothes — I made sure of that. He usually wore leisure suits, the newest trend for guys, in rust or brown, which matched my first fur coat, a red fox. His hair was appropriately long, and he was really good looking. Together, we were a perfectly matched couple, as they say.

Too young to be openly having sex, and with no secret or convenient place to have it, we couldn't keep our hands off each other, so we had a lot of sex with our clothes on. After school and drill team, he'd bring me home. Mom might be gone to the grocery store. Dad wouldn't be home from work yet. We'd turn the TV on low then run to the glassed-in sun porch where one of us could watch the driveway while we made out, kissing, touching, rubbing up against each other, whatever we could do while still dressed. If someone came, we'd pull our clothes together, dash to the living room, and turn the television up, oh so innocent. I still find it exciting to make love with some small piece of clothing on.

Practically from the day we met, Jim and I became an item. We enjoyed each other's families, and in no time at all he won my mother over. Long before we married, Jim became like a son to my parents, remaining a significant part of their lives even today. I adored Jim. My dangerously handsome, charmingly witty husband proved to be a stabilizing force in my life.

**Flash-Forward Again to 1976
and My Life-Changing Decision**

As I considered the pros and cons of Stan Malinowski's *Penthouse* offer, I recalled a recent occurrence. Jim and I attended a party at a bachelor pad he'd once shared with his pals, and among the group, we were the only married couple.

The rented, sparsely furnished apartment—accessorized with cheap candles and satin sheets, in case they got lucky—boasted no sense of style. The newest, biggest thing in the living room was a television tuned to a ballgame. Sports magazines littered the tables. Six-packs of beer were stacked against the cabinets, bottles of cheap wine open on the counter.

When one of the men brought out his latest issue of *Playboy*, the guys gathered round to ogle, crack jokes, talk about how "totally blazin'" the women were, especially the centerfold, and how awesome it would be to make love to a woman like that. Jim was sighing, salivating, conjuring up stories right along with his bachelor friends.

Listening to their banter, I felt myself fill with anger and jealousy. When we left for home, I asked Jim, "What's so special about the women in those pictures?"

"I don't know … they're not like regular women. Pretty but also sexy, and posing for that magazine with no clothes on."

"How could you and your pals act like such jerks with me and the other girls right there in the room?"

"I was just looking at pictures. I mean, all guys look. What does it hurt?"

"Maybe nothing. Maybe I'm being oversensitive. But how many of *those* guys will get lucky tonight — like *you would* have?"

"Vicki, we were just joking around. Making up fantasies."

"Fine, you can fantasize all you want, but not in *my* bed."

When Stan Malinowski called back to say the magazine had agreed to pay a three-thousand-dollar fee for my test shots, I couldn't help thinking about the photographs in *Playboy* that Jim and his friends had found so tantalizing. Having collected as many new and used issues of *Penthouse* as I could find — actually, I'd convinced Jim to collect them for me — I studied every detail of every photograph, shocked at first to find them so much more explicit than *Playboy*.

But the *Penthouse* shots also appeared much more natural, not so contrived, the women wearing filmy lingerie, or only a pair of silk stockings, or a man's white shirt open down the front. They might be in the process of dressing or undressing, for a man or for the camera, but this appeared to be their first time, and it was special. Or maybe we were peeking at them without their knowledge during a moment of personal intimacy.

Also, the lighting and photography in the *Penthouse* photographs were exquisite. Glowing seductively for the camera, seemingly absorbed in their own inner sexuality, they appeared, at least in the carefully staged photographs, to have only to crook a finger to set the world spinning around them. I couldn't envision these women ever washing dishes or taking out the garbage.

I identified far more with *Penthouse* models than with the air-brushed girls in *Playboy* with no pubic hair. The explicitness of the *Penthouse* photography made the women appear self-assured and confident in taking risks, in charge of their own lives, fearless in their decisions. They *chose* to give the world a glimpse of their most intimate moments.

Weighing my decision, I had to wonder: Didn't all women imagine being a sultry beauty who commanded devotion from men merely by their sexual attractiveness? Didn't most women imagine undressing for the camera and striking excessive passion in every man granted the privilege of gazing at her gorgeous nude body?

Not many would actually do it, but in the privacy of their own dreams, women wanted their bodies to be admired. It might be interesting to play such a sensual role for a few days, like playing the seductress in a risqué off-Broadway show. Three thousand dollars was a reasonable fee for test shots. I loved to travel, and I'd never been to Puerto Rico.

On an entirely separate thought plane, the timing for this opportunity seemed almost prophetic. I'd reached a plateau in my life where everything was working out as planned — an exciting lifestyle, a magnificent new home, a loving husband. My career was at a peak. The agencies called regularly with new assignments, and repeat clients and photographers were willing to wait for me to be available. I'd climbed the success ladder, if not to the top then certainly within a step or two of the highest rung. For an Atlanta model, I'd done it all. This might be a perfect time to step out and do something new and daring.

Anyway, the chances were slim that my photographs would ever actually be published. Stan had told me that hundreds of women sent in test shots. If the improbable *did* happen, if the pictures *were* published, then what a fabulously audacious and flamboyant "exit" statement that would make from the modeling world.

When I returned Stan's call, we chatted about what I should bring to Puerto Rico and what to expect when we arrived. While we talked, my mind wandered ahead to the actual photo shoot. Stan seemed like such a soft-spoken, normal guy, not your typical eccentric, neurotic, over-the-top hysterical, arrogant, strange, dope-smoking, gender-challenged, or blatantly sex-crazed photographer with ulterior motives — which I often encountered — prima donnas who wanted to trade sex for portfolio shots. *You need photos, I need sex.* While many photographers I'd worked with possessed one or more irksome qualities, Stan seemed, at least on the phone, not to have any of them. It was quite surprising, but was it possible?

And if Stan's professionalism was typical of the magazine's standards, regardless of the explicit content, then the company might be worth working for, should they actually choose to publish my pictures. I've always been somewhat drawn to the forbidden, with "Do Not Enter" warning signs often in my blind spot.

After Stan answered every question I could think to ask, I took a very deep breath and said, "Okay, let's do it. When do we leave?"

I believe in constantly pushing beyond conventional restrictions. By posing undeniably nude, in positions exposing the most intimate parts of my body, for pictures that might appear in the fastest-growing men's magazine in the world, I was about to prove it.

CHAPTER 4

A Moment in Time

Stan Malinowski, possibly the tallest man I'd ever met, forty years old and charmingly gawky — as if he wasn't quite comfortable in his own shoes — put me at ease the instant we met at the Miami airport. Nevertheless, the uptight business side of my mind was on edge, telling me I needed to demonstrate to this worldly photographer that he was working with a model every bit his equal in professionalism.

Meanwhile, my artistically inquisitive side became totally enchanted with the island setting. White sugar-sand beaches, brilliant turquoise water — I'd experienced these on other Caribbean islands, but the Spanish influence evident in Puerto Rico's architecture and culture appeared very old-world and thus different from any place I'd previously traveled. For me, this colorful US territory less than a four-hour flight from Atlanta was like visiting a foreign country. As promised, the hotel accommodations were first-class and the sun-buttered landscape was gorgeous.

We started shooting on the beach, Stan draped with half a dozen cameras. In early- morning sunlight, surrounded by the deep blue-green of the ocean, the earthy scent of seaweed and the roar of the surf, I shed my Georgia persona. My favorite wash-worn jeans, the softest ones, became soaked around my ankles as I walked barefoot along the water's edge, cool damp sand licking between my toes. I'd thrown a shirt on over my sleeveless tank top against the slightly chill breeze blowing off the water. That same breeze lifted my hair and whispered gently across my ears, "Shhhhhhhhh."

I wandered farther down the empty beach. For the moment

it was mine, no other soul in sight. I scarcely noticed the camera as the rising sun warmed my face, kissed my neck, and the shirt slipped from my shoulders. The wet jeans tugged at my legs with each step, so I let them drop, to be carried away by the waves splashing higher and higher against my bare thighs. My breasts craved the sun. The yellow tank top was off and gone with scarcely a thought, and then I moved deeper, the warm subtropical water caressing me, sliding between my legs, and I became purely female, as primitive as the sea.

Lingerie and Lip Gloss

After that first morning, I knew that life would not be the same for me when this trip ended. I'd come there expecting to feel a little nervous, but that never happened. Whether it was the natural surroundings, or the fact that I was far away from home and everyone who knew me; or perhaps it was Stan's ability to vanish behind his camera lens. Whatever the reason, I felt at ease.

Each morning, afternoon and evening, we chose a new location. Stan gave minimal direction, offering only occasional suggestions. As best I recall they went something like this:

"Imagine, Victoria, that you are undeniably female yet powerful."

Later: "Imagine you are a water sprite so completely captivated by sea and surf that you fail to notice how your curves affect the viewer's libido."

And as the camera clicked away, "A little to the left," or "That's perfect, perfect."

Still later, "Now pretend you're a goddess romancing the camera intimately with your eyes, suggestively with your open mouth. Smoldering with desire, you allow one breast to escape from behind your hands."

I began each shoot fully clothed, in swimwear, sexy lingerie, or a gauzy dress. The clothing came off slowly until I finished the scene wearing only my lightly applied makeup and a scrap or two of my original outfit. Whether we were shooting outdoors on one of the many private beaches, or in the hotel suite dressed with richly textured furnishings and luxurious bedding, I allowed the ambiance to seduce me into sexual arousal.

In the misty, humid rainforest, I heard sounds of nature foreign to me at that time in my life, as animals and birds called their mates in the rituals of seduction. Panthers' growls deep in the forest let us know we were not alone. I knew their keen eyes watched me, even though I couldn't see them — like the men who might view these photographs. Orchids growing on the ground felt soft and sensual, like velvet crushing under my bare feet. The rainforest made love to me. I just had to let myself go and be a part of it, give myself permission to feel its power, liberation, and sexuality. I knew intuitively that any emotions within would be reflected outward in the natural glow of my skin and the expression on my face. If these photographs could seduce a man the way Stan's camera was seducing me, well … I appreciated Stan's unwavering professionalism. The chemistry we shared was purely artistic.

Every setting was discreet and judiciously chosen, and with or without his cameras Stan remained a gentleman. During our breaks, I asked about *Penthouse.*

"The magazine doesn't exploit women," Stan assured me. "I know it might appear that way, but like Botticelli, the painter famous for his nudes, it honors women. On the photography, I usually deal with Bob Guccione at his home," he said. "Bob's exacting about the artistic aspects of the magazine and what he's looking for in a model. On business affairs, I talk to Joe Brooks, the art director. Dozens of people work at the office, but I only know the creative department."

From the copies Jim had brought home for me to analyze, I'd

learned that Bob Guccione was the owner, and that he was considered unconventional. Naturally, that word intrigued me.

"What is Bob like as a person?" I asked Stan.

"Smart. A perfectionist in his work, and it shows in what he's accomplished. He's given me an opportunity to explore a type of photographic art that isn't possible in more conventional venues. And Bob's always fair."

Finally, we began shooting the most explicit nude poses. Unlike the others, where I could imagine myself alone, interacting with nature or with the leisurely activity of removing my clothing, these poses featured the most intimate areas of my body. The camera came in close while I engaged in the pretense of orgasmic euphoria.

Surprisingly, I was able to disregard Stan and his camera. I'd studied those copies of *Penthouse*, and once I committed to posing for the kind of photographs they published, I was determined to do it to the best of my ability, just as I would any modeling assignment.

For the final shoot, Stan and I went to the hotel roof, and he snapped several hundred frames as the rusty glow of late afternoon sunlight silhouetted my body, my long hair blowing wildly in the wind. Then he took one last photograph, which I believe is the most beautiful nude shot ever taken of me to this day.

The sun had gone down and the light had just started to fade, the sensational colors of sunset draining away to darkness. I stood near the edge of the building with nothing behind me but the darkening sky and wearing nothing at all but the warm tropical night.

What a fitting end to a remarkable experience, to a moment in time I could never repeat, and to the awakening of a new outlook on life. The trip proved successful in many ways I never anticipated. Not only did I feel more comfortable in front of the camera than I'd expected, even with the candid nudity, I also felt strangely liberated, as if I'd crossed the hallowed boundaries of acceptability. I felt older, wiser, and unique for my twenty-three years.

Business as Usual

Back in Atlanta, I quickly became busy, not only with work but also with putting the finishing touches on our new house. One of my favorite quotes is by Italian poet Cesare Pavese, "We do not remember days, we remember moments." Shooting with Stan Malinowski in Puerto Rico marked a significant moment in my life, a moment in which I experienced notable growth in personal awareness. I intended to share that moment with no one. And until now, I never have.

Regarding *Penthouse* magazine, I didn't anticipate making any further decisions. My active career swept me up in the usual auditions and photo shoots. At night I retreated with Jim to the sanctuary of our home.

Two years earlier, Mom and Dad had bought a handsome Cape Cod in a fashionable residential area of Marietta. Jim and I immediately purchased the only lot left on the cul-de-sac. I was at the height of my career in Georgia. Jim and my dad were working together to build Dad's tire business. We were all making money, so it worked. At night, Dad, Jim, and I would sit at the dining room table laughing, sometimes mildly arguing, as we designed the new house. Dad, an artist with no formal training but an excellent eye and a steady hand, committed his napkin doodles and my extravagant ideas to paper. As a keen, proud observer, sipping on his rum and Coke, Jim kept the mood light. Creating the plan for our house was fun and exciting as we worked together late into the nights, and Dad's drawings were so good that the architect charged only a minimal fee for the blueprint. But the construction investment promised to be considerable, and we'd spent our savings buying the lot. It was Jim who figured out how to make it happen.

"With our combined incomes," he said, "there's no reason we shouldn't get a loan from my father's credit union." He was right.

From my point of view, everything about the house had to be as distinctive as my life — and even my wedding. I'd arranged to get married in Jamaica, long before it became a popular venue. We went in August, taking my parents, Jim's parents, and Carol Ann, his sister. From the Kingston airport, we drove two scary hours on narrow roads through the mountains and villages until we reached the spectacular tropical paradise of Frenchman's Cove. On the beach, the villagers had worked with the resort staff for days to create our wedding as if it were their own, building a grass hut, gathering flowers for bouquets and other decorations, placing hundreds of candles in the sand. We were married under a handcrafted arch of woven vines, with lilies hanging over us like bells and "Blue Hawaii" by Elvis playing on a record player. We hadn't anticipated guests, but the entire village turned out for our wedding, about 200 people, including lots of children. At one point during the excitement, I realized this was no longer just something clever and cool to do: this was for life. *Oh my god, this is really happening. I can't back out. I'm in Jamaica. Jim's family is here. My family is here. Ohmygod.*

Fantasy Island

Jim Arnold, from an email August 10, 2011

It was thirty-seven years ago this week. You're on the beach struttin' your stuff while I'm slaving on the golf course with your dad and gettin' my ass handed to me on the tennis court by my dad. The next day you took your vows with that stud in the white suit — I think Fantasy Island reported that suit missing. My god, Vic, we were one helluva beautiful couple, huh?

Happy Anniversary!

Not Another Like It

Our marriage license, torn from an original book dating back 200 years, described Jim as a bachelor and me as a spinster. After our old-fashioned ceremony, in which I promised to love, cherish, and obey, the celebration continued well into the evening. The workers had made a bonfire on a barge out in the water, and as the fire burned bright against the night sky, our limousine, a decorated golf cart, drove us to our cabin.

I couldn't imagine a more novel and distinctive way to begin our marriage. Now we were designing our home, which would be equally distinctive.

Tall windows, open beams overhead, every room on a different level, every wall at a different angle, and except for the thirty-foot stone fireplace and entertainment nook, it was built completely of natural cedar. The furnishings and fixtures were in shades of brown, cream, rust, or natural wood. Floor-to-ceiling bookshelves in the living room displayed our collections of handmade pottery, Native-American artifacts, and baskets handcrafted by locals living in the Georgia mountains. The wonderful cedar smell permeated every room.

What I loved most about our house was that it reflected Jim's personality plus a little touch of every part of mine: my contemporary, artistic spirit, my traditional upbringing, my romantic disposition in the bedroom, my love of nature, and most of all my desire to be unique. Traditional in one sense, the house was at the same time quite contemporary in its style. Our contemporary bedroom featured a traditional four-poster canopy bed. The stone-floored atrium was filled with tropical plants, some of which stretched up past the heavy crossbeams. The dining room featured an antique pine table and wall-to-wall sliding glass doors that opened to a modern deck and provided the feel of outdoor dining as we looked out into the woods.

One night I had the doors open to the balmy air, and I looked up to see a ceramic owl perched on one of the beams. It was about eight inches tall and quite lifelike. I suspected Jim or Mom had bought it and tucked it up there for me to find. That night, Jim and I heard a strange sound, and I learned that our owl was not ceramic. We let him out, but he must have enjoyed the atrium as much as we did, because he returned again and again, becoming part of our little family for a while.

Designed with only 2,000 square feet, our unusual home was ideal for two people and was quite an accomplishment for a pair of twenty-somethings. The builder laughingly told me later, "Every piece of wood had to be cut and fitted at a different angle. It's a show piece, not another like it in the city. I've built five-hundred-thousand-dollar homes that weren't as difficult to build as yours."

An Unexpected Offer

When the first call came from the promotions department of *Penthouse*, I couldn't help wondering if they'd mistakenly contacted the wrong model.

"Mr. Guccione's office asked me to phone you," the woman said, after introducing herself as one of the magazine's promotions directors. "He would like you to go to Rome and appear in the movie he's currently producing and filming there."

Bewildered, all I could think to say was, "What movie? And why me?"

"Why, *Caligula*! Malcolm McDowell, Sir John Gielgud, Peter O'Toole, Helen Mirren — it's the most spectacular film of the year, and the first *Penthouse* film production. Gore Vidal wrote the screenplay. I can't believe you don't know about it."

"I'm sorry. This is the first I've heard from *Penthouse* since the test shots I did for the magazine a couple of months ago, and no one has contacted me regarding those shots."

"But you're on the August cover and you're Pet of the Month. Surely someone called to tell you that."

"No." I'd been so sure I wouldn't be selected for the magazine. Maybe she phoned the wrong model. "Are you certain?"

By now the woman seemed completely rattled. "You *are* Victoria Johnson, aren't you?"

"Yes, of course."

She decided to double-check her information, apparently worried to have overstepped her authority by calling about the film before I knew about the cover and centerfold. She promised to get it straightened out and have someone contact me that afternoon.

A few hours later, a different woman phoned.

"Victoria, you are definitely on the cover for the August issue of *Penthouse* as well as the centerfold, and Mr. Guccione definitely would like you to appear in his film, *Caligula*."

Having had time to do my own checking, I'd learned that the August issue would actually hit the newsstands in July. This was nearly the first of June. Except for Jim, no one in my family, or his, nor the agency, knew that I'd done the test shots for *Penthouse*.

"Before I make any decisions about going to Rome, I need to know more about the movie and the role I'd be playing," I said. After reading off a list of questions I wanted answered, I added, "I need to talk to Mr. Guccione."

"You want to talk to Bob Guccione?"

"Actually, I'd like to meet with him."

"Victoria, nobody talks to Bob. I'm in charge of the magazine's promotions, and *I* don't even talk to Bob."

"Why not?"

"All communications go through his assistant. Mr. Guccione is incredibly busy and a very private man. He rarely speaks to anyone personally, other than his family and, when necessary, his executives. After he chooses the models, the office handles any details."

"Please understand, I don't want to talk to an assistant. I need to talk to Mr. Guccione, if he's the one who made the decision to send me to Rome. And I need to *see* this August issue." I vividly remembered the photos Stan had shot, but now they were no longer merely test shots. They were about to be published in a hugely popular and sensational, if not borderline scandalous, men's magazine and distributed worldwide. Including Marietta, Georgia.

"Going to Rome is a big commitment and totally unexpected," I added. They wanted me in Rome? I didn't want to talk to them about movies while I was still trying to grasp the image of a *Penthouse* magazine with *me* on the cover. "I need more information, so yes, I'm requesting a call from Mr. Guccione."

The woman promised to get back in touch soon with the information I needed, and now that they had me on their radar, the magazine continued calling. The next phone call was about the copy that would accompany my photo layout. They wanted to know what I liked to do, how I liked to make love, my measurements, my astrology sign, where I'd most like to live, and how I felt about the beach where my photographs were taken. With every question I realized more fully that my boundary-pushing whim was becoming a reality. I cooperated, providing the information while suspecting I had no control over how it would be written. I'd probably never recognize myself. By now I'd read several issues. The women on those pages might be real, but the story the magazine spun around them was clearly pure fantasy.

Then she asked, "Are you going to use your real name?"

I'd been trying to get the South to call me Victoria since I could remember. No such luck, but now was my chance.

"Victoria Lynn," I said, but before adding "Johnson," I got spooked and dropped my last name. By the time the issue hit the newsstands, I was sorry I'd made that decision.

The next day, when the phone rang again, I knew exactly

what I was going to say about Rome. "Thank you very much, but no thanks." If a department head from a major magazine could mishandle communications so completely for a single issue, how could I let them send me to Italy?

"Hello, Vicki. This is Bob Guccione."

His deep, resonant voice conveyed, in those six words, all the reassurance, comfort, and confirmation I needed.

"I understand you have some questions," he added.

"I do." For the life of me, I couldn't remember a single thing to ask. "I understand I'm on the August cover."

"I've looked at your photographs, Vicki, and they're beautiful. The centerfold is lovely. I understand you'd like to come to New York and meet with me. When would you like to come?"

Serious Is Not in My Vocabulary

Jim Arnold, from an email to Victoria, July 12, 2010

When this whole Pet of the Month deal came up, and you talked about shooting test shots with Stan, I was petrified. I had the perfect life and the perfect wife, the perfect house in the perfect neighborhood. This was a perfect time in our lives, an absolute dream world. It wasn't difficult to see over the horizon what was about to happen to that dream.

I supported it because you wanted it badly. I hoped we could maintain our lives together in Georgia while you excelled in your career, including this terrifying new twist in that career. Then you'd come home, have babies, and maybe learn to cook, like me. (Sorry. Got sidetracked with a little humor. I'm trying to be serious here, and you know serious is not in my vocabulary.)

Giving up the perfect home and probably the perfect marriage was devastating. But more important to me was your desire and motivation to go after something you wanted so much, I guess to validate your existence. You were number one in my life, for sure.

You held that spot long after the divorce and through numerous other relationships, until my daughter, Dottie, swooped into my new life and stole my heart.

Love you always,
Jim

CHAPTER 5

NYC: Pavement Pounding to Pampered Pet

When I stepped from the taxi to the New York City sidewalk on that hot June afternoon in 1976 and mounted the steps to Bob Guccione's townhouse, I truly had no idea what lay ahead. My earlier experience in New York, a grueling career-building venture, had been the most miserable six months of my life.

Any model, whether commercial or fashion, who expected to get into the top echelons had to do it in New York. Gary White, a former partner of Peachtree Models, where I eventually made the coveted "Top Ten" list that had awed and intimidated me at age nineteen, was with Zoli, now, a powerful New York modeling agency, and he'd invited his favorite models to join him. Every couple of weeks I commuted back and forth, leaving Jim and the comfort of my home to stay at Gary's Manhattan apartment with him and his friend Artie. I slept in a spare bedroom, with no furniture, no air conditioning, just a mattress on the floor, and with other models coming in and out, sleeping on mattresses in the living room. Most of the girls had just arrived in the city and were nine feet tall. I'd never felt so short in my life until I lived in New York.

Gary and Artie loved their night life. They'd work until five p.m., sleep until ten, then go out partying, dancing, and doing "poppers" — amyl nitrate, which produces a head rush, euphoria, and sexual arousal. Pop one, sniff it, get high. Never enough time to eat a proper meal, they'd order pizza and leave the empty boxes around the kitchen. The apartment always smelled of stale pizza and poppers. In mid 1970s, this was the life of many agents, models, advertising executives, Wall Street stockbrokers, and other swinging singles. But not mine, at least not then. My party days came later; I was too busy trying to carve out a piece of New York's modeling world.

I didn't know how to ride a subway, and I hated buses, so I took taxis, an expense that put a huge dent in my modest New York budget. And try to get a taxi when it's raining at five o'clock and you're in Midtown Manhattan. The taxis vanish, so you're standing there with a dripping umbrella wearing your best designer suit and brand-new Charles Jourdan high-heel shoes. My feet throbbed painfully at the end of every day.

For six months, I shuttled back and forth from Atlanta and pounded the New York pavement carrying a huge portfolio filled with photographs and tear sheets of print ads, because that's how you got the high-paying ad campaigns and TV commercials. Gary put me in touch with agencies that created television advertising, where I discovered I wasn't very good at delivering copy. Determined, I started taking acting classes. My delivery improved quickly, and I did get quite a few commercial assignments, mostly regional.

Gary also continued to promote fashion layouts, and every so often he'd send me on a go-see to this photographer or that. Usually, they wanted someone taller. I modeled for several book covers and a poster for one of the publishing houses, promoting the latest historical romance novel by Rosemary Rodgers. Small jobs as well as more substantial jobs, and finally, one photographer said, "You'd be great for my Konica shoot next week." He hired me for a national Konica Camera advertising campaign, a highly lucrative assignment.

But no matter how much experience and advancement I was gaining in my career, it wasn't worth the agony of living under such miserable conditions.At night, I'd lie on my mattress in Gary's apartment and wonder why I was putting myself through this madness. I was lonely. I missed Jim. I missed my house. I missed breathing fresh clean air, without automobile fumes or poppers or pizza smells.

Physically and emotionally depleted, I returned to Georgia, grateful for the comfort of my home and family. And now, no matter what Bob Guccione or his magazine had to offer, I vowed I'd never repeat that wretched experience.

Publisher, Producer, Artist
From Biography.com

While his company went on to develop many different publications, Bob Guccione is best known as the founder of the raunchy men's magazine, *Penthouse*. It was an unusual career choice for someone who once studied for the priesthood. Growing up in a Catholic Italian-American family, Guccione had been an altar boy. He even spent several months in a seminary before dropping out. Instead of attending college, he decided to pursue his dream of becoming an artist.

For years, Guccione traveled around Europe and Africa. Unfortunately, he could not support himself with his art alone so he took odd jobs and received some funds from his family. In 1960, Guccione moved to London and eventually became the managing editor of the *London American*, a weekly newspaper. After that venture folded, he started a mail-order business before coming up with the idea for *Penthouse*.

Judy Garland's Canes

It's my nature to be prepared, because I don't like to be caught off guard, so before boarding the airplane to meet with Bob Guccione, I read everything I could find about the man, the magazine, and the movie he was making. The internet was not yet invented, so research wasn't as easy as it is today. Everything I

"Victoria is one of the most successful centerfolds, if not the single most successful centerfold, we've ever had ...

She was Pet of the Year like (snaps fingers) that! ... There was a constant demand to see more and more of her ... she's been enormously successful for the readership ... She's beautiful to look at ... The issues that carry her on the cover sell better normally than the issues that don't have her on the cover ... I tell her it's the time of the year, state of the economy, the weather, I never tell her how great she really is (laughing) ... Vicki represents a lot of what Penthouse stands for ... She's educated, a very ambitious young lady, a very bright girl ... Very representative of what the best of feminism has brought about in this new era."- *from a video produced by Penthouse Productions about Bob Guccione shooting the centerfold models. He chose Victoria as the model for the video.*

learned reinforced what Stan had told me, that regardless of the magazine's content, the company had an excellent reputation for treating its employees and support staff well.

Penthouse, I discovered, was rapidly gaining on *Playboy* as the leading men's magazine and had been the favorite, two-to-one, among American servicemen in Viet Nam. Its allure was not only the titillating photographs but also its award-winning journalism and the active support Bob Guccione gave to soldiers fighting overseas. *Penthouse* photography was praised as being more realistic and artistic than that of its rival. *Penthouse* readership rated higher on an educational level, and its twenty-five-plus age level was higher than *Playboy's* eighteen-to twenty-five. Most impressive, to me at least, was that Mr. Guccione had been named Publisher of the Year in 1975 by Brandeis University, which cited him as a "new force in the world of publishing."

Preparing to meet this "new force," I wore my favorite cinnamon-colored designer suit from Saks Fifth Avenue and carried a slim briefcase. A security guard opened the door and led me to a sitting room, dark, very European, draped with a ton of red velvet, furnished with Victorian sofas and other antiques, and cluttered with strange, beautiful objects. Apparently, the townhouse had belonged to Judy Garland at some time in the past. The canes holding up the staircase banister were the actual canes from Judy's concert tours.

It was a little scary sitting there on a sofa, my legal pad and pen in hand, my legs crossed appropriately to one side, waiting. People told me later that Bob Guccione quite commonly kept individuals lingering for two hours or more, yet that didn't happen to me. I'm not sure I would have stayed two hours.

A woman came in first and introduced herself as Kathy Keeton. I'd read about her and had spoken with her on the phone, so I knew she was Bob's partner. They lived together but were not married, and she ran the business side of the company. Together, Kathy and Bob made the magazine happen.

Tall, slender, in her late thirties, I guessed, and rather imposing, she wore black lounging pants and a silk spaghetti-strap top with sparkly appliqués across the front. Her straight blonde hair hung in a single ribbon-embellished braid that fell across her shoulder. When she smiled, I could tell that her intention was to be warm and welcoming, but I got the feeling she might be made of steel.

"Bub will be down," she said, as if such occurrence was both unusual and special. "Until then, we will have time to get acquainted."

She'd said "Bub" not Bob, I noticed, trying to place her unusual accent. I discovered later that she'd grown up in South Africa. As we talked, she asked about my modeling career, the types of ads, promotions, and publicity I'd done. She seemed impressed to see me taking notes.

When a rumble of thumps and heavy footsteps sounded from outside the room, higher than where we were sitting, I took a second or two to realize someone was descending the stairs, not just some-*one* judging by the sound, but a whole *herd*. A giant dog bounded into the room, followed by more dogs, each a replica of the first. In the midst of them stood a man who, for a moment, literally stole my breath away.

Dressed impressively all in black, he wore a form-fitting jacket of shiny, wavy, fur-like fabric, belted at the waist. A black shirt, half-unbuttoned, black pants, and English boots completed the outfit, and at his neck hung a wealth of gold chains. He looked to be in his mid-forties with well-defined muscles, black hair, beautifully tanned skin, and intensely handsome features. His eyes brought to mind a phrase from my childhood. "He has bedroom eyes," women my mother's age said when describing a particular actor. Now I understood what they meant. Bob's eyes had an alert but languid quality, as if he could spend an eternity gazing at you, taking in every curve of your face without tiring or losing interest.

And in that moment, while his eyes locked on mine and I forgot to breathe, something passed between us, some tiny sensual preview of what lay ahead for us. Was it chemistry? Pheromones? Animal magnetism? It lasted only an instant, but when he spoke, in that same deep reassuring voice I'd heard on the phone, all my concerns about this meeting melted away.

"Vicki, I'm so glad you've come. I'm Bob Guccione."

He sat in a chair across from me, a twin to the chair where Kathy sat. I counted seven large dogs, which I learned were Rhodesian Ridgebacks. The largest was named Grundy, Kathy told me, and his mate was Fia. Grundy settled at Bob's feet, while the others spread out around Kathy's chair, eventually covering most of the floor. It occurred to me that the dogs were probably responsible for Judy Garland's staircase canes looking battered and broken.

I thanked Bob for taking the time to meet with me, all the while thinking, *This is a truly beautiful man.*

"As you can see," he said, handing me a page he was carrying, "your cover photograph is exquisite."

What he showed me was an advance copy of the August cover of *Penthouse* magazine. I remembered Stan taking the shot, but this was my first time to actually see it. In the photo, I wore a black lace bra and matching bikini panties, two fingers of one hand tucked suggestively beneath my low-riding elastic waistband. I gazed straight into the camera, signature red hair framing my face, moist lips slightly parted. A picture, they say, is worth a thousand words, but somehow the single word *Penthouse* spread in lavender type across the page above my photo screamed "porn" at me, and a little voice in my head responded, *Are you really sure this is what you want to do?* But the magazine was printed now. There was no turning back.

"You are a beautiful centerfold," Bob murmured.

In the centerfold pictures, I would not only lose the black panties, I would lose all semblance of modesty.

As Bob continued to talk, telling me how much he loved the photographs Stan had taken, and that he personally had selected twenty-nine in addition to the cover shot, and what a stunning layout they made, and how magnificently I was going to represent the magazine, I found myself mesmerized by his resonating voice and slightly British accent, by his presence, and most of all by a soothing assurance he exuded. Instead of worrying whether my friends and family in Georgia would be horrified to see my legs widespread, showing what Southern women are really made of, I was absolutely at ease, feeling relaxed, calm, fascinated by the exotic new world awaiting me, and certain that I'd done exactly the right thing.

In Kathy's opinion, too, I would be an outstanding addition to the *Penthouse* "family." She talked about a weekly retainer program, mentioning a significant amount of money, plus health and life insurance, a wardrobe allowance, and extra pay for any extra days I worked. The national recognition would benefit both me and the magazine, she said, and I would be free to take on other assignments, as long as I reserved two days a week, if needed, for *Penthouse* promotions.

"Come to the office tomorrow," Kathy said. "Meet everyone. See what we do."

We talked for a while longer. Bob wanted to know where I was staying. When I mentioned the Sheraton on the West Side, where the magazine had made my reservations, he made an odd face and asked if I wanted to move to a better place. I wasn't about to say yes.

"My room's fine," I assured him. But I never again stayed at the Westside Sheraton.

After the meeting, he called his driver to take me back to the hotel or wherever I wanted to go. Sliding into the spacious limo, I felt somehow changed and lightheaded, as if I'd been in the presence of royalty. Silly to think it now, but that's exactly how it felt. Atlanta suddenly seemed very small. My new opportunities as a *Penthouse* centerfold promised to be as big and as boundless, as mild or as wild as I wanted to push them. Elated by Bob and Kathy's compliments, my self-doubt quashed, I was completely enthralled.

But what about Jim and my family?

My life with Jim was the fairy tale that little girls dream of from the first time they watch *Cinderella* or *Snow White*. Many women never find such an ideal mate, a man who is fun to be with, thoughtful, amusing, supports her most outrageous notions, an attentive lover, not to mention handsome. The sexual chemistry between us made our lovemaking perfect. And, my god, we'd just moved into our new home. Kathy had made it sound as if I'd be traveling all over the world for *Penthouse* if I accepted their offer. Yet, here I was sitting in another man's limo, enthralled after an hour in his presence, and realizing that the decisions I was about to make could jeopardize my ideal marriage.

For the first time it also struck me fully that I might be putting Jim and my parents in a position to be humiliated or embarrassed when the magazine came out. Until now it also hadn't occurred to me how it might affect the children, my fourteen-year-old sister, Carla, and ten-year-old brother, Stacey. I knew I was not the one to address it with them. It would have to be my mom's job. Because of our age difference, I'd overlooked this most obvious potential problem, and I didn't know how to solve it.

What had started as a flash of curiosity about the sexier side of modeling had exploded into change for all of us. It certainly could have a damaging effect on Jim's life, on my family's provincial bubble of existence, and perhaps on my dad's business.

In the past, I'd always been proud of my decisions as well as my thought process for getting to them. Now I began to seriously question what I'd done. I may have made the right decision for myself, but I wasn't at all sure I'd made the right decision for the people I loved, especially Jim.

Kismet

Only after reaching my hotel room did I realize no one had mentioned *Caligula*, the movie Bob was filming in Rome, or my flying there to take part in it. The phone call about that movie had prompted me to request the meeting today. Was the phone call a mistake? Had they decided not to offer me a role? Or had I said something during today's conversation that changed the direction of my relationship with *Penthouse*?

In years to come, the controversial film would be a moderate box office success, especially in New York, but would be panned by critics. Eventually, I previewed *Caligula* with Bob in London, before it premiered for the public, and was secretly relieved that, for whatever reason, my role in it never materialized and, thankfully, I never had to say no.

Today, as I look back on that meeting, it seems in many ways inevitable, like destiny or fate. If not for that errant phone call about flying to Rome to appear in *Caligula*, my meeting with Bob might have never happened.

A Family Business

When Kathy and Bob spoke of joining the *Penthouse* family, I didn't realize how literal they were being. The *Penthouse* offices at 909 Third Avenue proved to be impressively chic and modern, with plenty of wide windows, plush carpeting, classic, expensive furnishings and art, but I was equally impressed by the fact that so many of Bob's family members worked there. His father was the company accountant, his sister, Jeri Winston, the administrative vice president and director of merchandising. Kathy Keeton headed up the advertising department, and Bob's oldest son, Bob Jr., interned there as he pursued building his own publishing business. In this way, *Penthouse* magazine was more like a conservative mom-and-pop business than a major corporation, yet it was extremely professional in its operations. Rumors I'd heard of a dark, dingy office with half-nude girls hanging around and couples having sex anywhere, anytime, couldn't have been more wrong.

Equally notable, most of the executives were women. At a time when feminists were clobbering major corporations with lawsuits and unfavorable publicity for gender discrimination, Bob Guccione had hired smart, savvy women at the highest levels of his company.

Over lunch, Kathy and I discussed promotions I might do, including numerous print campaigns for their major clients, mainly liquor and tobacco companies, as well as for ads that promoted *Penthouse* and its various divisions. She told me I'd have the option of saying no if I'd scheduled a better shoot on my own. She clearly was impressed with me, believed I'd be an asset to the magazine, and I was impressed with her. I came away convinced that Stan Malinowski's assessment was absolutely true: *Penthouse* believed in taking excellent care of their models.

Back at the office, I overheard Kathy tell someone, "Vicki is a smart woman. She arrived at the house with a pen and legal pad, ready to take notes. No centerfold has ever done that before. She's a businesswoman." Even though I'd yet to sign the contract that would make me an official representative of the magazine, Kathy sent me to fittings for various outfits I'd wear in the promotions we discussed, and for fashions I'd wear in an editorial piece for *Penthouse*'s sister publication, *Viva*.

Forging a Friendship

A number of people I met at *Penthouse* became my friends for life, but I connected instantly with Jeff Zelmanski. Jeff and I were both new to this world of magazine publishing. Exciting and less demanding than the modeling career I'd known in the past, the *Penthouse* world included the best makeup artists, hairdressers, and photographers in the business. Working in such a supportive environment would prove an absolute pleasure.

Jeff's job, the one he'd soon be promoted to, was keeping the Pets busy doing national promotions and sending them to Manhattan's most popular restaurants, clubs, and events, where they could be seen looking gorgeous and photographed by media journalists. In years to come, my job would mushroom into a cloud of activity, travel, publicity, and along the way, it would prove entertaining and fun. Jeff would make it more so.

During those three days in New York City, I felt a tidal wave building behind me, a wave that would carry me into a fascinating, fast-paced, and highly public lifestyle that other girls growing up in Georgia — and indeed many other models — would only dream about.

Imagine Custom Blended Shampoo
Jeff Zelmanski

New York City was the most exciting place in the world in the late seventies and early eighties. And Victoria was one of the most beautiful women, I mean simply breathtaking.

Seriously, everyday people just don't look like that.

You see her on the street and she looks like she's somebody *or* should be somebody. *Like an aura around her. People like Vicki have that special thing, that* je ne sais quoi *that can somehow immediately win you over.*

There was a woman in charge above me at Penthouse, *and*

Vicki immediately knew she was scatterbrained. Vicki would tell her, "I want to talk to Jeff," and then she'd explain to me what she wanted or needed. Vicki does not suffer fools gladly and she can size up a person pretty fast.

I graduated from the University of Detroit, a Jesuit school yet, and moved to New York looking for a job. I had one interview set up with The New Yorker, but they said, "Everyone here starts in the mail room." I couldn't make it in New York on that kind of low salary. Prestige is nice, but you need money to live on, so I interviewed with Penthouse. And it wasn't like, "Ohh, this is dirty." On the contrary, the magazine had status. The office was in this gorgeous building on Third Avenue, and it was a very competitive magazine with good advertising. So I started in a very low position that paid well.

Before long they switched me over to the department that handled promotions for the centerfolds; they were called Pets as an endearing term. I kept working for a number of different women until they each got fired, then someone finally told me, "Jeff, we're going to give you a chance." I said, "Great!" And so then I wanted to see if there was some way I could work the department like a real business.

Previously, reaching out to the centerfolds to make public appearances was not routinely done, so I started getting in touch with all of them. We did events, conventions, and the Pets became popular with the public, and I became friendly with the Pets. I talked to them and got to know them as people.

I credit Vicki with so much. She made me feel important. We enjoyed spending time with each other. Her apartment was right behind the office, Midtown East Side, in a beautiful high rise. Once she called me from who knows where and asked me to go to her apartment and listen to her phone machine messages for her. She said, "Just go, it's all arranged. The doorman and the concierge will let you in and give you a key. And don't be surprised at what you might hear." I remember her saying that like it was yesterday.

I was so nervous. I took a paper and pen, went right up there, into this fabulous apartment that was decorated in black and peach and grey, and it really was unique and pure "Vicki" at that moment. This was her style. It had well-placed mirrors for accent and such soothing colors. It became routine: I would take these messages down, call her, and read them back, trying never to sound shocked or surprised, just giving her the rundown of her calls. To this day, I've never divulged the names of anyone who called her.

Sometimes I went to her apartment for lunch. People would ask me, "How was lunch?" "Lunch was fine." Nobody knew I was at Vicki's. Nobody knew what a special relationship we had. We trusted each other.

Some evenings she would say, "What are you doing tonight?"
"Nothing"
"You want to go out for dinner?"
"Okay." I was twenty-two years old, and Vicki was twenty-four, but she was a star. People looked at her on the street, and for me it was still amazing that I was her friend. It hit me like "wow."

One morning she made me grits. I'd never had grits. How cool was that?

I love theatre. I have no talent, but I moved to New York so I could go to the theatre. And I love movies, especially silent. So Vicki and I would talk about film and theatre and acting. We connected. She was giving me this kind of New York sophistication, and I was giving her an earful of the New York culture that I loved. I remember her doing a play in one of her acting classes, Lu Ann Hampton Laverty Oberlander, a Texas play by Preston Jones. Vicki read me some of her lines and you could see she knew what she was doing. She had a sense of theatricality and had studied her craft.

And no one had to teach her how to dress. Vicki had more stockings than anyone could imagine — textured and plain, in every color and shade. She had a collection of gloves, scarves, shoes, and belts, everything to go with whatever she chose to wear. She knew what looked good.

Vicki had this dress that was white gabardine with black lizard lightning bolts. Real lizard. I mean fabulous! At that time in New York, there were two amazing drycleaners. She took the dress to Jeeves of Belgravia, who could clean anything.

The manager called to inform her, "We cannot clean your dress."

"But I have to get it cleaned," she said.

"Madam, if you can afford a dress like that, you can afford another one."

That was New York in the golden years, when your drycleaner could insult you over the phone. She wore the dress until she couldn't.

The idea that someone would design this dress that couldn't be dry-cleaned — and Vicki owned it. She always had fabulous clothes that you couldn't tell where they came from, and always with amazing belts, huge, unique designer belts. Every day, going nowhere, she'd still look fabulous.

The other models didn't have that fashion sense or that eye for detail. Some girls looked like Frederick's of Hollywood; to them a boa was haute couture. *Vicki came along and knew what looked great and what fashion worked on her. No one had to show her about hair or makeup. To this day, she thinks it was no big deal that Philip Kingsley created her shampoo for her. Nowadays, celebrities expect personalized treatment but back then, it was so rare. I would call people in Ohio and tell them, "Imagine custom-made shampoo. Vicki has it!"*

Vicki's hair, after all, was her trademark.

CHAPTER 6

The Tidal Wave

Flying back to Atlanta after my meeting with Bob and Kathy, it hit me again that the August issue, with my cover and my centerfold, would actually land on the newsstands in late July. That was barely a month away. The only person in my family who knew about the magazine, the test shots, and that I'd flown to New York to meet with the magazine's owner, was Jim.

In every phase of my career since high school, Jim had been supportive, and he'd been equally so with my *Penthouse* madness. Was it real? Or just an act to encourage me in my career? I hoped he really meant it.

Being familiar with *Penthouse*, Jim had to know what sort of pictures of his wife would be floating around Marietta. But my parents led a much more sheltered life. I suggested to Jim that we take them to Hilton Head Island, one of our favorite vacation spots, and break the news there.

Meanwhile, I also saw the month ahead as the time to reap full benefit from any advance publicity the magazine created. My personal manager in Atlanta jumped on the opportunity, arranging appearances at upscale Atlanta nightclubs and trendy restaurants for after my return from Hilton Head. Only later did I realize these local appearances were wetting my feet with the beginnings of the tidal wave about to sweep me up. They helped attune me to dealing with people's reactions, and those reactions were not quite what I expected.

Naturally, I had my share of snooty, finger-pointing prudes, but for the most part people were respectful. I discovered that when men come face to face with a girl slated to appear in a national magazine such as *Penthouse*, in full nudity and, supposedly, full sexual arousal, they often turn into a different kind of creature than they are with women they see every day. Suddenly you become a sort of goddess in their eyes: desirable, out of reach, and somewhat revered. The experience, for me, was at times a little scary. They treat you with the respect they'd show a famous actress or a work of art. Those same men might see me walking down the street in jeans and T-shirt, not recognize me, yet start whistling and catcalling, acting like a bunch of animals.

A Quick Stop at Hilton Head

Because of the sudden whirlwind of attention, Jim and I knew we needed to take my parents out of town before the local newspaper got word of my sexy centerfold. With the magazine coming out so soon, it was time to act fast.

Getting away together was a big thing for my family. We enjoyed Hilton Head because it had plenty of activities for children. Carla and Stacey stayed with my parents in one condo. Jim and I stayed in another. Dad loved the golf course, Mom loved going for walks. The kids loved the swimming pool, and Jim and I enjoyed the beach and the much-needed rest.

Although my intention was to tell both my parents about the magazine while we were vacationing, the timing had made me antsy, so I broke the news to my mom a day or so before we left. I felt on stronger ground with Mom. She came over in a great mood to chat while I was at my dressing table, getting ready to go on a shoot. At some point in the conversation the moment seemed right, so I told her.

My mother was, and still is, a modest woman, not uptight but private about such things as sex and nudity. In an era when nude beach parties were becoming popular and students were "streaking" naked on college campuses, my mom never left her bedroom without being fully covered. What I didn't know back then was that Mom might have been more like me, more independent and free-thinking, if given the same opportunities. But like other women her age, she carefully repressed such ideas in favor of her husband's.

After I finished telling Mom about the test shots, about going to New York and, finally, about the photographs that would soon be published in *Penthouse*, she thought for a moment, stunned I suspect, and speechless. I'm not certain she'd ever seen a copy of *Penthouse*, but I'm sure she'd heard of it.

Then she said in her soft, Southern manner, "If that's your decision, Vicki, then we'll support you. You've always made your own decisions. I hope this is a good one."

"What do we do about Dad?" I asked.

"I'll tell him while we're in Hilton Head." Her lips trembled slightly, and I knew the prospect worried her.

"How do you think he'll react?"

"He won't get angry, but …." She gave a big sigh. "You know that disappointed thing he does."

"He doesn't read *Penthouse*," I said, my desperate mind grasping at straws of hope. "Maybe if we don't tell him he'll never find out."

Did the conversation she intended ever take place? I don't know. Near the end of our trip, Jim and Dad went to a local quick-stop to pick up a few groceries. All the men's magazines, such as *Playboy* and of course *Penthouse,* were displayed on shelves behind the clerk. Whether it was because the issue had just come out — two weeks early — or whether the store had been notified that the Pet of the Month was from the neighboring state of Georgia, I never learned, but the shelf space allotted to *Penthouse* for that issue was more than twice what *Playboy* and the others occupied.

So there I was, in full color and mostly bare skin, positioned at eye level, with *Penthouse* blazoned in lavender above my photo. A bold subhead in the same color read: *Getting a Grip on the Great American Organ.*

Calm as a Cucumber

Jim Arnold, from an email, July 2010

Vicki and I had been married for two years the summer her issue of Penthouse hit the 7-Eleven magazine racks in our small town. Marietta, Georgia, known for its strong Bible Belt supporters, was thus introduced to a "local girl making it big" in modeling.

A few months earlier, when she told me she was going to Puerto Rico for the test shoot, I remember her saying she'd be in competition with a couple of hundred other girls who were submitting test photos.

"There's very little chance I'll win, Jim. So don't worry," she said.

"Is there any talent involved in this competition?" I asked.

"No."

"You'll win," I told her.

Not long after the centerfold came out, she began shooting for the Pet of the Year competition. Vicki was one of four models selected from the twelve centerfolds as finalists. The winner would be chosen by Penthouse *readers.*

Once again she said, "Jim, there's very little chance I'll win. So don't worry."

"Is there any talent involved?" I asked.

"No."

"Then you'll win." Later I told a friend, "My God, have you ever heard her sing?"

With all the nude modeling, you'd think we'd be able to bank a lot of wardrobe money. Anyway, getting back to when the centerfold issue first came out, Vicki was on the cover as well as inside, which turned out to be a problem. Our customer base in the automotive business was primarily NASCAR and dirt-track racing fans, all of whom believed that "NASCAR" was derived from the redneck remark, "That's a nas car you got there, buddy!"

Naturally, they all knew Vicki Lynn, not only because of her daddy's business but because at the local mud-hole tracks popular at the time, Vicki held most of the Miss Dirt Track Racing titles. The boys sure did love that Vicki Lynn.

Vicki informed me that the magazine was coming out with her picture on the cover just about the same time we were finishing our new house.

"Don't worry," she said. "I don't think the cover picture even looks like me. It'll pass with no one even knowing about it."

"Have you told your father?" I asked her.

"No." She and her mother had talked about it, she said, but believed he'd never find out.

Wrong. Conveniently, there was a Hilton Head 7-Eleven, where her dad and I went to pick up groceries. When we went to the counter to pay, there was the magazine rack dead ahead — and this gorgeous redhead staring back at us from the cover of Penthouse.

Her dad, calm as a cucumber, turned to me and said, "Did you know about this?"

"Wow," I said, still staring at the cover.

"Why didn't you tell me?"

"Carroll," I said, "not my place to tell you."

He was so cool. And that was the last time I ever heard him say a thing about it, good or bad. After I kicked his butt at golf and we returned home, Carroll found a surprise waiting in his mailbox. Someone had left him a copy of the magazine, with the centerfold unfolded, wrapped around the outside, and held in place with a rubber band.

CHAPTER 7

The Road Not Taken

J im told me later that Dad didn't say a word in the car but was visibly shaken. When they arrived back at the condos, Dad went inside, closed the door, and never mentioned the magazine again, not to me, not to Jim, not to anybody. My parents must have discussed it at some point, because later my mom told me Dad's greatest fear was that the magazine might destroy my career, my marriage, and my life.

This was at the end of our trip, so we left Hilton Head and traveled back to Marietta, where Jim and I finished moving from the apartment into our new house. Life continued rushing forward for me, the curl of that wave growing higher and higher as men in the Greater Atlanta area realized they had a genuine centerfold living in their midst. Yet when Jim and I were at home, snuggled together in our apartment or working on our new house, it seemed nothing at all had changed.

A Blush of Color

Making appearances for the magazine, I traveled considerably during those first months after my issue hit the newsstands. One day I returned from out of town, dropped my luggage off at home, and drove around the cul-de-sac to my parents' house. Still wearing my traveling clothes, including my new fox coat that matched my hair, I talked to Mom for a while. She said Dad was painting the apartment, so I walked over to say hello.

For my dad, painting was therapy. He enjoyed not only the way it made everything look new again but also the actual process of running the paint roller back and forth, back and forth over the walls. When I walked in, he stood on a ladder, painting near the ceiling. I knew he heard me come in, but he didn't look down, he just kept pushing the roller back and forth, slow and easy. The motion had a soporific effect, even on me.

"That's a beautiful color," I said.

A long moment passed as he continued painting as if in a vacuum where only his own thoughts could be heard.

Finally, while still slowly working the roller, he said, "You like it?"

"Yes, I do, Dad. It's really nice."

"I chose it just for you." He never once looked at me, but I detected a slight smile. "It's called 'Nude.'"

It's Not a Twin

Life accelerated unbelievably. Not only was I still booked with modeling jobs in Atlanta and making the appearances my personal manager had arranged, but also the *Penthouse* promotions department sent me on assignments. Around Atlanta, my fame skyrocketed.

One day I went to the bank to make a deposit. This was my first time going inside to the window since the magazine had come out, and while the teller was handling my transaction, I noticed a security guard watching me. After a moment, he came over.

"I hope you won't be offended," he said, speaking low and stumbling over his words, "but if you want to see your twin, take a look at the August issue of *Penthouse* magazine."

I smiled, not embarrassed but also not accustomed to being face to face with a man who'd seen me naked in twenty-nine explicit photographs. I had to make an instant decision: *Am I going to own up to this? Or should I change banks?*

"It's not a twin," I managed to say with a semblance of confidence. "It's me."

The effect was the same as if someone had hit the man with a hammer. As he stood there totally speechless, I stuck out my hand to shake his in a friendly but business-like gesture.

"Victoria Lynn Johnson Arnold," I said. "For the magazine, I dropped the last two names."

His mouth opened, but he apparently couldn't think of another word to say.

"Don't be shocked. It's just another modeling job." I smiled again, picked up my deposit slip from the teller and said, "I'll see you guys later."

By the time I opened the door, the place was buzzing like a beehive. Wishing I could hear what they were saying, I walked out with knots in my stomach but a little more confidence in my step, feeling happy that I hadn't weaseled out.

Celebrity Husband

Men coming up to ask for my autograph were fascinating to watch. Some smiled suggestively, others stumbled for words, their self-confidence toward women suddenly gone. Having modeled since I was sixteen, I was accustomed to getting attention, but the way men reacted now was completely new.

And as fascinated as my fans were with me, braving their way forward, carrying a copy of my *Penthouse* issue, and asking for an autograph, I was equally fascinated with being asked. Locals too shy or embarrassed to inquire directly if that was me in the magazine secretly asked our friends. Jim's best friend was questioned fifty or sixty times, he told us, within two weeks.

In addition to signing photographs and copies of the magazine, I also autographed napkins, both paper and cloth, drivers' licenses, hands, arms, bald heads and abs, T-shirts or whatever a fan wore, even if it was silk, from the waist up — that's as far as I'd go. I signed one magazine six times, because the six guys who pitched in to buy it planned to cut it apart and split it between them. A girl asked if I'd sign a magazine for her fiancé. One guy at an airport bought two copies, one for himself, another for his father.

Through all the commotion, Jim remained supportive and enjoyed people treating him like a "celebrity husband." One day he took his car to a shop for repairs.

"How much is this going to set me back?" he asked the mechanic.

"Not more than a million or so," the man replied, grinning. "And if you'll get your wife to sign a copy of *Penthouse* for me, it'll cost you nothing."

"You got a deal," Jim said, his business mind already calculating other bargains he might strike with my centerfold as currency.

So Jim took orders, I signed the magazines and he delivered them, all in fun. Years later, Jim told his friends, "It was the biggest thing that ever happened in Cobb County."

Action Before Thought

As a teenager, I loved any social or physical activity — drill team, Homecoming events, making floats, setting up parades, anything that would take me outside the boring classrooms — and one of my favorite extracurricular activities was Drama Club. How I became president, I have no idea, because I'd cultivated no particular talent. I didn't sing, dance, or play a musical instrument. When one of the pageants I entered required having a "talent," I took singing and dance lessons to prepare. Pageant day came. I wore a green and yellow outfit festooned with flowers. My hip version of "Singin' in the Rain," with my plastic umbrella, didn't bring a standing ovation, but I did receive polite applause, and I placed in the finals.

For better or worse, one of my overriding personality traits is action before thought. I tend to say "yes" to a challenge, then figure out later how to make it happen. This was as true in acting as in any other part of my life. And for whatever I took on, I'd do the best I could to prepare. I'd practice, practice, and practice again until, despite any inadequacies, I somehow managed to shine.

Before *Penthouse*, and around the time of my six months of misery lugging my model book along the streets of Manhattan, film producers discovered me. Some of the acting jobs came through modeling agencies; others I got by word of mouth.

Anytime I had a break in my schedule, I took a class at the Estelle Harmon Acting School in New York or a seminar at the New York Academy of Theatrical Arts. I enjoyed acting, got glowing reports, and one of my prizes when I became Pet of the Year was a scholarship to the Academy. Admissions told me I was the only winner who'd ever used that prize.

Screaming Comes Naturally

On October 29th of 1975, a few months before the call from Stan Malinowski about the *Penthouse* test shots, I found myself once again standing before a panel of men who expected me to perform. This was my first movie audition.

"We're looking for an actress to play the role of Gail, a forest ranger," one of the producers told me. "We'll be filming in the North Georgia mountains, and it will be a fairly long shoot, so we'd like to use local talent as much as possible."

A forest ranger — did that mean I'd get to keep my clothes on? Where was the script? What were my lines?

Instead of giving me pages of dialogue to read, one of them began laying out a scene.

"You're deep in the forest, and you know two women have been horribly ripped to pieces. Along with the other rangers, you've been searching for the killer grizzly, but you're certain it has moved on. So when you see a crystal-clear mountain brook and a waterfall, you decide to stop and rinse off. Under the silvery veil of the waterfall, you suddenly see a huge black monster in front of you. You're stunned, terrified, panicked."

He described the scene so well, I was actually feeling the fear he wanted to invoke. Faking it might not be a problem.

"What would you do?" he said. "How would you scream?"

No script, just a scream. In an office. Who knew what people outside the door might hear? It seemed weird.

"Take a moment to imagine the scene," he said, pointing me toward a corner of the room. "Then do exactly what feels right at the instant you see the monster."

Going to the corner as directed, I closed my eyes and tried to get into the eerie mood of tracking a grizzly. Imagining the shadowy forest, the inviting brook, the silvery waterfall, I took a deep breath, clenched my fists, and, "AHHHHHHHH!"

Over and over and over again I screamed, feeling like an absolute idiot, until they told me to stop.

"Thank you," they said. "We'll be in touch."

I don't remember ever reading a line of dialogue, yet the next thing I knew, I had the co-starring role of Ranger Gail. *Grizzly* began shooting on November 17th, 1975, with several name actors on board. Andrew Prine, who started on Broadway, had become popular in Hollywood, especially in Westerns. A bit of trivia: Andy posed nude for the May 1974 issue of *Viva*. Richard Jaeckel was best known for his war movies and for *Sometimes a Great Notion*, for which he received an Academy Award nomination for Best Supporting Actor. Christopher George, the handsome leading man, had won a Golden Globe for his TV series *The Rat Patrol*, and had posed nude in the June 1974 issue of *Playgirl*.

Having a co-starring role in the company of such admirable Hollywood talent was an experience most actresses would covet — even if I did get killed twenty minutes into the film. At the time,

I didn't fully realize the importance of the opportunity. This was my first time on a movie set, and I was merely concerned with doing it right.

In the film's opening scene, I'm driving into the forest. In the next scene, the other rangers are being briefed about two missing girls, and I'm late. After the girls' bodies are discovered, we begin scouting for the killer, which we've now determined is a giant grizzly. As the search winds down, we're hot, tired, disappointed, and this, of course, is where I meet my demise — in the film and almost in reality.

The director warned me that the waterfall scene would be difficult. In the movie, the sun is shining and it's supposed to be summer — but this was November. It's remarkable that even in the role of a forest ranger on the hunt for a crazed man-killing grizzly, my character decides "Oh well, strip off and get wet." So once again, I was in the Georgia mountains, taking my clothes off, only this time I had the added torture of being soaked and frozen stiff.

At any time of year, the mountain streams are too cold for swimming. After peeling off my uniform, I strolled across the rocky landscape in my bikini panties and bra and ventured under the waterfall, all the while worrying about getting it right, not screwing up the scene. I was already cold, and the shock of the water took my breath away. In truth, I didn't really need to act because the water was so cold that my body started to shake, tremble, and cringe. Screaming came naturally.

In the film, you don't see the monster grizzly, just a huge black arm that comes out and grabs me. Then you see my face contort in a scream, and the water turns red with my blood. Sadly, I'm gone.

The crew had oxygen waiting for me, along with blankets, heaters, smelling salts, and a thermometer. I have a photograph that was shot seconds after they brought me out of the waterfall, my face white with shock, the heat lamps on, and people holding

Such a small roll. Park Ranger in the movie, Grizzly. But low and behold... in 2016, a close friend brought me a t-shirt she had purchased at a popular store in the local mall. Apparently, my little known movie had developed a cult following! On the front of the shirt was an image that bore a striking resemblance to ME! I was shocked!

me to get me warm. After a while, I warmed up enough that we started all over with the next take.

Coming hard on the heels of the blockbuster *Jaws*, this little film was produced for less than $1 million and managed to gross $39 million. It also spawned a sequel, *Grizzly II*. For such a small-budget film, I was paid well, and I developed a deep respect for my fellow actors. The townspeople appreciated our bringing the excitement of Hollywood, as well as the revenue, to their community, and despite the difficult waterfall scene, the entire experience was one I'll always recall with fondness.

Grizzly opened in theaters in May 1976. Around that same time, I was making the test shots for *Penthouse.*

Extraterrestrial Sex

Film producer Ken Gourd saw my credits for *Grizzly* and my centerfold in *Penthouse* and passed them along to his co-producers, Ed Hunt and Norman Glick. Together, they were making *Starship Invasions* for Hal Roach Studios in Canada. The magazine's film department got a call and put me in touch with Ken Gourd.

Again, I worked with two impressive stars. Robert Vaughn took time off from his starring role in the TV series, *The Man from U.N.C.L.E.* British actor Christopher Lee, so elegant, so proper, such a lovely man, was hard to imagine as *Dracula,* Fu Manchu, and *The Mummy*, the villainous roles that made him famous. For me, this was another coveted acting job squeezed in between appearances for *Penthouse* and my modeling assignments. We filmed in Canada periodically for about eight weeks.

Captain Ramses, the bad-guy alien played by Christopher Lee, comes to our spaceship under the false pretense of gaining information for his planet. He sees me, Gazeth, a good alien who's trying to save Earth, and he's attracted. We meet in a common area of the ship and, surrounded by walls of mirrors, engage in an extraterrestrial love scene. The film crew shot it two ways, of course, with clothes and without clothes, although it was never meant to be a fully nude scene. Alien lovemaking required no actual touching, and I never took off the most important items of alien clothing, my long black gloves.

In my last scene, I'm at the spaceship's controls. The bad aliens rush in and zap me with their lasers, and I die.

If you're fortunate enough to get a death scene, it's all about how you die. I died gracefully in a perfect curve of body, face, and hair, so that my corpse could lie on the floor, my hair spilling out around me in a lovely auburn fan, while they finished shooting. For several days, my job was to go to the studio in full makeup and my skimpy black-and-brown costume and lie on the floor while the other actors stepped delicately over and around my dead body. Occasionally, one would acknowledge that I was dead and there was nothing they could do. Oh, my, how tragic.

Again I received a costar billing, which looked good on my résumé, I was paid well, and I especially enjoyed working with such outstanding actors. During our nightly dinners at the hotel, as Robert Vaughn and Christopher Lee reminisced about their amazing careers and lives, I soaked up every word.

Six Famous Words

In the future, I would appear in other minor films and on several popular television shows, but the movie everyone most remembers, and which was shot during this same 1975-1976 period, was *Smokey and the Bandit*.

This time we were shooting in the warmer areas of Georgia. The racetrack scene was filmed at Lakewood Speedway, part of the old Lakewood Fairgrounds on the south side of Atlanta. The roller coaster, "Greyhound" in the movie, had long been out of operation and was refurbished especially for the film.

My scene wasn't with Burt Reynolds, although he was on the set that day. Nor did I appear with Sally Field. The stars in my scene were actor-comedian Pat McCormick and Oscar-winning song writer-actor Paul Williams.

McCormick, six-foot-eight, two-hundred-fifty pounds and sporting a handlebar moustache, played Big Enos Burdette. Williams, five-foot-two, played Little Enos. In the scene, I'm standing next to my trucker boyfriend and his eighteen-wheeler when Big Enos and Little Enos walk over.

Big Enos asks, "Where's the Bandit?"

And I deliver my famous line: "He's over there by the rig."

That was it. Six words, and there's not a person in my life who doesn't give me credit for being in *Smokey and the Bandit*. It doesn't seem to matter how little time I spent on screen. Blink and you'd miss me. But there's rarely an article or a conversation about me that doesn't get around to "And she was in *Smokey and the Bandit*." Since its release in 1977, when it grossed $126,737,428, it's been running continuously on network stations or cable stations, and I still get residual checks. Every time it runs somebody will call and say, "I just watched *Smokey and the Bandit* again, and there you were!"

I can't help wondering if *Penthouse* hadn't come along when it did, and in a big way, would I have taken my movie career more seriously? I enjoyed acting, but who knows?

I do know that I worked hard to become more than just a model. While at college, intent on eradicating my Georgia accent, I'd listened carefully to my roommates' northern dialects. I read vocabulary books and took speech classes. I strived to overcome my lack of formal education.

When I read about myself in press articles, I scanned quickly past comments about my clothes, my makeup, my fingernails, my high-heel boots, how "pretty" I was, or that my photos were

My scene in Smokey and the Bandit unfortunately did not include Sally Field or Burt Reynolds.

beautiful or sexy. When a writer said, "She's surprisingly articulate and witty," or "She's incredibly smart and talented," or "Despite her success, she's a normal, down-to-earth woman who comes from a good, loving family," I paid attention. Those remarks resonated with me. They focused on accomplishments I was most proud of and validated my need to be seen as a woman of substance.

You Belong on Stage

Philip Nolan, director of the New York Theatrical Academy of Arts, followed Victoria's career and graciously wrote this letter after her appearance on the David Susskind Show in February 1983. She appeared that night with spokespersons for the Women's Liberation Movement: Bella Abzug, lawyer, congresswoman, social activist; and Gloria Steinem, feminist, journalist, social/political activist, and co-founder/editor in chief of *Ms.* Magazine.

Dear Vicki,

I should like to extend my compliments to you for your appearance on The David Susskind Show, which pleased me no end, last Sunday.

The aplomb and élan with which you presented yourself was a delight to my eyes and ears.

I am justly proud of your articulate Speech Delivery as well as your Poise and Stage Presence. Indeed, you offered a marvelous rebuttal to those non-entities who tried to denigrate Bob Guccione, Penthouse *and its objectives.*

Of course, I've always been Bob's fan and an advocate of the Magazine. And Vicki — you belong on Stage. Do stay in touch.

With warmest regards,
Philip Nolan

A World Apart

Even before making my film debut as Ranger Gail in *Grizzly*, I found acting much more interesting than modeling and discovered I was good at getting into roles. To overcome my lack of commercial experience with copy, I practiced often. My goal was to work continuously, whatever the assignment, and although I was still relatively unknown to national advertising agencies, I was a frequent presence in the Atlanta media.

Photographers enjoyed working with me because no matter what the situation I arrived on time and well prepared, and in an era studded with perky blondes — Olivia Newton-John, Farrah Fawcett, Cheryl Tiegs — a fiery redhead attracted attention. One day I went to an audition that promised to be a challenge. Kathy, from Atlanta Models and Talent, admitted she was sending me as a last resort.

"Don't give me any hassle about this, Victoria." Always gruff and bigger than life, Kathy sounded even more stressed than usual. "I know you're not right for it. Just go."

"Okay. You've got the address?"

After Kathy rattled it off, she added, "It's for Shake 'n Bake. You *do* know what that is?"

"I've heard of it." Growing up, I'd heard their obnoxious TV commercials, but I was too health conscious for Shake 'n Bake.

"You need to pull your hair back. Wear some kind of white shirt, not too much makeup. You're supposed to be a mother of twins, about thirty-two years old."

"*Thirty-two?*" A model's glamorous career is over when she's old enough for "mother" roles. "Kathy, I'm a decade too young, and I've never worked with kids. Can I pass for a thirty-two-year-old mom?"

"These people are determined to find a talent in Georgia with authentic Southern style. I've sent everybody I know, and they've rejected them all." When she paused, I could hear her shuffling papers. "By the way, you'll need to fake that Southern accent you used to have."

I covered the mouthpiece so Kathy wouldn't hear the exasperated sigh that hissed through my teeth. Having spent time, energy, and money on ridding my voice of "ain't," "y'all," "fixin," and the elongated vowel sounds that marked me as a Georgia native, I wasn't eager to revisit that ground. But Kathy needed me to do this and do a good job of it. I swallowed my resistance and decided to think of it as acting more than merely modeling.

The client was Ogilvy & Mather, a prominent New York advertising agency. Dressed as Kathy directed, I arrived at their local office, temporarily rented for auditions, feeling slightly annoyed to be presenting myself as a dowdy housewife, so different from roles I normally played. *Penthouse* was not yet on my résumé, and these talent scouts hadn't seen me frolicking naked through the woods as "Eve" on Walnut Mountain. I was merely another local talent.

In my white shirt and sweater, hair tied back with a ribbon, I got into the role as directed, determined to make this video reading the best it could be. Each of my lines followed an off-camera voice blandly reciting the parts of my "husband" and two "children." As I read the script, my voice oozed the syrupy Southern drawl I'd so painstakingly drummed out of it.

Suzie: *Can we help you fry chicken, Mama?*

Sally: *I want to help!*

Victoria: *I don't fry chicken anymore. But you can both help me with the Shake 'n Bake. Suzie, you shake, and Sally, you bake.*

Husband: *Fine fried chicken, honey. Real crispy. Moist and tender, too.*

Suzie: *Mama didn't fry it, Daddy.*

Husband: *It's crispy like fried.*

Out of character as the "Shake N' Bake Mom"

Sally: *It's Shake 'n Bake.*

Both girls: *And we helped!*

Victoria, voice over: *Shake 'n Bake coating mix — it's better than frying.*

A week later, Kathy phoned again. "You got a call-back on Shake 'n Bake."

"Oh, god." Of all the parts to get a call-back on, this was the worst.

"I'm as surprised as you are. Just think about the money, Victoria. This is a national commercial with an eighteen-month initial run."

I reluctantly returned, wearing the same dowdy look, and read through the entire commercial again. Another week passed before the announcement came from Kathy — I was the new Shake 'n Bake mom.

At the time I'd not heard of photographer Stan Malinowski and had no idea of what lay ahead with *Penthouse*, but the magazine came out while the commercial was still running. The two images couldn't be more at odds.

One Big Explosion

Knowing I might encounter someone from the press when I arrived at the shooting for such a prominent commercial, I dressed professionally and glamorously. I stepped from my gold Mercury Cougar, hoping that anyone watching might think I'd arrived straight from a major Hollywood movie studio.

And indeed, the location looked more like a movie set than the setting for a television commercial. Five movie trailers and a crew of thirty-something had transformed an idyllic traditional home in a posh Atlanta suburb to a confusion of activity. Inside the house, set designers, lighting crews, sound crews, camera crews, gaffers, go-fers, and various administrative types rushed in one door and out another.

I'd learned that the agency was actually doing a remake of the popular black-and-white commercial from the late 1960s, and the intention was to recreate in color the original pure Southern hokum in every way possible. People darted in and out with cameras and film canisters, scripts and supplies, no one clearly in charge. Finally, a woman wearing baggy jeans, sweatshirt, and loafers, with coral lipstick chewed off to a ragged outline, noticed me and approached.

"Who are *you*," she demanded, looking down at her clipboard.

"Victoria Johnson."

The woman jabbed her pencil at her board, glanced at me then flipped pages. "This says you're the *talent*."

"That's right."

Her scowl darted from my hair to my clothes, shoes, then back to my hair again.

"No, huh-uh, no. You're not the Victoria Johnson we hired."

"Yes, I'm Victoria Johnson from Atlanta Models and Talent."

"You didn't look like *that* on our audition tape. You did *not* have red hair."

"My hair has always been red. It was pulled back, and I wore different clothes — which I have in my bag."

"You *can't* have red hair. We cannot use red hair." She walked away shaking her head. "Wait there. Don't *move*. I'll be back."

As it turned out, the local film crew had used black-and-white video to tape the auditions. The New York agency execs took my red hair for brown, which was the color they wanted, and no one had asked about the actual color. Listening to them, I felt totally unwelcome. With seven years of modeling behind me, I'd established a level of excellence. I brought a variety of clothing and accessories, and I tried to immerse myself in the mood of a moment with very little coaching. Yet my hair was frequently the main reason I was hired. With Shake 'n Bake, this apparently wasn't the case.

After a while, the stylist came in to determine what to do about my hair.

"We could dye it," she told the line producer.

"How long would that take?"

"We can be back on schedule in a couple of hours."

Realizing what they were about to do brought me to the edge of hysteria. Before they could whisk me away to a bathroom sink and a bottle of Clairol, I spoke up.

"No! We are absolutely *not* going to dye my hair." I was willing to go along to a point, but that was a deal breaker.

"All right, no problem," the stylist said in a consoling tone. "Next best, we'll spray it with Nestlé's. It comes in dark brown and will wash right out."

They lacquered my hair. It was like wearing a helmet, but the agency got what they wanted — the clothes, the hair, the makeup, the setting, the twins, and my "authentic" Georgia drawl. Eight-year-old twin girls, much like the pair used in the original, played the role of my daughters. The shoot went extremely well. Most important, the agency was happy, their client was happy, and Kathy was elated.

This was my first big SAG commercial, and it turned out to be my most financially successful commercial ever, running day in/ day out on national network television. Walking through my living room, where the TV was playing, I'd hear that famous line — *And we helllllped!* I'd cringe and keep going, happy that the next residual check was on its way. Although I'd never tasted Shake 'n Bake, it was furnishing my new house.

Because of the lacquered-down hair and the clothes, few people realized that chic, red-haired Victoria Johnson, known for Atlanta's most provocative ads, was also the Southern mom touting Shake 'n Bake during the breaks between their favorite TV shows. The two images of me were a world apart. Otherwise, my most successful TV commercial and most transformational magazine layout might have clashed in one big explosion during that summer of 1976.

CHAPTER 8

Frequent Flyer

When an airplane takes off, everything has to come together perfectly, every screw, wire, and instrument in unison. Meanwhile, the air controller, baggage handler, runway personnel, and pilot do their jobs. When everything comes together, you go.

The bits and pieces of my new life were coming together. At twenty-four and already a top working model in Atlanta, I was far from aging out, but I hadn't intended to take up modeling as a permanent profession. What was next? And what could I do better than *Penthouse* to bid an audacious and memorable "goodbye" to the industry. If an opportunity to do the roles I enjoyed and excelled at had come along, or if I'd been more secure with my undeveloped talent, I might have pursued acting further. I didn't believe anyone would take me as a serious actress until I proved myself, which meant devoting time and study to the craft and sacrificing the life I'd already made for myself. Yes, I took risks, but only those I felt confident in pulling off. Even more than I feared failure, I feared the pressure of success. What if I acquired a starring role and couldn't bring enough talent to the screen day in and day out?

In any case, I hadn't yet climbed the acting ladder when *Penthouse* came along, plucked me out of Atlanta, and opened new doors for me in New York. Once my centerfold was published, my new life came together, and I took my new commitment seriously.

All Within Two Months

Determined to make my overnight celebrity legitimate and acceptable, I focused my best efforts behind my controversial decision, pouring all my skills, talent, and intelligence, which no one knew I had, into validating a job that many considered less than reputable. Taking the initiative to circulate my résumés and apprise myself of articles or blurbs written about me, I began putting a better frame around this slightly tainted photograph.

Penthouse sent me on appearances, but I wanted to balance that work with jobs I acquired on my own, and since the phone rang constantly with modeling offers, I could finally be choosy. All manner of media called — newspapers, radio, television. I made appearances all over Georgia. Then I was off to New York again for meetings with Kathy Keeton and other executives at the magazine, fittings and photo shoots. After doing fashion layouts and editorials in both *Penthouse* and *Viva*, *Penthouse* catalogs and covers for *Forum* magazine, I flew back to Atlanta, then to Foley's Department Store in Houston for a *Penthouse* promotion, followed by an appearance at a convention in New Orleans for *Penthouse*, and finally back to New York to attend the party for the 1976 Pet of the Year — all within two months.

In that brief time, I discovered, and appreciated, that *Penthouse* was accepted across a broad segment of society, including well respected family markets. Between traveling, packing for travel, making myself beautiful for assignments, working the assignments, and occasionally crashing for a few hours so I wouldn't get bags under my eyes, my calendar was packed — forget having a social life.

You Don't Look Big Enough

It was hard work but it was also exciting, and every new event was in some way eye-opening. Being a centerfold automatically comes with admiration from some, criticism from others, and the occasional lewd remark.

Just before my centerfold was published, I visited my dentist in Atlanta, Ronnie Goldstein. I'd been going to him since my first modeling job. Ronnie was great, but his uncle, who was an orthodontist in the same building, was your typical dirty old man. His comment when he heard that I was slated for the centerfold was, "You don't look big enough to be a centerfold." After publication, he said, "You know what I liked best about your layout? Your facial expressions. They looked real, like you're having a real orgasm. You looked so big. I suppose you do look big enough to be a centerfold." He didn't mean my height.

In good days, with great friends, Myself and Dr. Ken Horwitz, and Judy and Dr. Ron Goldstein. Houston may have been a new adventure, and Ken made it warm and welcoming

I never told Ronnie what his uncle said, but I did go upstairs to his office and mention that I was only twenty-two days into my centerfold and already getting sick of all the questions about *Penthouse*. Ronnie said, "Victoria, it seems like old news to you, it seems repetitious and tiresome, but it's still new and exciting to everybody else."

Storing his comment in the back of my mind, I vowed to appreciate every fan for caring enough to buy the magazine and to treat every question as if it was the first time I'd been asked. Around this same time, I remember being in an airport, picking up a copy of *Cosmopolitan* to read on the plane, and seeing a man in front of me purchase my issue of *Penthouse*. I can't deny feeling a little thrill of fame when he turned and saw my face. He looked down at his magazine and up again with that glimmer of recognition in his eyes. He wasn't certain enough, or maybe bold enough, to ask for my autograph, but in future travels, my fans would become bolder.

A Better Frame

Where *Penthouse* originated, in England, "pet" is an affectionate term for a woman or sweetheart. My English friends might say, "Hello, pet" or "Oh, she's such a doll, such a pet."

So it's not a derogatory term at all. The Penthouse Club also originated in England. And just as Playboy Bunnies wear their cotton tails and ears at the Playboy Clubs, the Pets at the Penthouse Club also had a uniform.

For one of my earliest appearances with three other centerfolds, Kathy Keeton sent costumes from London for the four of us to wear. Mine was blue velvet with a white organza apron and hat, sort of an R-rated version of an old-fashioned English bar wench. The other girls' costumes were the same, only in different colors or patterns. In a photograph, the four of us are walking down a hallway together, looking ridiculous, in my opinion, certainly not chic.

Tattered from being worn by many Pets at the London club, the outfits didn't fit well. After wearing mine a second time, I approached Kathy and told her I thought we could do much better than that.

"Instead of trying to fit all the girls in these same costumes, why not allow everyone to dress stylishly according to the event, appropriate day or evening wear. Sexy without being risqué."

I could see Kathy considering it, but I hadn't quite won her over.

"These costumes are rather adorable," I said, "but we look as if we're trying too hard to be like *Playboy*."

The key word was "*Playboy*." I'd planted the thought, but it had to be Kathy's idea. Regardless of her decision, I planned never to wear the ridiculous costume again. It was outdated, overdone, and embarrassing.

Kathy never acknowledged that she agreed, but the costumes disappeared and were never again used for promotions. Instead, we wore clothes appropriate for the occasion.

A short time later, I also requested the magazine provide me with a New York apartment. I was commuting so often from Atlanta, spending so much more time in New York, that the cost wouldn't be nearly as much as hotel rooms, and having my own place locally would save hours of time packing and unpacking.

Making this request was bold, but it was also necessary. To do as much for the magazine as they had in mind and put as much of my energy into being the best centerfold Kathy or Bob ever encountered — as I had in mind — having a New York apartment was simply crucial.

Vicki Came to Penthouse *with Her Own Rules*
Jeff Zelmanski
Previous to Vicki, the magazine didn't give the centerfolds special treatment. People treated Vicki well because she expected it. She

showed me that it was important to treat all the centerfolds well because they represented the magazine. When Vicki came to New York, she came with her own rules, and she was a tough negotiator. She wanted an apartment. A car service. She initiated the possibility of the girls getting a clothing allowance. Vicki's Pet of the Year party was at Rockefeller Center's Rainbow Room. In previous years, we held parties in smaller venues.

Later, when Vicki was selling her apartment, the magazine's lawyer was the one helping her. I met him when he came back from one of the loan meetings.

"Vicki's incredible," he said." The way she was wheeling and dealing, she should work here. *It was amazing."*

Vicki was also the only model who ever paid the magazine back.

Jeff Zelmanski never failed me. I knew from the moment I met him when we were just starting out in our careers. So very young in New York City... both with Penthouse Magazine, the friendship we forged would last a lifetime. And it sure did. He accompanied me to my 50th high school reunion.

Dinners at "The House"

Often, when I was in New York, I'd get a call from Jane Homlish, Bob's assistant.

"Kathy and Bob are having a small dinner party. They would like you to come."

No longer living at the rented Judy Garland townhouse, where I'd first met them, they'd renovated two townhouses on East 67th Street into one nine-level, forty-five room, 27,000-square-foot mansion. When completed, "The House," as it was dubbed by office and staff personnel, as if it was the only house in existence, became the largest single dwelling in Manhattan.

In addition to Bob and Kathy's expansive residence, it held abundant office space, and Bob shot most of his photographic layouts in the various bedrooms and living areas. Strategically placed skylights provided natural lighting. Bob rarely visited the magazine's corporate offices. He worked his own schedule, and people came to him.

Invitations to The House made me feel like part of the magazine's extended family. A "small" dinner party might include Bob, Kathy, me, Bob's family, and any visiting models, or it might be a collection of Who's Who in New York politics, art, and business. At various times, I recall dining with artist LeRoy Neiman, designer Pauline Trigere, actors Peter Ustinov and Michael Douglas, sex expert Dr. Ruth Westheimer, infamous attorney Roy Cohn, governor of New York Mario Cuomo, and a diverse host of other famous artists and local dignitaries.

At my first occasion to dine at the Guccione table, my place was set immediately to Bob's left. The table was long, with Bob sitting at the head, Kathy on his right, and I sat directly across from her. That became my seat anytime I was in town. For all the years I was with the magazine, Kathy was always on his right, I on his left, and no one ever got my chair. Ever.

If I came down to dinner, and guests were already in the process of sitting down, Bob would say, "This is Vicki's chair. I would like Vicki to sit here."

The other girls, of whom there were usually two or three living at "the house" while being photographed or interviewed or between residences, would disperse themselves among the other invited guests around the massive table. Throughout the years, many of the girls vied for my chair — not for Kathy's, no one would try to cross that line — but they thought my seat was fair game. They never got it.

Commute from Atlanta

In Georgia, Jim experienced the first amazing year of *Penthouse* publicity, both good and bad. Married for almost three years, we were still very much in love, and while we'd never had serious money problems, my current success as a model and actress was providing a lifestyle far above what we'd known in the past. Supplementing my continuous and generous *Penthouse* fee, and other modeling fees, residuals came in from Shake 'n Bake and movie contracts. Except for my frequent absences, we couldn't ask for a better life.

Jim didn't mind at playing bachelor while I was away. Our new house was fabulous, and my traveling gave him an opportunity to play golf, ignore chores, and hang out with his buddies, who eagerly awaited the latest about *Penthouse*. Jim was having just as good a time with it, I hoped, as I was, and he certainly kept his sense of humor.

Penthouse Magazine, the Golden Years
From Penthouse *Historical Resource Material*

Sharp reporting on timely and controversial issues brought *Penthouse* magazine and its writers an impressive collection of editorial accolades, honors and awards. In 1981 the American Society of Journalists and Authors named *Penthouse* "Magazine of the Year," and in 1985 the magazine received the prestigious New York Art Directors' Club "Gold Medal in Photography." *Penthouse* also received numerous citations from the Overseas Press Club.

Besides being a force to be reckoned with on the newsstands, editorially *Penthouse* never shied away from controversial issues and First Amendment causes. *Penthouse* became famous for its monthly column, "The Vietnam Veterans Adviser," which explored the treatment vets received after returning to the United States. This was the first of its kind, a regular forum dedicated to such a controversial issue in a national publication. *Penthouse* received hundreds of thousands of letters and devoted itself monthly to fighting for veterans' rights.

Did these and similar articles reflect the views of publisher Bob Guccione? It's widely known that he was a firm believer that conspiracy groups controlled many of the country's most notorious decisions and actions. Judging by the magazine's popularity, a large portion of the American population agreed with him.

While the magazine's journalistic slant was debatably contentious, the interviews were more mainstream yet noteworthy. Between 1969 and 1982, interview subjects included such diverse luminaries as: Fidel Castro, Reverend Jerry Falwell, Germaine Greer, Robert Redford, Henry Kissinger ... Jimmy Carter, Raquel Welch, Steve Martin, Gore Vidal, Jackie Mason, Rajiv Ghandi, John and Yoko, Pierre Cardin, Pete Seeger ... Gene Roddenberry, Stevie Wonder, Vincent Bugliosi, Ted Turner, Reverend Jesse Jackson, Lee Marvin, Willie Nelson, and Charles Schultz.

Bob Guccione created national headlines in 1983 when nude photographs of the current Miss America, Vanessa Williams, appeared in the magazine, causing her to relinquish her crown. "I didn't ruin her career. I made her career," Bob commented. And indeed, today Ms. Williams's own website bio admits, "The controversy that followed only left Vanessa stronger and more empowered in her commitment to a career in the world of entertainment." *Penthouse* followed up this coup with never before seen nude photos of both Madonna and supermodel Lauren Hutton. The Vanessa Williams issue was so popular it became one of the only two magazines in history that ever went back to print because of public demand. The other was *Atlantic Monthly*.

During the golden years, an international array of stunning women graced the pages of *Penthouse*. As testament to this unique source of beauty and award-winning journalism during those years, the magazine sold 3,100 copies per hour, 24 hours a day, 365 days a year.

Moving Forward

Days I spent at home in Atlanta became my downtime, a chance to relax, give my mind a rest, and regroup before returning to my busy life in New York. During these periods, I enjoyed taking care of the house, cooking, and having small dinner parties. Jim loved going to nightclubs where we could listen to live music. We both enjoyed getting out and about, going to movies and our favorite restaurants. These daily activities most people take for granted gave me strength to sustain my two lives.

Mom and Dad came to terms with my infamous new lifestyle. Jim's father was okay with it—he had a wild side—but I was never sure about Jim's mother. Nevertheless, it was our life, mine and Jim's, and they loved their son.

Most women would have found this an intensely satisfying way of life. Great parents, great job, a totally devoted husband who supported my wildest whims, and I *did* love my life.

But I also needed to keep going forward, doing something new and different, gaining new knowledge and new experiences. No matter how perfect my days and nights might feel when I was at home, I was always driven to do more, to move on. Something was always pushing me, whispering to me: This is not forever.

Pet of the Year

Of the twelve models that appear each year in the coveted centerfold, four are selected as finalists for "Pet of the Year." Photos from the original shoot accompany the announcement in the June issue. During the years I modeled for *Penthouse*, mid 1970s to early 1980s, Bob Guccione photographed the four finalists individually in anticipation of announcing the winner. Millions of *Penthouse* readers voted, Bob's "Pet of the Year" photo layout of the winner appeared in a special fall issue, and the lucky model received "a queen's ransom" in cash and prizes.

Penthouse was as professional an organization as any I'd ever encountered. During my tidal wave months, it quickly became evident I was a finalist. No one had to say it. The reality floated subliminally as Kathy selected me for the more elite ad campaigns, Jeff sent me to appear at the most desirable functions, and high-profile media interviews focused on my career. Anytime a model was expected to represent the magazine as more than a sexy mannequin, to speak and interact with fans, public officials, or with the general public, I was called upon.

More than actually posing for photographs, I loved being involved in all these spectacular events, meeting stimulating new acquaintances from places I'd never been or learning about fascinating occupations I'd never encountered. It was such a compliment to be chosen. For the first time since my modeling career began, a client looked beyond my physical appearance and gave me an opportunity to use my intelligence. Who could have imagined it would be *Penthouse* Magazine?

Bob Came to the Office in Spirit

Irwin E. Billman, Former Executive Vice President, Chief Operating Officer, Penthouse Group

Before I started at Penthouse *magazine, on October 1, 1971, I was given two weeks in England to learn more about the magazine and company background. My first job was to efficiently raise the print order. We were selling around eighty percent of the copies we printed. For the Christmas issue in 1971, I raised the print order to a million copies and the cover price from seventy-five cents to a dollar. We sold 700,000 copies. It did very well.*

Every couple of months we would look at the numbers and raise the print order again. When we cracked the million at one point we had a big celebration, then we kept going to over six million in the second half of the 1970s.

In the early days after coming to New York, we rented an office at 1560 Broadway, a large space with two desks. Bob Guccione's name was on one desk, my name on the other, and he never showed up. So it was my office and secretary, but Bob was there in spirit. He and I were very close friends for a long period of time.

The success of Penthouse *was its publisher. The magazine was superb, and we rivaled* Playboy *in every way, yet we were the up-starts. Bob coined the phrase, "We're going rabbit hunting" and published it in a full-page* New York Times *ad. The artwork depicted the* Playboy *bunny caught in a rifle's crosshairs. The phrase caught on and hung on. We introduced pubic hair in the magazine in the early '70s, showing a lot more of a woman's physical anatomy than* Playboy. *It was obvious from our sales that's what people wanted at that time in America. Cigarette advertising, automobile advertising, all the major advertisers wanted to be in* Penthouse. *In fact, when the first 7-Eleven store opened in Manhattan, Bob and I cut the ribbon with their CEO. That's the status* Penthouse *had in those days.*

If I Won …

During that hectic time in New York City, I applied my talents to making the most of my new "celebrity" status. Meanwhile, my home in Atlanta kept me grounded. Between these two worlds, I was living the most exciting and emotionally gratifying years of my life.

In December 1976, I attended the celebration party for the current Pet of the Year, and for me, the entire evening was like peeking into a crystal ball, previewing what I could anticipate a year later — if I won. Looking around that room, I focused on previous centerfolds, all attractive, talented, equally positioned to be the next Pet of the Year, and tried to discern the quality that established one of them as the favorite.

A few had mastered the chastely innocent girl-next-door look. Some appeared overtly sexual, and several among those girls would appear in the upcoming *Penthouse* film, *Caligula*. I assumed that gave them a certain status. None of them looked like me.

CHAPTER 9

London Bridge

Flying to London for a photo shoot would be a first. As a Pet of the Year finalist, I would be photographed by Bob Guccione himself. The two of us would stay at his London apartment above the Penthouse Club, unchaperoned except for occasional visits from housekeeping and Security. For me, married three years, this was another first.

It delighted me that I was traveling to London in the company of someone who knew the city intimately. But on a more private level, Bob and I were becoming attuned to each other in a way I'd never experienced. Beginning the moment we met, when he mesmerized me with his dark Italian eyes and seductive, slightly British voice, Bob had a mysterious way of quietly including me in his inner circle, no matter how many friends, family, clients, famous or influential people crowded around us. That inclusionary manner could make me feel we were the only two people in the universe. Although extremely different in personality and behavior, on some mental-spiritual level we were exquisitely in harmony.

On the day we flew to London, May 28, 1977, Bob picked me up at my apartment in his limo. I was nervous about that. This was the first time we'd ever been alone together, just the two of us, and a sexual tension had been building between us since that first day. Now, cocooned in our own luxurious space separate from the driver, embraced by the comfortable black leather seat that matched Bob's black-on-black clothing, and surrounded by the muffled sounds of Manhattan streets as we drove to the airport, I felt the tension intensify.

Despite the undeniable attraction, it hadn't occurred to me until now that this trip might take us beyond our professional relationship. I was married. Bob was devoted to Kathy Keeton. He was my employer as well as the photographer that would shoot nude poses of me as Stan had done in Puerto Rico. Stan and I never came close to crossing that professional line, and I felt certain Bob and I could be equally objective.

With Stan, however, there was an artistic intimacy but no physical attraction. Within the enclosed atmosphere of the limo, the sexual tension I'd endured during these six months of professional communications and friendly camaraderie with Bob crackled insistently, and I became aware that I *wanted* to cross that forbidden line.

In an effort to relax, I released my nervously clasped hands, put one in my lap, the other on the seat beside me. It was Bob's nature to set others at ease, and I believe that was what prompted him to reach over and place his hand on mine. At least, that's what I told myself. Had I made the first flirtatious overture, or was it as innocent as I believed?

Regardless, his touch ignited the pent-up tension. A look passed between us filled with scorching energy, chemistry, magnetism — whatever it was, it created a tangible bridge that we seemed destined to cross. The feeling continued to intensify throughout the limo ride and the flight to London.

An Affair to Remember

We flew the Concorde, a futuristic supersonic airliner famous not only for its speed but also for its delta-wing design and unique drooping pointed nose. The Concorde had begun flying commercially in 1976 and, sadly, flew its last in 2003. Only twenty were ever built. While commercial jets were taking eight hours to travel from New York to London, supersonic flight time — twice the speed of sound — fell just under three and a half hours.

The takeoff was so fast, I felt like I was in a rocket ship.

"We've just hit Mach 1, flying at thirty-six-thousand feet," the captain explained. When the plane surged, as if taking off again, he added, "Now we'll proceed to Mach 2. You'll begin to see a difference in the light as it starts to darken."

Breaking the sound barrier in the Concorde was an experience that marked the initiation of an entire week of new experiences. The next thing I knew, Bob and I were entering his private residence.

A cozy living space, small by American standards, the apartment was furnished in English antiques and tapestries. The light streaming through the windows at midday was absolutely gorgeous, ideal for painting or photography, and was probably what attracted Bob to this apartment originally.

We would be shooting here for the entire week. We also would sleep here, not together but certainly in close proximity. It was not my habit to sleep with photographers. Other models did so quite frequently, and the expectation that sex was an unspoken part of a model's contract was one of the things I hated most about the business. But the sexual tension that had heated up during the trip was now smoldering. I knew we would make love before the week ended.

Back in New York, in the limo, I'd quieted my conscience, left behind my Georgia-bred inhibitions, and mentally accepted that my physical and emotional needs would prevail.

Perhaps a brief affair far from home, far from my small-town morals, would cool down this unrelenting fire inside me.

An Orgasm Without Touch

The day after our arrival, we began shooting in the early afternoon. Bob used the elements of the room as props — luscious velvet chairs, fine wood tables, ivy and other greenery, pillows, flowers, fruit, the paintings, the crystal chandelier. On the balcony, he used the brick wall, the wrought-iron furniture, the terracotta tiles.

My room had an ornate antique brass bed, embroidered linens, translucent sheers on the windows. Bob wanted his photographs to appear unstructured, so fresh flowers might be casually arranged in a vase or strewn among the rumpled sheets. He wanted the space to look natural, in casual disarray, as it might be if a woman had just awakened, hair tousled, eyes heavy and languid. As she dressed for the day, donning sexy French lingerie — camisoles, lacy garter belts, stockings — or removed her clothes to step into a hot bath, or secretly pleasured herself, she should be totally unaware of the camera and the man behind it. Bob wanted the reader to sense that this was a first-time experience, that he was seeing what no one had seen before.

Bob wouldn't like the models of today. They're too harsh, constructed, enhanced, and skinny. He preferred his models to be feminine, sensuous, and genuine — real women — unpretentiously attractive with soft, delicate skin and a natural body. He didn't need them to be perfect. He wanted them to be real in their expressions, in their awareness of themselves, in their comfort within themselves, and in going through the motions he suggested. He didn't want a model's actions to look posed.

Bob's photographic technique and attitude, as much as the magazine's journalistic content, made *Penthouse* unique among popular men's magazines. Yes, he adored women, all women, but not merely for their sexual beauty. Valuing their strength and intelligence, he entrusted the running of his company chiefly to women.

As a photographer, Bob captured the way women changed visually, outwardly, as they dealt with various emotions. He had an instinct for detecting deep, personal feelings, coaxing them into the light, where they tugged sensuously at a woman's lips or softened the dark pupils of her eyes or brought a rosy flush to her skin. He could reveal that emotion on film like no other photographer of his time.

I discovered immediately that I loved being photographed by Bob. It was the most sensual and romantic experience one could have without actually making love. The settings were soft and billowy. The natural lighting was warm. His husky voice guided me through the movements. His handsome presence behind the camera was seductively erotic. I felt I was moving in slow motion, gently and delicately touching, stroking, caressing my body as if it was the most natural experience in the world. Bob made me feel I was the most beautiful woman in the world. Shooting photographs with Bob was an orgasm without touch, a love affair without sex.

Our lovemaking that first night after shooting evolved from the activities of the day as naturally as two dancers on stage fold fluidly into each other's arms. Throughout the week, we lived and worked in the same space, days flowing into nights. I slept in the same bed I'd be photographed in the next day. And every minute of our lovemaking was as effortless as breathing. Yet that first morning afterward, I awoke a nervous wreck.

The Morning After

Bob was already outside on the terrace when I awoke, crawled quickly out of bed, jumped in the shower and tried to figure out how not to let him see me before I pulled myself together. I felt way too insecure to meet him barefaced and unpolished.

Washing my hair, I tried to calm my jitters. When I turned off the water and stepped out, I heard my name.

"Vicki?" Bob always called me Vicki, never Victoria, no matter how I tried to convince him. "Come join me out on the terrace."

I did as much as I could in sixty seconds, threw on a terrycloth robe, combed my wet hair, and walked back through the room, through the open doors to the balcony. With no makeup, no armor, no camera between us, I felt naked and exposed. Apprehensive. My world had taken a sharp, irreversible turn.

Wearing a tan warm-up suit bearing a *Penthouse* logo, Bob looked as if he'd been awake for hours.

"Good morning," he said. Then he smiled and added, "You look beautiful."

"Good morning." My mind raced with anxiety. Why had I done this? Had I made a mistake? Had he expected to sleep with me, or had I jumped to that conclusion? Did I meet his expectations as a lover? And what must he be thinking? He was a confident, mature man in his forties. I was a married twenty-four-year-old woman with limited sexual experience.

"Coffee?" he asked. "You'll find it different from any you've tasted."

"Yes, I'd love a cup."

All my insecurities must have shown in my expression. Bob's eyes met mine with the same calm intensity and intelligent approval he'd expressed from the day we met, and my jittery fears settled.

"Baby," he said in his huskiest voice, "you were great last night."

It was such an old-fashioned thing to say, and such a cliché, but like everything with Bob, it was perfect. While he went downstairs to the kitchen to make my coffee, I walked back inside and finished dressing. Somehow, it no longer seemed important to put on makeup.

A few minutes later in the kitchen, his secret coffee ingredients turned out to be fresh cocoa and heavy cream, so typically British. He meticulously placed our cups and a carafe on a tray; then we went back upstairs and sat on the terrace.

The morning was wispy with fog, the sun barely beginning to shine through, and the balcony was high enough to have a delicate breeze. We conversed as comfortably as we would in a room filled with family and friends, sharing no covert glances, no awkward sense of betrayal. Bob was as committed to Kathy as I was to Jim, and I believe neither of us at that moment expected our week in London would be more than a one-time affair to be fondly remembered. I secretly examined my conscience for any hint of shame or regret. I found neither.

Borderline Acceptability

The Penthouse Club was in an older part of London, the Mayfair area, and down below I could see people milling around on the street. Bob said he liked coming back to England, where things were simpler. I remember studying him that morning, thinking that he was truly an enigma. The more questions I asked, the more he opened up, as if I were stirring memories and drawing them out.

He talked about his family and his background. He'd gone to art school in Rome and sold paintings on the street. He'd also been a newspaper publisher, a painter, cook, actor, private eye, writer, cartoonist, even a drycleaner. In the very early years of starting the magazine, he'd lived in this apartment, painting, writing articles, and taking photographs. Once he got the magazine up and going, he bought the building and opened the Penthouse Club, a private dining establishment.

Talented, smart, but more than anything else, Bob Guccione was a sexual man. It came across in his voice, his unusual and distinctive personal style, his presence. Everything about him was distinctively different from anyone I'd met at the age of twenty-four, and that still holds true three decades later.

Bob constantly stretched the borderline of acceptability, which was what led him to start *Penthouse*. He was interested in science and political intrigue, in probing the limits of human knowledge and the depths of human consciousness, boldly going "where no man had gone before," though perhaps his explorations tended toward darker, more secret realms than any starship captain's.

A Gentleman in Many Ways

Albert Zurof Freedman, former Managing Director of Penthouse International in England

Through my work as a television producer for NBC, I had a lot of publicity, and Bob Guccione heard about me. Los Angeles, I felt, was becoming too dicey because of the drug situation, so I decided to raise my family in London instead, arriving there in 1964.

Bob invited me to a press conference where he was making a big announcement. At that time, in Europe, there was nothing equivalent to Playboy. *The magazines for men were very shoddy. Bob was working in London as editor of a weekly newspaper, and he had decided it was time to start a legitimate, first class, elegant, sophisticated British men's magazine in London to be published throughout Europe.*

Dressed all in white, Bob announced the beginning of Penthouse *at this press conference. Afterward, we talked, and he hired me as his managing director.*

Starting with basically no money, Bob took a gamble. He sent brochures in the mail to get subscribers, hoping the publicity about the magazine would be extensive, that people would get excited and subscribe, and that he'd make enough money from subscriptions to pay the printer. Fortunately, it worked. Frantically, Bob opened all those subscriptions, pulling out checks and money to pay for his first printing of Penthouse *magazine in September of 1965. Seventeen years later, in 1982, he was listed among the*

Forbes 400 Richest Americans.

But some of the subscription letters he sent out went to uptight British spinsters and Lutheran ministers, and there was a law in Britain, hundreds of years old, stating that it was not legal to send anything by mail which the government declared to be indecent.

The word "indecent" in the 1960s had yet to be defined. What was indecent to a 90-year-old virgin lady was quite separate from what was indecent to a 23-year-old fellow. Nevertheless, the police heard about these mailings that were asking for subscribers to a men's magazine headed by the American, Bob Guccione, and featuring pictures of semi-nudes. Just a few years later, in 1972, The Sun, a British tabloid, would feature, on page three, its first photo of a woman topless, but in 1965, this was still unheard of. Bob's brochure presented basically the types of photographs of topless beauties that would eventually appear in the magazine. What Bob sent through the mail was considered indecent, and the police tried to arrest him.

While it was all being sorted out, he had to stay sequestered in his home, a little townhouse. We'd meet there, I'd work with him there, and he'd have to get someone to go pick up the mail. Bob, to his credit, was the first to see the power of people helping people, writing to the magazine and participating in the sex revolution by telling their stories, asking advice. The 1960s column was spun off into Forum magazine.

Bob kept to himself that part of his life that he shared with women. He was a gentleman in many ways. Although we talked about everything, and were very close, he did not divulge personal things.

A Strong Life Force

Eventually, as we became more acquainted, Bob's insecurities emerged, and I wondered if he was really so different or was just very good at disguising the fact that he was an ordinary guy from New Jersey. Another thing we had in common was the desire to transcend our simple beginnings.

The week we spent shooting photographs in London, living in the Penthouse Club apartment protected by a private elevator and security guards, was like being in dreamland, far from the reality of our everyday worlds. Bob's assistant began treating me as an integral part of Bob's life, often asking if I needed anything. I felt in awe of this fairytale lifestyle. It was an amazing experience but not a life I would want to live every day. It didn't feel quite real.

Yet the connection Bob and I shared was genuine. Bob represented everything I had imagined since my earliest childhood — to be successful, to see the world, to live life to its fullest, to love deeply and with abandon. During that week, Bob became indelibly entwined in my personal and professional life while at the same time remaining completely separate from my hometown existence. I was already becoming aware that I couldn't live the lifestyle I enjoyed in New York and continue with my life unchanged in Georgia. Yes, it was certainly possible to close my eyes to the exciting possibilities of my unfolding career, put my *Penthouse* encounter behind me, chalked up as an incredibly successful, thrilling, financially profitable learning experience with a romantic tryst thrown in. Was that what I wanted to do? If my marriage should end, which I couldn't yet imagine, I had no desire to have Bob replace Jim in that role. Even if Bob didn't have Kathy, his long-time partner and a woman I respected, he was not a person I would choose for such a committed relationship. He was the realization of secret, sensual desires, but not husband material.

What I didn't realize during that London tryst was how much more we would ultimately mean to each other, despite my love for Jim, Bob's bond with Kathy, and my assumption of his sexual escapades with other women. I admired Bob, trusted him, enjoyed everything about him as a friend and as a sexual partner, and eventually I came to love him. An air of invincibility enveloped Bob, a sense that no matter what life threw at him, he was going to win. Much later, after he lost the magazine and all his millions, after he lost his beautiful voice and his health, that spirit was still alive in him.

Near the end of the shoot, Bob set up a scene, put the camera on delayed action, then stepped into the frame, behind me and loosely embracing me. Very sensual, it was a remarkable shot, even among the 3,000 or so photographs he took that weekend, and he chose to use it in the Pet of the Year layout. Looking at that photo today, I believe the connection between us is evident.

I don't know if having a strong life force in the face of debilitating illness was another quality he and I shared or if I acquired it later on my own. I do know that I wouldn't be the woman I am today if not for Bob Guccione.

He Didn't Sleep with as Many as Was Rumored
Bob Guccione, Jr., Bob's eldest son

I was twenty-one when Vicki was Pet of the Year, just a couple of years younger than she was. I remember Vicki first as sort of rumor, and as part of the accepted circle. I was never really around when Vicki was with Dad. No one was, except at dinner parties and other social gatherings.

I was actually publishing my own magazine then, we called it Poster *magazine. It was five years later in the early 1980s that I got really involved with Dad's business. I ran the circulation department for a couple of years. In 1985, I started* Spin *magazine.*

So even though I was very close to him, I rarely saw my dad and Vicki together as a couple. Part of that was because he was not a person to boast about his girlfriends. He was the exact opposite. He was prudish. My dad was an interesting dynamic in himself.

He always had beautiful women around him, and he didn't sleep with as many as was rumored, but he certainly slept with a lot of them. He was basically a single man, even though he was officially still married to my mother at that time, and he was living with Kathy. So he had a common law wife, a real wife, and he still considered himself single.

But having said all that, he was very prudish, and I think that's an interesting dynamic. His magazine, a naughty, sexy book, established a world he himself did not live. So there was an unexpected dynamic, but I think an essential one, because it mirrors most people. Most people aren't purely hedonistic. That dynamic struggle between the puritan and the decadent was always present. His personal life embraced the concept of a big Italian family.

He Kept Pushing Me Through the Crowd

Bob and I stopped in Rome for two days on our way home from London, and stayed at the legendary Hassler Hotel, which managed to be both glamorous and charming at that time. I was so infatuated at this point that it's amazing I noticed anything around me, but the location alone, with its breathtaking view, carved a place in my memory.

The Hassler is at the top of the Spanish Steps. Scalinata della Trinità dei Monti is the longest, widest, and most majestic staircase in Europe. It forms a steep slope dominated at the top by the Trinità Church. Below, the Piazza di Spagna, a park-like common area with picturesque fountains, attracts tourists as well locals who come there to walk, read, or just to have lunch and enjoy the day. Bob had spent a lot of time there in his younger days, painting and selling his art. While he was showing me around Rome after dinner, pointing out the historic landmarks, the sun began going down. We drew closer and closer to our hotel, and when we finally arrived at the Spanish Steps, it was dusk.

People clustered around shouting and gesturing. We couldn't see what was going on, and I didn't understand the language.

"I think we should go around them," Bob said, "and get to the other side."

Before we could move, the crowd engulfed us. Not a happy crowd of boisterous partiers and jovial citizens, it was some sort of demonstration. The mob grew louder and rowdier, getting out of control. Within seconds, people around me were all elbows and angry voices, pushing and shouting.

Bob grabbed me and covered me with his arms. "Come on, we're going this way."

We started running down an alley. Suddenly, a barrier of rifles appeared in front of us, the men holding them wearing full assault armor, including face masks. They obviously intended to shoot anyone trying to pass.

Then just as suddenly, I was drenched. My first thought: *Acid!* Or some kind of chemical.

"It's water," Bob said, "Just water." Pulling me close to him, he called out in Italian, "Wait! Wait! We need out!"

He kept pushing through the crowd and down the little alleys between the old buildings, where another wall of policemen stood with rifles and clubs. Bob spoke to them, and finally one stepped out of rank and escorted us to safety.

I never learned whether the crowd was fighting with plastic bags full of water or if the police were dumping water on them, but that sudden deluge soaking us was terrifying, one of those horrendous moments when you feel totally unprotected in the midst of insane brutality, and you can't believe what's happening. Only later do you realize how fortunate you were to escape unharmed.

The next morning I looked out from our hotel rooms and saw the Steps were a mess of mud and clutter. The story was all over the papers, and obviously political, but since I didn't read Italian and Bob was busy checking on the progress of *Caligula*, I never discovered what the crowd was protesting. I did hear that it became a full-fledged riot in which a number of people were hurt, including several policemen who moved in and broke it up.

We got out just in time. Thinking back on the experience, I'm still impressed at how calm Bob remained. Most celebrities I've dealt with, on either a personal or business level, are worthless in a calamity. They depend so completely on their assistants, their managers, and their agents that they can't do anything for themselves. Many who knew Bob would say he was like that, too, that he couldn't hail a cab.

But the Bob I saw in Italy that day, and the Bob I came to know, was entirely capable. He never got caught up in being a celebrity. If anything, he was an anti-celebrity. His protectiveness, and knowing that he could take control like that while at the same time reassuring me, made me feel even more connected to him.

One of the Great Loves of My Dad's Life
Bob Guccione, Jr.

Vicki was one of the great loves of his life. His great loves included, of course, Kathy, his long-time partner, and my mother. Like many people who are brilliant, creative, and successful, he had a capacity to love more than one person. He certainly had the curiosity and the appetite. So Vicki was a great love, and in many ways, she could have been the one he wound up with. I think Kathy just did a good job of hanging on.

Dad wanted the whole family to stay with the company. While I was there, I learned from him, and the one quality I always tried to emulate was his work ethic. Pure and simple, it came down to the fact that you just had to work harder than anybody else, as hard as you could possibly work. It was a matter of persistence. This is true in life: there is no simple stroke you hit and then everything falls into place. You pave the road, you pave it stone by stone, and it's a great equalizer of talent. Talent and inspiration are magic, but the execution and the manifestation of the talent is pure hard work. I saw how hard Dad worked. It was not a fluke. He did not wave a magic wand.

I also learned respect; to respect people, and to have good manners. The most he ever got upset with me were the times I displayed bad manners at the dinner table. Once I put food I was finished with on my grandmother's plate. He punished me for that severely. I was about ten years old, so that was forty-something years ago, and I remember it like it was yesterday.

He was a good father, he was a good guy. One thing he was very smart about was keeping us away from the Penthouse *Pets. He realized that when we were young and horny we were very susceptible to gold diggers. Vicki was never like that, but many of the girls were. If we messed around with them, the girl got fired and we got in trouble. It was serious.*

Dad was smart in his own life, though I think he screwed up a few times, but he was particularly smart in trying to minimize the number of times his kids screwed up. He taught us also to be humble. If you had something go right for you, you weren't the cat that got the cream, you were blessed. And you have to be patient when things go backwards.

Mostly what he taught me was to be my own man.

Mutually Acceptable

Returning from that trip to London and Rome, I felt a little shaky on my feet. My life had changed 180 degrees from the week before. No, I didn't suddenly consider myself a "cheat," even though technically I'd cheated on Jim. What happened with Bob in no way altered my love for Jim or my desire to have a life with Jim.

I was brought up in a world where equality was never tested. My parents never discussed their mutual roles in our family; they simply fulfilled them. Television shows I grew up with, *Leave It to Beaver*, *The Brady Bunch*, showed marriage as thirty minutes of cute couples playing house. Commitment was taken for granted but never discussed.

Variety programs, like *Laugh-In*, or *The Smothers Brothers Comedy Hour*, brought stars into our homes. About the time I was making my mark in Atlanta as a model, Cher was glamorously taking her act solo and Farah Fawcett was on her way to her break-out series *Charlie's Angels*.

These stories and images impressed in me the attitude that life was a worldwide feast of experiences. Deep down, I craved to spread my wings and fly far away from Atlanta. I wanted to see, hear, smell, taste, and touch the *world.* But like a homing pigeon, I wanted to know I could return at any time to the sweet sanctuary of the cozy nest I'd created.

My marriage to Jim and my dalliance with Bob in London were, in my mind, a conflict I had to resolve. On those many nights when I wasn't at home, I never imagined or questioned whether Jim was with other women. I certainly assumed that Bob had multiple women in his life.

CHAPTER 10

The Awakening

An underlying fear often dictated my choices, a fear that I wouldn't measure up. Nothing I did came as easily to me as my friends and family believed it did. I tried so hard to be perfect for everyone. Being nice was seen as a sign of weakness, so I tried to be strong, but being strong was seen as bitchy and aggressive.

Growing up, I often attracted people who treated me like a local celebrity — and that was embarrassing at times. Some of my girlfriends were sincere and honest, and I gravitated toward the few I trusted. Other girls were outwardly nice to me, yet I sensed a desire to use and destroy. To these fake friends, I was useful when they needed me. Boys, and eventually men, often became my best friends. Right or wrong, I felt they were more honest than the girls I knew. Although I had a loving and supportive family, I hungered for acceptance and recognition from the world at large.

In New York, I had no idea whether a romantic relationship between Bob and me would continue or what path it might take. We didn't discuss it. Nevertheless, I couldn't help feeling "released" from commitments established by earlier times. In my heart, I'd never have wanted Jim to do to me what I'd just done to him, and in my desire to experience life, I had to face this conflict. The 1970s was a time when America was sampling a less structured, less prohibitive version of family values, but that wasn't me. In actuality, though, I spent little time dissecting my feelings after I returned home. I hit the ground running.

The next day I had a *Viva* fashion shoot with, as Fate would have it, Stan Malinowski. I honestly don't recall the thoughts going through my head as I posed for what turned out to be an extraordinary fashion spread. Faced with the man who had first photographed me nude in thousands of poses, with no sexual connection between us, and just having spent a week with Bob photographing me nude while sexual tension crackled in the room like a freshly lit fire, how could I not have been embroiled in emotions?

Perhaps like Scarlett O'Hara, the ultimate Southern heroine, I put blinders on and set my concerns aside to deal with "tomorrow." Today was for business, and my business was modeling.

Untamed

At the office, there was no denying a change in the way I was treated; I soon realized it had nothing to do with what had occurred between Bob and me. No one knew about that. Did they suspect? Given Bob's reputation, of course they did, but he was suspected of bedding all the *Penthouse* centerfolds.

Bob was such a private man that people filled in the gaps of actual knowledge about him with every piece of gossip, envious supposition, mystery, or publicity hype they could gather. What I realized only later was that executives at the magazine had already positioned me in their minds as the next Pet of the Year. They'd been publishing centerfolds long enough to predict how the votes would sort out. I wondered if the fact that Bob had taken me to London for the shoot solidified it. He photographed all the finalists, and they all felt "special," but how many did he select to photograph in the London apartment? I had no idea.

Kathy Keeton, from the first day we met, had pegged me as an asset to the magazine, and now Jeff Zelmanski was sending me on most of the high-profile assignments. Despite having a large selection of centerfolds to choose from, he kept me either booked or flying every day.

Consequently, I had little time to *feel*; the shock and reality of that week with Bob were overshadowed by sheer activity.

Interestingly, no one at *Penthouse* ever acknowledged that I had a husband. They didn't say, "Oh, no, you can't be married and be a Pet of the Year." Or "Will your husband be okay with your traveling so much?" There's no law that you must be single to be a centerfold. It's not Miss America, where you have to pretend never to have had sex. *Penthouse* was run by women, and a number of the centerfolds were married, which was fine, as long as husbands didn't stomp into the office and interfere. *Penthouse* was all about fantasy and illusion. That's what made it work. The illusion that centerfolds were available to the readers had to be maintained.

In truth, however, even before London, the magazine *was* having an adverse affect on my life at home, if only in subtle ways. In Atlanta, I may have clung even tighter to my comfortably normal lifestyle with Jim, our families and friends, which was the flip side of my Manhattan life, where I was moving from my tiny studio apartment into a larger one-bedroom in the same prestigious building. But the less domestic, untamed side of me craved the excitement I so far had only glimpsed.

Did You Break Bob's Heart?
Jeff Zelmanski

Vicki asked me, "When did you know about me and Bob?" In some ways I always knew. But I kept it to myself. Bob would say, "Is Vicki available?" "No, she has this event or that." Then I'd get a call from Bob's secretary. "Vicki doesn't have to attend that event. Bob needs her to do a live interview for a news show." Okay. But the centerfolds got paid for doing things for the magazine, and Vicki's checks kept coming.

Every time Penthouse *opened an International edition of the magazine, like the Spanish edition, Bob would say, "Vicki will cover it." Bob took Vicki because she looked great. She spoke well.*

She was presentable. I had to teach girls how to get a passport. *Vicki* had *a passport. So when Vicki went to other countries, we didn't have to make those arrangements. Slowly I picked up that something was going on. Vicki was only for the special things. Bob didn't have that kind of relationship with the other Pets.*

Bob had full-time security, cameras at the door, three assistants, a bodyguard, and a chauffeur, so we always knew where he was twenty-four-seven. We knew he was at the country house, he was in the city, he was in Europe. People kept tabs on him. When Vicki and Bob would spend the weekend working together, and he was unreachable, I knew it was special. The way Bob Jr., Kathy Keeton, and everyone talked about Vicki, I knew that relationship was hands off. It was sacred, not to be touched, not to be talked about.

Vicki would talk to models, photographers, never let on that Bob and she had any kind of relationship at all. She was so professional.

I asked Vicki once — it came out of nowhere — did you break Bob's heart? I think maybe she did. Maybe she was his last chance to have a normal life. And she never realized. He was an Italian, a man's man, and he loved women, but this woman he loved so much left him. Left him. *After that it was all business. Vicki was his chance to have a real life. I don't think she knew it was that serious. But again, I don't think she knows her effect on people.*

I knew girls who slept with Bob after Vicki. They always told me, whether I liked it or not. In fact, Bob would ask them, "You don't tell Jeff anything, do you?" "Oh, no." Then they'd tell me. Beautiful girls, sometimes enchanting girls, with amazing skin and features, but his interest ended after the publication. He wasn't a party guy at all. We'd have parties at "the house," a magnificent home, which they used often for cocktail parties. Bob would be upstairs, come down for five minutes, just to say hello, then disappear again. Bob was everything that Hugh Hefner was not.

Not that he didn't love women, God knows he adored women, but he had a mother, sister, girlfriend. He said, "I would rather be with the ugliest woman in the world than any man in the world." He loved women. He loved the art of the woman, how beautiful women are. The gender. He was an artist. He brought that love of art and of women to his photography.

Penthouse was the first magazine to show everything. To show the complete body, and Playboy followed soon after. I learned that in Japan showing a woman's vagina is not censurable, but if there's hair it's censurable. So they have to be shaved. In middle Eastern countries they would always make sure the centerfold would not be Jewish. They would ask.

But because of the natural lighting, Bob's work had this wonderful texture, like Renaissance art. Also, when Bob photographed, which was rare after the magazine got busier and busier, but always Pet of the Year, you would know the photographs were his, because Bob and the girl had a rapport. That's what you're seeing. She knows she's special. "Bob's photographing me, and that's going to be something." Some of those girls turned out not to be Pet of the Year, but he still photographed them, so there was a disappointing moment after they realized, which I had to deal with. And they would go, "But he photographed me." And I'd have to say, "Well, he photographed the other finalists, too."

With Vicki he got to work with a real model. With the other girls, he'd have to show them how to do this, how to do that. Vicki did it naturally. Bob loved photographing Vicki because she did everything naturally.

Fame and the Craziness It Brings

The sleek Connaught Tower, where my apartment was located, marked the beginning of the new high-rise condominium era in Manhattan. An architectural marvel of glass and steel, the building was startlingly and elegantly modern against its older neighbors of stone along Second Avenue in midtown's trendiest section. It had every convenience an urban resident could ask for: a full-time doorman, good security, an atrium garden, a health club, a full-service garage, and a private drive so that people didn't have to exit taxis and limos on the street. One of the most progressive amenities for the time was a year-round indoor pool with an outdoor sundeck on the roof.

One day in the early summer I was lying on the roof by the swimming pool, catching the morning rays in my latest bikini and Christian Dior sunglasses, when suddenly my light was blocked. This annoyed me: somebody was standing in my sun. Opening my eyes, I found a very tall, handsome man standing over me.

"Hello, Ms. Johnson," he said with a beautiful English accent. A well-modulated voice with an accent gets me right away. "Welcome to the Connaught Tower. I'm with Benenson Realty, project manager for the building."

I said hello and he introduced himself as Shaun Henderson.

"We're pleased to have you as a resident of the building," he said, then added, "I know that you have been in the public eye recently."

Oh, really, I thought, wondering how he knew so much and why he was bringing it up.

"I brought you a copy of today's newspaper," he said. "I wanted to introduce myself, but also I thought you would like to know that you are in Liz's column today."

He showed me the article in the *New York Daily News*, and sure enough, Liz Smith had announced in her column that I was one of the finalists for Pet of the Year. Reading it awakened me to the realization that any anonymity I had retained at my New York residence was now gone, and the building either had an excellent PR staff or I had a fan in Mr. Henderson.

Easthampton Fun

The Connaught Tower residents, it turned out, were like a little family. Shaun and I became friends first. Charming and interesting, he repeatedly told the story of his origins, and as I heard it retold with a few important variations, I realized that Shaun, like many others, including me, had come to New York to reinvent himself. He was smart, rose quickly in the real estate market, and as an executive of Benenson Realty had secured himself an apartment in the building. As my New York career absorbed more and more of my life, I began losing hold on my life in Atlanta. But I was caught up in this new world and loving it, so I reached out for an anchor. Shaun became that anchor.

What I liked most about Shaun was that he had an interesting mix of friends in New York, and he loved being with them. When we combined our collections of friends, they were the greatest. On hot weekends, everybody went to the Hamptons, the summer respite for old New York money, new Hollywood money, and New Yorkers who want to be known. Shaun, through his real estate connections, found us a huge old mansion in Easthampton for the summer, with about twenty rooms, no furniture, many mattresses, electricity but no hot water, and situated on a bluff overlooking the ocean. It was our personal version of Grey Gardens, without any help from Jackie Onassis.

Most weekends a dozen or more friends would hang out there together. Other guests would come and go. Gary White, now a top agent at the super-hot Zoli Modeling Agency, brought with him the cover girls of *Vogue* and *Cosmo* and *Harper's Bazaar*. I still have a photograph of a group of us traipsing across the bridge in ball gowns just as the sun is rising.

Sometimes we'd take the seaplane to the Pines section of Fire Island, where we might see Calvin Klein, Rudolph Nureyev, or other New York notables. Fire Island was free, fun, gay, and the music was the best in the world. Those were crazy times. We never thought about how long they might last. Young, frivolous, we each expected a long lifetime ahead.

My Three Lives

Our group, and indeed all of New York in those days, was gay, straight, or confused. Straight people wanted the freedom they saw in gay people, and gay people wanted the acceptance that straight people had. This was all pre-AIDS, of course. Friendships bloomed between models and makeup artists, hairdressers and their clients, drug dealers and their buyers.

Even the clothes were losing their gender specificity. Men as well as women enjoyed showing off their bodies. Never before or since has sexuality been so fluid. Although I stayed true to my attraction purely for the male of the species, most of my new best "girl"-friends were men.

Shaun and I spent a great deal of time together for nearly two years. *Penthouse* gave me a New York career and Shaun showed me a New York social world. In many ways, he was my grounding force in a city with more intriguing distractions than I'd encountered in my entire home state. My new life of limitless possibilities and adventures awakened as my primary life began shifting from the family comfort of my Atlanta home to my sophisticated New York career with *Penthouse* and the modeling world. And I can see now that my social time with Shaun and our friends, and their fascinating mix of fun and entertainment, provided the secure bridge I needed between my other two lives.

CHAPTER 11

Seven-Year Stretch

I'm sure most husbands would never have been as understanding as Jim. Not that he knew about Bob. I'd compartmentalized the London episode as another of those singular moments in time. Bob and my New York life rarely entered my thoughts when I was at home in Marietta, Georgia, and nothing much changed regarding my personal life at home. To his credit, Jim never voiced having a problem with the magazine, and in Marietta, he was in the spotlight almost as often as I was.

When I was traveling, Jim got all the attention. In many ways we felt united in this daring venture, and I believe he enjoyed those years of notoriety. To have more time with Jim and my family, I asked my handlers at the magazine to please send me back to Georgia for every publicity opportunity happening there.

In New York, I spent more and more time working for *Penthouse*, although my agents continued to get modeling jobs for me and I took the ones that fit my new perspective. That tidal wave kept pushing me forward. The business of modeling, including many hours of publicity-related activities, absorbed most of my time. Bob and Kathy considered me an integral part of *Penthouse*, treating me like family when I visited The House, and those situations were more business than social. At that time, I was too people-oriented to simply shut down after my modeling duties were done and spend my off hours alone in my apartment, so I was grateful for my little family at the Connaught Tower.

From the perspective of three decades later, I notice that I seemed to reinvent myself every seven years or so. It had been seven years since I met Jim and began dating seriously for the first time. During that same period, modeling became more than a part-time summer job, and the day of my centerfold signified the most dramatic occurrence in my life as a model and a wife. Moving into my new, slightly larger, extravagantly and elegantly decorated Manhattan apartment signified the beginning of my next seven-year reinvention of Victoria Johnson, even though I didn't fully realize it at the time.

One thing that changed markedly was my loss of privacy. In Marietta, where I valued privacy most, men climbed telephone poles to try to catch me sunbathing on my balcony. In New York, I was expected to bare my life for the media. Being "seen" at the best restaurants and clubs was part of what *Penthouse* paid me for, and frankly, I loved being in that limelight.

At the same time, though, I began to appreciate what real celebrities must go through when they want to shop at the grocery store or have a quiet dinner out. The truth is you can't. You're always "on." You have to look great every time you step out the door, because you never know when a camera will be pointed your way. In this high-tech day and age, with cameras on every cell phone and the internet only a click away, privacy must be nonexistent.

In Good Company

At *Penthouse,* seventy percent of the executives were women, and many used their positions to launch spectacular careers. Dawn Steel, who left just before I arrived, climbed the ladder at *Penthouse* from receptionist to director of merchandising for *Penthouse* products. In 1976, shortly after leaving the magazine, she made a quick name for herself by printing the Gucci logo on toilet paper and selling it as a gag to gift shops. Her designer TP garnered a lot of press, and Steel got enough notoriety to land a position at Paramount Studios, where she became the marketing and merchandising expert for *Star Trek, Flashdance,* and *Fatal Attraction.* While working on the merchandising for *Star Trek: The Motion Picture*, she came up with the first-ever tie-in products between movies and fast-food chains. In her biography, Ms. Steel, who went on to become president of production at Paramount, the first woman ever to run a major US motion picture studio, states that she recalls *Penthouse* as a company which "supported women's rights ... long before it was fashionable to do so."

Marianne Howatson started as a waitress at the Penthouse Club in London, then sold ad space and came to New York as the magazine's advertising director. She moved up to Publisher and Vice President of General Media and was still at *Penthouse* when I arrived. Marianne and I worked well together, but she and Kathy Keeton had an odd rivalry. Marianne thought of herself as above it all and Kathy saw her as someone the magazine had nurtured. Later, Ms. Howatson moved on to become president of *Playboy* Enterprises, publisher of *Travel and Leisure* and *Self* Magazines, was involved in such varied publications as *Parents, YM, Expecting,* and *Baby Care,* and served as president of the Magazine Publishers Association. Few people know, however, that she appeared as *Penthouse* centerfold Marianne Gordon during those early London years.

Before Patricia Bosworth became a contributing editor at *Vanity Fair,* she was managing editor of *Viva*, the women's adult magazine started by Kathy Keeton as a *Penthouse* companion. Patty and her art director were instrumental in putting my photograph on the cover of *Viva*. Previously, centerfolds had not graced *Viva*, which was an international magazine for women that explored feminine sexuality and fantasies. After leaving *Penthouse*, Patty wrote bestselling biographies of actors Montgomery Clift and Marlon Brando, and photographer Diane Arbus. Although she doesn't mention her time at *Viva* in her bio, in 2009 Ms. Bosworth featured Bob Guccione in an extensive *Vanity Fair* article, "The X-Rated Emperor."

Another famous publishing diva, Anna Wintour, came to *Penthouse/Viva* the same year I did, 1976, and stayed until *Viva* closed in 1980. Her fashion layouts were amazing, culturally and stylistically fast-forward. In one dress shoot, the models' skirts are being blown in a windy, Marilyn Monroe/*Seven Year Itch* manner, so that the models' faces are not seen. She openly admits that her position at *Penthouse* was the first for which she was be able to hire a personal assistant and was the beginning of her reputation for being a demanding and difficult boss. Editor-in-chief of *Vogue* since 1988, Anna Wintour is widely believed to be the inspiration for Lauren Weisberger's fictional character Miranda Priestly in *The Devil Wears Prada*.

How Did It Feel?

Penthouse consistently promoted women to positions of responsibility, and I was no exception. The months before I became Pet of the Year were only a sample of what I could expect during my tour the following year. Afterward, I continued to represent the magazine, billed often with the unofficial title of "Pet of the Decade," until the mid-1980s, when I was eager to reinvent myself again.

I've never been treated better or with more respect than in my years at *Penthouse*. But when this book comes out, I will still be asked the same question I was asked in 1976. "How did it feel to do those photographs?" And a few self-righteous people will not ask it as a neutral query, as in merely wanting to talk about it. A few will ask in a condemning and adversarial tone, lips pursed in disgust as they look down their sanctimonious noses. "Oh! How could you *DO* that?"

I'm pleased, actually, that I chose to do what I did. All in all, the positive effects of my years with *Penthouse* far outweigh the negative. I'm happy that Stan Malinowski came along at the right time, when I was at the right age and at the right moment in my life. I was looking to make a statement, which I definitely accomplished, and I knew I was going to make the best of it no matter what anyone thought. While I may not have fully internalized my intention, I know now that I set out to prove that an intelligent woman with personal values and morals can appear in a magazine like *Penthouse* and still remain "normal."

It worked for me. It worked for the magazine. And it worked for the times.

The Art of Being Seen

The late seventies were also the beginning days of Studio 54 in New York. Steve Rubell and Ian Schrager opened Studio 54 on April 26, 1977. Instantly, it developed a following of Manhattan celebrities.

The "in" place to party, the club soon transformed the lives of many notable New Yorkers. They became obsessed with being "seen" at 54, where diamonds, disco, and cocaine were *de rigueur*, and you might rub elbows in the VIP section with Calvin Klein, Andy Warhol, Bianca and Mick Jagger, Elton John, Cher, Diana Ross, Liza Minnelli, Halston, Truman Capote, Michael Jackson, or newlyweds Donald and Ivana Trump.

Part of the success of the club was its nineteen-year-old doorman, Marc Benecke. He held the power of New York nightlife in his white-gloved finger, which he pointed at each lucky guest he allowed to enter the club. No one was guaranteed admittance, not the rich, the beautiful, the powerful, the famous, or the infamous. The "bridge and tunnel" crowd from Brooklyn or Queens might stand outside the door for hours in the cold and rain, or the heat, and once in a while Benecke would point, and a fortunate couple would become a legend in their own community. *Not* getting in could be the most horrible, devastating, humiliating moment, with everybody standing around you, scrutinizing, judging.

Once inside, you stepped into wall-to-wall glitz and glamour, from the parquet dance floor, decorated with a giant Man in the Moon "inhaling" cocaine from an animated spoon, to the strobe-lit columns descended from the ceiling, to the mirrored, diamond-shaped main bar located beneath the balcony. Music throbbed nonstop, mixed by the most popular New York DJ's and played through a world-class sound system. While giant mirrored disco balls spun overhead, sending colored lights darting around the room, handsome waiters in butt-hugging short-shorts and bowties served the guests.

The dance floor was filled with hot sweaty bodies, mostly naked, rubbing against each other in a dancing frenzy. Smells of sex, sweat, sin, and amyl nitrate permeated the air. When the intro to Donna Summer's "Last Dance" started playing like a pounding heartbeat, it sent a shot of adrenaline; everyone knew it was coming and surrendered to the hedonistic decadence.

Studio 54 was a cutting-edge disco in the same way that *Penthouse* was a cutting-edge publication. The magazine held spectacular events there, or sponsored events for our top advertisers, and invited guests never had to wait outside in the crowded line. Being "seen" at Studio 54 usually meant getting a mention in the next day's columns, which made the magazine's publicity agent, Sy Presten, a very happy man. Even when I wasn't attending a *Penthouse* event, my friends and I always zipped past the line and walked right in. But I usually worried right up to the instant Marc Benecke pointed his arrogant young finger.

Those were the good days of Studio 54, before the club turned sort of dark and desperate. In June 1978, a new disco opened in Manhattan; Xenon quickly became the only club popular enough to compete with Studio 54. In a fabulous Fiorucci woven ribbon skirt that barely covered my bottom, worn over a tank-top leotard, I was among several centerfolds who attended Xenon's opening night. Andy Warhol, arriving at the same time, spied us getting out of the limousine and came to have a photo taken with us, then politely escorted us inside.

Show Up, Look Fabulous, and Speak Well

Being "seen" at Mahantan's hottest hangouts was a significant part of my career. Reporters cruised the city, taking note of who was where and what we were wearing, then published the blurbs and photos in the next day's gossip columns. So even when I had no actual "date" and no official event to attend, I'd call my New York friends and go out and flash my smile around. Rarely did a day pass that my name didn't appear in print.

At this point many of my jobs were photo shoots for fashion editorials, lingerie layouts, or covers for *Penthouse* and the various magazines and catalogs published under the corporate name, General Media. These assignments took place in New York. I still traveled quite a bit, but unlike the other centerfolds, I wasn't asked to go on a grueling convention trip every week.

Instead, Bob would send me, or take me with him, on radio and TV interviews, especially when they involved women's rights. One reason he liked having me along was that he could count on me to always show up looking appropriate and to represent the magazine articulately. Bob was not a media hound. He never frequented the "in" places, and he appeared in person for the media when a topic touched on subjects that interested him, such as first amendment rights, women's rights, or veterans' rights. In my hometown of Atlanta, congressional hearings were taking place involving the First Amendment. When Bob was called to testify, he flew in with several lawyers and I met him at the Atlanta courthouse with a representative from the magazine's distribution company to show our support. The hearings proved interesting but also dangerous, with rowdy protesters from both sides of the issue furiously picketing. A few months later, at this ongoing hearing, Larry Flynt of *Hustler* magazine was shot by a sniper outside the courthouse and was paralyzed.

Bob Rarely Left the House
Irwin E. Billman

Bob was an interesting man, a sort of Renaissance man, constantly changing, pushing for the literary, artistic, and political freedoms he believed in. But he was always a photographer first. He designed the sets with the girls. He used his own residence most of the time, and rarely left it, which was why he had such lavish facilities, and he would dress the girls in pearls and jewels and silky lingerie.

Bob's artistry was visible throughout the magazine. He looked through every pictorial with his spyglass, his loupe, and went over every picture. In the early days I occasionally watched Bob shoot a pictorial, or we would hire a photographer and I might go along, help him oversee the photos being taken — not the hardest thing to do.

Money was never really Bob's prime objective. After he accumulated so much, I'm talking many millions of dollars every year back in those days, in profits to the company, that wasn't where his head was. I or the English accountant, Gerald Kreditor, would sit in on the tax meetings to help minimize taxes. Bob was very trusting, and he didn't always use the information his paid consultants provided. He would listen to the wrong people. He'd have meetings sitting at a table with this person or that, whoever was around, and too often whatever those people told him he would believe. Right or wrong. Gerald and I would tell him it was wrong.

"Don't go to Atlantic City," we told him. "Don't get into the movie business. Stick with what you know."

"Why not get your pictorials in on time," I asked him more than once, "so it doesn't cost you a quarter million dollars a month in overtime?"

Constant overtime dollars going out, a quarter or half a million dollars a pop, just didn't bother him. More than once he told me, "When everybody says I'm wrong, I know I'm right."

I didn't function as an accountant, though. His father, Anthony, was the treasurer, and he and I signed all the checks. Anthony had loaned Bob $5,000 to start the magazine, and he became quite involved in the operation of the company for a number of years.

During that phase of the business, I would look at every invoice that was signed. I also handled everybody's expenses. A pictorial never went by without Bob examining it; an expense report never went by me. I would act very mean and tough. We had some 300 employees at that time, only twenty employees when I started, counting me, Bob's father, and Bob's two sisters. His son, Bob Jr., came in and oversaw circulation in the later years, after we'd made that big move. His daughter, Tonina, was involved in the '80s, and his middle son, Anthony, in the '80s and '90s.

Kathy Keeton was the dominant business head of the family, the one you had to worry about. I was her supervisor, yet I had to worry about her, too. I wasn't her friend. She was giving me some trouble one time, and Bob said, "Don't worry, you have a job for life. Just control the company and control Kathy. That's your job."

I couldn't do it. My demise came in 1981 because of that. She was vice chairman of the company at one point, he was president, and she wanted to control everything. She did control advertising, publicity, promotion, the Pets, except for Victoria. Victoria controlled her own life. But Kathy also wanted to control the purse strings.

While Bob was president and CEO, I was chief operations officer, COO. People came to me with their problems, and I'd try to work them out. I'd always check with Bob in the background. When Victoria began commuting more and more often from Atlanta, he put her into an apartment. On the road, he would somehow manage to take Victoria to certain events.

"Always take care of her," Bob said. "Make sure she's comfortable."

CHAPTER 12

Just the Two of Us

The spinning of events following our trip to London and Rome kept me too busy to think, for the most part, except on those evenings when Bob's assistant, Jane Homlish, called to say, "Bob and Kathy would like you to come to dinner." On those evenings I spent just a bit more time considering what to wear — would Bob like it? — and a bit more time applying my makeup to look entirely natural yet perfect, and a bit more time fussing with my hair until it tumbled gently around my shoulders in its most appealing style, but with a few charmingly errant strands escaping to suggest I'd come straight from a deliciously decadent afternoon. In other words, creating the look I knew Bob loved.

Sitting there in "my" chair on Bob's left, I had no problem at all making small talk with Kathy and others at the table, but inside I churned with emotions. His presence made my heart race, my temperature rise, and every inch of my skin yearn for the touch of his fingers and mouth.

Bob remained the gentleman host, parceling his attention in fairly equal amounts to all his guests. Then occasionally his eyes would rest on mine a second longer than was necessary and with a secret intensity that told me more than words ever could that he, too, was fondly remembering our passionate week together.

One day that summer my phone rang. This time it wasn't Jane Homlish calling to invite me to The House. It was Bob, calling to ask if *he* might visit *me* later that week. He'd love to see my apartment, he said.

"Don't go to any trouble," he added. "Perhaps we could have

dinner sent in for the two of us. A quiet evening together.''

His call surprised me on so many levels. First of all, despite my ongoing fascination with Bob, I had not expected our overseas tryst to assert itself on home ground. I'd secreted the memory away like a favorite photograph in a treasure box. Second, in the weeks since our return he'd given no indication that we might pick up where we'd left off. Third, I hadn't yet fully given up on my marriage.

I believe Jim understood, as I did, that our relationship was in a serious state of unrest, just as my dad and several others of our families and friends had feared when my centerfold was published. Jim didn't want to admit any more than I did that the marriage might actually end. It wasn't as if I loved someone more than I loved him. I didn't.

My enthrallment was with the breathtaking wonders of the life I'd stumbled into, like Alice down the rabbit hole, and to the exploration of fresh experiences awaiting me with every new day. Bob was part of it, because not only was he the most complicated and unusual man I'd ever known but also because he represented the forbidden world I longed to explore.

The fourth reason Bob's call surprised me was that I'd never known him to visit *anyone*. He liked the world to come to him.

Ripped from the Pages ...

Looking back, I know I shouldn't have been entirely surprised. For weeks we'd exchanged those heated looks any time we found ourselves in the same room.

Don't go to any trouble, he'd said. With fittings and fashion shoots and appearances, I hadn't time to do much more than pick up a six-pack of Tab, which was about the only thing Bob ever drank, and order Chinese food, which was fast and easy and different from the meals either of us usually ate. Naturally, I rushed home from my afternoon assignment in time to slip out of my day clothes, freshen up, and put on something sensually appealing, but not overtly sexy, opaque enough to be unassuming yet alluring enough to make him want to see more — an odd notion, since he'd already seen everything.

The fact that Bob rarely left The House was well known and often commented on in articles written about him. When he did go out, three people accompanied him: an assistant, a driver, and a bodyguard. Bob's closest friends often joked that he wouldn't know how to hail a taxi because he always took his limo, nor would he have money for a taxi. He didn't carry cash or credit cards. He depended on his driver or his assistant. I knew from our experience in Rome that Bob was entirely capable of taking care of himself, yet on home turf it seemed out of character. And getting out of the mansion without anyone knowing, past the dogs, the help, the bodyguards, and the numerous other people surrounding him, would be impossible.

Yet he magically left his bodyguard and the limo at home that night and arrived at my building, where he announced himself to the doorman as "Mr. Roberts." Looking the way he did, dressed all in black with his extravagant collection of gold chains, wearing his English boots even in the summer, there's no way he could have pulled it off without being recognized.

The doorman phoned my apartment to announce him.

"Ms. Johnson, Mr. *Roberts* is here," he said, emphasizing the name in a judgmental tone. My living room was designed with built-in platforms and banquettes of various sizes and at various levels to define the seating areas. The carpeting was a soft, luxurious slate gray. Everything else was black or gray with touches of peach, complemented by mirrors and glass shelves that made the space appear much larger.

While the living area was starkly contemporary, the bedroom

could not have been more romantic, with everything in shades of peach and ivory — peach-carpeted platforms, peach-and-cream bed linens, peach walls with more mirrors. You walked up the platforms and down into a queen-size bed covered with dozens of pillows made of lace or satin and embellished with handmade silk roses.

So Bob left his Italian mansion with its forty-five rooms, some as large as ballrooms, and its massive antique furniture, and arrived at my cozy 675-square-foot apartment.

"I like it," he said, glancing around. "It's chic yet sensual. Like you."

We talked about our day as I spooned steaming portions of Mandarin Chicken and Mongolian Beef from their white carry-out cartons onto our plates. We talked about the magazine as we ate. We laughed about the funny things that had happened during the week. I drank wine. He drank Tab. While I cleared the dishes, he smoked a joint. As always, he managed to calm my jitters and, for two nontraditional people, we enjoyed a quiet, traditional evening together.

As naturally as breathing, we started toward the bedroom.

"Vicki," he said, and when I turned to look at him, I stood on a higher platform, bringing our eyes and lips to the same level. The aromas of wine and marijuana mixed in the air between us. His curly black hair glistened in the lamplight. A hint of those same curls peeked from the V of his partially unbuttoned shirt. I could feel the heat from his body and the intensity of his dark eyes drinking in every detail of my face. "I've missed you," he murmured.

I studied him as if for the first time, as if London had never happened. That magical week was merely a lark, a delicious fantasy, after all. This was real.

Despite anticipation clouding my head, I saw what I'd never seen before: the desire so evident in his eyes was overshadowed by a deeper emotion. For him, too, the fantasy was behind us. Tonight was real. And along with the depth of feeling I saw a trace of … was it fear? What could this bold, brave icon of a man fear from the likes of me?

No one who knew Bob Guccione would believe he was capable of being hurt. Insults from the most acerbic journalists, political activists, and others who attacked him for the graphic content of his magazine rolled off his shoulders like rain off a tarp, eliciting only a level-eyed stare of pity for such narrow-minded contention. Yet I realized at this moment that even the strongest man can have a heart of marshmallow.

He could crook his finger and summon practically any woman he'd ever met. It wasn't his money or position that attracted them. Bob had an inherent sensuality that women couldn't resist. A bevy of girls floated around him like honeybees.

I didn't float. I didn't hover. Although I was twenty-two years younger, Bob and I had come together as equals, in business and in bed. Yes, I'd been eager for the experience, but the attraction had been as mutually respectful as it was mutually intense. He wasn't accustomed to that sort of relationship. And he didn't quite know what to expect from me, nor I from him.

I touched his face, following the fine line of his cheekbone to the corner of his sensuous mouth. My thumb lightly traced his beautiful lower lip. Placing my mouth on his, I transferred all the affection, admiration, and devotion I felt into a tender kiss more loving than passionate.

He placed his hands on my shoulders. His thumbs stroked my throat then slid from my neck down over the front of my filmy blouse. Feeling the warmth of his hands on my breasts, every sensation in my body centered on those few square inches, and I leaned in to him, wanting more. Somehow, he measured his touch to my need and instead of allotting me the firmer grip he knew I wanted, he pulled away just enough that his fingers scarcely brushed the tips of my nipples. Suddenly, I was in an agony of longing.

He let one hand slide to my hip, lighting a fire there, then slowly stroked my lower back while his fingers at my breast traced feathery circles. His hand on my back dipped lower until it cupped me from behind, drawing me against his hard thrust. His tongue danced across my lower lip, teasing my mouth the way his fingers teased my breast.

My arms hung limp beside me, but now I brought them up and around, until my hands urgently clasped the back of his neck and pressed his mouth hard against mine. When he finally took my breast fully in his grip and squeezed it in firm but gentle massage, I gasped.

Reviewing what I've written, it seems as though I might have ripped a scene from the pages of a romance novel. But this was how I always felt with Bob, completely comfortable and at ease, yet passionately attracted to each other and detached from the reality of ordinary life, as if we floated in a time bubble of our own making.

"You haven't begun to know me, Vicki," he said.

"I want to," I whispered. "I want to know all of you, everything you think and know and feel."

"You will."

Love and Respect

This handsome black-haired, dark-skinned Italian looked totally out of place in my tiny peach bedroom, lying against the pile of fluffy silk pillows he'd propped up behind him to watch TV. It was funny to see him there, and all these years later I wish I had a picture, but we never took personal pictures. We had enough of that during the day.

My physical relationship with Bob remained deeply sexual

but somewhat traditional. No kinky role-playing. In my life and in Bob's life, sex was all around us all day. Bob examined sexy photographs for hours on end, and I posed in them. We didn't have to create a fantasy. Compared to normal people, we *lived* a fantasy. Our relationship was loving, passionate, fairly simple, and built on mutual trust. We never talked about how we should act around other people, because we trusted that our time together was private.

Our evenings gave Bob an opportunity to get away from The House, where he was constantly besieged by people, telephones, staff, bodyguards, the dogs, and the demands of being a hands-on publisher of a rapidly growing international empire. My apartment was a sanctuary. He could relax, slow down, actually watch TV. He could literally disappear for a few hours, as we all want to do at times, and his sense of humor always emerged.

Our clandestine evenings typically started with talking, laughing, and dinner. After the first night, Chinese food became our "thing," a distinctive choice for our secret meetings. We remained acutely attuned to each other, and our lovemaking would last for hours. Bob never called to say, "I'm coming over, I've got two hours." We never rushed. Our evenings never started with a deadline, and they didn't end until we were both too sleepy to stay awake another minute.

I usually drank a glass or two of wine, and he might smoke a joint. After dinner we might watch television, but certainly we would cuddle, and in the flickering glow of the screen we would gradually become more and more passionate until our foreplay spontaneously and effortlessly turned to intercourse orchestrated by our intense mutual desire. There was no part of my body that was not touched or caressed, then Bob languished as long as possible in the softness of my bed. We would have sex, then talk and still be having sex, entwined with each other, stroking and kissing and touching for hours on end.

He had exquisitely soft skin, a gorgeous body, and his own distinct scent. I don't think he used cologne. I don't think Bob did anything that wasn't natural. Like the lighting and props when he was shooting photographs, he liked everything to be unpretentious, genuine, nothing artificial. He had this scent, somewhat but not precisely like cinnamon with the underlying aroma of musk, not cheap-perfume musk but a purely erotic smell that, like animal pheromones, affects women subliminally.

Two things that have always attracted me to a man are voice and scent, those primitive elements inherited from our ancestors, I suppose, which influence our behavior with members of the opposite sex. I need that instinctive physical attraction. I'm not drawn to men merely by their looks or by who they are or what they stand for, certainly not by where they come from. There has to be carnal male-female magnetism. I've had that with the men I've truly loved and was acutely attracted to. And I had that with Bob.

He was a great lover. Merely being around him created sexual energy. He knew exactly how and when to sensuously touch every part of me and make me feel I was being loved as well as aroused. And he taught *me* to be a great lover. He taught me how to truly love a man back.

Making love was about my pleasure as sincerely as his own. I believe much of the pleasure Bob felt was from giving it, and I believe that was because he truly loved women. Not just me, he loved the essence of women, which I believe is a rare but important quality for a good relationship. To sincerely love one woman, a man must love and respect all women. And Bob did.

Letting Go

The fact that I was still married was not a fact I ignored, but it was hard for me to deal with ending my marriage. By fall of 1977, however, Jim and I were drawing apart, and in my mind no matter how much I wanted to hold on to both lives, the end of my comfortable, secure little world in Atlanta was inevitable. I was moving on.

I'd hoped that Jim would recognize the changes in me and initiate a conversation, some sort of conflict even, that he would say, "I'm not going to take this anymore." That's the scenario I was hoping for, because I was reluctant to bring it up myself. I didn't want to let Jim go, or the life he represented. He was my best friend, my first love, and my stabilizing force. I was torn.

Yet I knew I had to take the hard step. It wasn't fair to him that I was outgrowing our relationship.

Saying goodbye would be painful, because I truly cared about him, and I truly cared what I was doing to him. That's why I procrastinated. I couldn't say I loved another man more than I loved Jim, because it wasn't true. I loved Bob differently, not more.

Also, as my new world was wooing me away from Atlanta and all I loved there, Jim was just as surely committed to Atlanta. He would not be happy living in New York, nor would he have enjoyed my New York City lifestyle. Yet I'd passed the point of no return: I could no longer live in Marietta.

When I'd moved to my first small apartment at the Connaught Tower, my heart was still in Georgia. I was an Atlanta girl working in New York. After moving into the larger apartment, I felt my loyalties and interests changing. My heart was divided. I chose to go toward the thrills and wonders of learning new things and being with people who would challenge me.

But not only was it hard letting go of my one and only husband, my one and only real marriage, it was also hard letting go of what we had accomplished together in such a short period of time, and what we'd brought to our families. My job had created excitement and abundance all around. Our strikingly handsome home was scarcely completed. I could still smell the "new." My father's business was flourishing largely because Jim was part of it. I didn't know how all that would change.

I sound like a vacuous, starry-eyed twit, tossing away the solid foundation of a devoted husband and family, a home we built together with love and joy, and a thriving career many women would die for in exchange for cheap thrills. All I can say is that I felt compelled to keep moving forward. The significant men and women in my life, including Jim, have always been people I could learn from. With Bob, that was also true. Our relationship was never simply about sex.

Jim never asked me how I spent my free time in New York. And I didn't tell him. I waited until it was unmistakably apparent that my life was accelerating in a new direction. I suppose we both wanted to avoid a confrontation. Through the toughest times and our occasional arguments, Jim never criticized or demanded I reconsider. He kept his cool, dealt privately with the pain as only a man of his superb caliber would. I tucked my own sorrows out of sight, out of mind, and set my face toward the future.

Over the next year, our marriage quietly dissolved.

CHAPTER 13

A Grand Prix Whirlwind

In typical *Penthouse* style — everything first-class and some-times over the top — the official announcement that Victoria Lynn Johnson was the new 1977 *Penthouse* Pet of the Year went out to a crowd of thousands at the United States Formula One Grand Prix. The race took place in Watkins Glen, New York, that year, with every racecar-loving ear in the nation tuned in to the broadcast.

By now, more than a year after my centerfold issue, I'd become centrally connected to the *Penthouse* family. I knew the event would be significant by anyone's standards. Yet until that day I didn't realize how monumental a name *Penthouse* was becoming.

Before and during the race, Toyota teamed up with the maga-zine to give away the Watkins Glen pace car, a Celica GT Liftback. On Saturday, a week before the race, Bloomingdale's, a New York City icon, teamed up with *Penthouse* for an in-store promotion. *Penthouse* Pets inside the store dazzled patrons with their beauty as they passed out promotional material for the race and directed buyers to the signature Grand Prix racing jackets. With each jacket purchased, eager customers received a free copy of the *Penthouse* October issue.

Penthouse was sponsoring a Formula One team in the interna-tional Grand Prix circuit. The magazine was always looking to ex-pand their brand, and racing was a natural match. Rupert Keegan, winner of the 1976 British Formula Three Championship, and who later became one of my best London pals, was scheduled to drive the car at Watkins Glen. For two weeks before the event, the magazine sponsored a promotional radio blitz in fourteen cities

I presented the trophy to the winner of The Watkins Glen Grand Prix in October of 1977. The year I was named Pet of the Year. What an honor to be a part of the event, and to meet Niki Lauda and James Hunt.

to announce their involvement and to boost interest across the country.

And to top off the day, the 1977 Pet of the Year would award the trophy to the winning driver of the US Grand Prix at Watkins Glen. That Pet would be me.

Twenty-five centerfolds wearing the Watkins Glen jacket with black turtlenecks, *Penthouse* emblazoned across the front in silver, boarded two chartered planes at LaGuardia Airport at 7:30 a.m. My black turtleneck, of course, was framed by a gold lamé racing suit.

Including *Penthouse* executives and important advertisers, eighty-six of us in all arrived a half-hour later at Elmira Airport to be shuttled by helicopter. My friend, Dottie Meyer, or more recently centerfold Dominique Maure, and I rode together along with our chaperones, and our helicopter set us down dramatically right on the track.

My First Official Appearance

As if there's not enough tension surrounding a major auto race, the weather turned cold, raining, and muddy. The media volleyed the question of whether the race would go or not. Marshaled by a National Guard unit for security, the audience, according to reporters, was the biggest ever, and more than a little boisterous.

VIPs from all over the world gathered at the exclusive Paddock Club, where Pets acted as informal hostesses for our *Penthouse* guests and served as grid guides behind the drivers. Every time *Penthouse*, the Pets, or Toyota was mentioned over the public address system, the crowd cheered noisily. The most thunderous ovation of all came with the long-awaited announcement of the new Pet of the Year, Victoria Lynn Johnson.

Just hours into the day, and despite the nasty weather, I could see my winning tour was going to be a fantastic ride. The flag went up. The race took off on schedule. With mud spray so heavy we could scarcely see the cars, James Hunt pulled ahead of Mario Andretti and Jody Scheckter in the final lap, winning by a margin of 2.2 seconds.

In the winner's circle, I joined James Hunt and Niki Lauda, who had just regained his title as Grand Champion, and draped them both with garlands of roses. At every move I made, someone was snapping a photo or taping video. Television and newspapers around the world covered the race, so I received tons of media attention, right along with the Grand Prix winners, their sponsors, and *Penthouse*. It would have been a heady experience if I'd had time to think.

Around the press circle, a temporary fence separated the crowd from the winners being interviewed and photographed, and now that the race was over and the trophy awarded, people seemed to be even rowdier than they were during the main event. Fans shouted questions and pushed forward for a better look or to get closer to the drivers, to other celebrities attending the race, and to me. I suppose no one wanted the day to end.

The only thing keeping the crowd from rushing up to us was the insubstantial fencing, which began swaying and leaning. As the mob pushed in, I saw the fence posts tilt toward us, ready to give way at any moment.

Then I saw National Guardsmen headed my way.

"You ladies have got to go," one of them said, quietly but convincingly.

Our escorts herded us into a small group, and with the Guardsmen surrounding us we navigated through the mass to a waiting helicopter. The crowd closed in behind, shouting and groping — good natured yet a little frightening in their determination.

I climbed in with Dottie, and the helicopter lifted off. Looking down at the throng of fans, high on excitement and testosterone, maybe also on wine or beer, and all reaching up, waving wildly to get attention, cheering, I realized that this was *it*.

This was the payoff for my years of hard work and for making those hard decisions. After all the doubt, the contemplation, my reservations before doing the shoot with Stan and after seeing the cover at Bob's house, not to mention the shock of seeing the first issue at newsstands and knowing it held twenty-nine nude photographs of me between its covers, this is what I'd accomplished by deciding to go for it — and keep going for it. My first official appearance as Pet of the Year, the first day of my tour, the first official announcement to the press, and it happened at a US International Grand Prix.

What a great moment. Every negative thought vanished as I marveled silently in the roar of the helicopters' rotors, *Wow, so this is what it's going to be like as Pet of the Year!*

From Mobs and Mud to Diamonds and Dancing

Preparations for my Pet of the Year party, scheduled for the following night, would consume the rest of the day, so after warming our shivering bodies with coffee, sandwiches, and celebratory champagne at the Elmira Airport, we flew back to LaGuardia.

Kathy Keeton had introduced me to Il Makiage, an exclusive boutique that had opened only a few years earlier but was fast becoming the salon of choice for New York's fashionable women. Naturally, after getting my hair done that Saturday, an Il Makiage artist was the only person I trusted, besides myself, to give my face the perfect shimmering glow for the most dazzling party of my life.

Bob had flown Mom and Dad in early and put them up at the Drake Hotel. Knowing I'd be busy after the race, I'd spent some time with my parents while I could and had taken Mom shopping at Bloomingdale's to buy the dress she would wear. She was quietly beaming. I could tell she was thrilled with her first visit to

New York, plus maybe a little bit proud of her daughter.

Among my prizes were two designer gowns. The one I chose for the party was by Larry LeGaspi, a futuristic version of what a Grecian goddess might have worn. I'd exchanged the one I received for this even more stunning gown. Extraordinarily beautiful and unusual, it draped across my shoulders and down to my toes like gossamer, the silky white fabric flowing and floating, billowy sleeves slit from shoulder to wrist, the bodice similarly slashed from neck to navel. Decadent while remaining amazingly modest.

Bob and Kathy picked me up in the limo, so I arrived with them at Rockefeller Center. We entered the Rainbow Room to find the *Penthouse* executives and advertisers among another throng of people lined up to shake hands and offer congratulations. The Grand Prix winners and other drivers attended, adding color and festivity to the room and thrilling the girls. Several of the New York Giants had come, including star quarterback Joe Pisarcik, along with quite a number of celebrities I don't recall because I was so caught up in enjoying the moment.

Three years earlier, the Rainbow Room had undergone a $25 million-dollar restoration and expansion. The new space was incredible, and mine was the first and only Pet of the Year party ever held there.

Forsaking his customary black on black with gold chains, Bob wore a more traditional tuxedo, and despite his usual reserved demeanor, he couldn't have looked more like a proud father. When I say that, people think, *She must have seen him as a father figure.* But I didn't. Kathy looked just as proud as Bob did. The celebration was theirs as much as mine, as special to them, individually and as an accomplishment together, as it was to me, as it would prove to be the biggest day of the magazine's history. For *Penthouse*, my Pet of the Year issue marked the beginning of a growth surge that would last for several years.

Crowning Glory

In a daze of wonder and amazement, I walked onto to the stage. It struck me then, but even more now as I look back, that the entire Pet of the Year event resembled a beauty pageant.

The other centerfolds, wearing Pet of the Month sashes, flanked me on both sides like runners up as Bob made the announcement; then kisses, congratulations, prizes, speeches; someone handed me an enormous armful of roses. A parody of the traditional Miss America pageant, so conservative in those days that a two-piece bathing suit was considered risqué, and *Penthouse* exposing everything, yet it's funny now to think that I could have gone either way — if only I'd had a stage talent.

Mom and Dad sat in the center of it all at their own table, and I couldn't have been prouder. Dad loved to travel, a holdover, probably, from his Navy days, so his coming to New York at Bob's invitation didn't surprise me. Dad wanted me to be happy, and I knew he'd accepted that I would make the best of whatever came about from my unsettling decision. Coming to the party, though, must have caused some anxiety. *What might those people be wearing — or not wearing?* He didn't say it, at least not to me, and in fact, didn't seem to have a problem at all enjoying the party.

Jim, of course, hadn't come. From the beginning, he understood the magazine's desire to maintain the illusion that centerfold girls were obtainable. Although we were still on excellent terms, all things considered, the subject of his coming to New York simply never arose. Just below the surface of my parents' acceptance and happiness for me lay a measure of sadness for what they suspected would be the end of my marriage. Jim was their son, now, almost as much as I was their daughter. Although we hadn't talked about separating, and the dreaded "D" word never crossed our lips, everybody felt it happening. Typical of my parents, they focused on the positive aspects of my new life during the celebration. I think they arrived at the Rainbow Room even before I did.

"Well, Hello, Mr. Bob."

At the crowning moment, Bob presented me with the *Penthouse* Pet of the Year key, a 14K gold pendant, specially designed with six full-cut diamonds and one oval Burmese ruby. Because I was expecting the pendant, which Bob had shown to me earlier, I'd worn minimal jewelry.

"I will place it around your neck at the party," he'd said at the time.

As he fastened it, I realized how many prizes I'd collected since entering the room. A thick gold-clasped, multi-strand rope of gorgeous freshwater pearls was already draped around my neck. On my arm sparkled a gold-and-diamond Mathey Tissot watch, and on my finger an emerald-and-diamond ring. Not part of the prize package, the ring was an early Christmas gift from Bob.

So much of the evening remains a blur. So many people to greet, hands to shake, cheeks to kiss. I smiled and smiled and smiled, and that was okay, because this was a good night. For me, for my family, for the magazine, for Bob and Kathy, it was an all-around breathtaking event.

I recall Bob handing me the microphone. I'd written out my speech, but it was short enough that I could deliver it easily without notes, honestly and from my heart.

Back in May, while Bob and I were in London shooting the Pet of the Year photos, he received word that *Penthouse* had caught up with *Playboy* in newsstand sales. Now, in October, *Penthouse* had overtaken *Playboy*. At an opportune point in the speech, I announced to a room filled with the magazine's key advertisers and executives, and with more press than had ever attended a Pet of the Year party, that *Penthouse* was officially the bestselling men's magazine in the country.

The crowd jumped from their seats into a standing ovation of cheers and applause. I saw a couple of columnists head for the phone lobby. When the room quieted down, Bob took the mike again and said, "Victoria's proud to have her family here tonight."

He motioned for my parents to stand, which they did, taking a blushing bow. That seemed to be the cue for everyone to relax and start milling around. Bob and I walked to my family's table, and I introduced him. He hugged my mom. Then my dad put his hand out, and Bob accepted it.

"Well, hello, Mr. Bob," Dad said, "it's really nice to meet you." He didn't attempt to pronounce Bob's last name.

That was the moment Dad accepted Bob Guccione. I'd made a good decision, Dad seemed to acknowledge, and quite possibly Bob was a man of integrity after all and had not taken advantage of his young daughter. Obviously, Dad's daughter was a happy and successful girl these days.

It's not well known, but there was never a better person than Bob when it came to parents and family. If one of the girls had a family member with any sort of problem, Bob would help them. I don't know exactly what he did, and my family was doing well at the time, so that never came up for us, but Bob did make my parents feel special that night. I saw them glow with pride as Bob praised my work in making the magazine a shining success.

One of my prizes was a fur coat, which had to be fitted. Having a particular soft spot for mothers, Bob whispered to me, "When you go to pick up your coat, choose one for your mother. I would like to give it to her for Christmas."

My party at the Rainbow Room was the crowning moment of an eighteen-month transformation of my career, my personal commitments, and my world view. After the helicopter swept me away from the Grand Prix racetrack at Watkins Glen into a whirlwind of nonstop events, we flew from one glittery, glamorous, media-marked event to the next, and I never landed until the end of my tour two months later.

If Vicki Knew What She Had, She'd Be Dangerous
Jeff Zelmanski

Unlike the other girls, Vicki was a real model. She did so many covers for Penthouse.

There's one shot of Vicki that became iconic for Penthouse, *one of the great photographs of all time. There's no nudity, it's just the face, but there was something about it — I know this from straight men. It's so hard to find that sexy kind of redhead. You see red auburn or carroty red, but this certain red that's kind of erotic is so rare. Bob loved redheads, but we had very few in the magazine.*

Previous to Vicki, women who appeared in the magazine were waitresses and dancers. There was no cachet *to them. They didn't have a modeling history. Then Victoria came, and she starts making the columns.*

New York was unbelievable in those days. We were breaking ground in the world of sexual liberation. Women at the office would show up the next day in the same clothes after a night at the new singles' bars.

My job promoting the Pets was to send them where they could be seen, especially by the media. I never had to set Vicki up on dates. She dated. In fact, she dated Engelbert Humperdinck. She kept that quiet. She kept it quiet about Glenn Frey of the Eagles. I never knew that for the longest time. Unlike other Pets, you never had to send Vicki someplace important, because wherever she was going that night was better than wherever you were hoping she'd go. She'd say, "I'm going to Regine's." Only the best private club in town, and she's going there. "Oh. Okay."

The magazine ran fashion layouts for men, and we'd get some good celebrities once in a while. There's this great shot of Vicki with the whole New York Islanders hockey team. The players are all wearing colored underwear, and Vicki's wearing the team jersey, with all this ice around. That's the kind of thing where we'd talk to the PR person, and they wouldn't want to do it. They'd say no. Then we'd mention Vicki. "Oh, well we might do it if you send Victoria." We send Vicki and it's done. It's a great shot, they love it. When the team pulls out a secret player, a ringer — Vicki was our ringer.

At the beginning, she would go on a ten-city promotion, and she'd spend a weekend in Vegas signing pictures, do whatever had to be done. But I could see we needed to save this girl for something special. Like when Vicki did commercials for Jordache jeans. Penthouse couldn't have paid Jordache to do that. We would have loved the connection and the advertising. Vicki got it on her own. Even years after she was Pet of the Year, if someone could get Vicki for a promotion, they'd be delighted. She'd say, "All right. I'll do one circulation promotion. Pick one, Jeff. I'll do one city."

I remember being in an airport with Vicki, and she looked at someone and could see they recognized her. I'd see people gawking wherever we went. "Don't look them in the eye," she'd say. She didn't want to make eye contact, never could be comfortable, because anyone could come up to you and might be a nut. But she was always so present, so friendly, so nice. Women were not threatened by Vicki because she was really warm. If people had a baby, she'd pick up the baby.

She was like a normal person who looked like she came from another planet where people are too beautiful to be real. If she knew what she had, she'd be dangerous.

CHAPTER 14

25 Cities

In one amazing three-weekend rush of parties, the New York event repeated itself in Los Angeles then again in Chicago, each magnificent and unique in its own way. In LA, Bob, Kathy, and I entered the party with a number of notable celebrities, including the always glamorous Zsa Zsa Gabor.

Parked on display out front was the sleek white Lotus Esprit James Bond drove in *The Spy Who Loved Me*. Mine, a duplicate and the Pet of the Year grand prize, had not yet arrived — and would not be equipped with anti-aircraft missiles, nor could it turn into a submarine — but it would be equally sleek, white, and extremely fast.

Television crews crowded in everywhere. Sports idols mingled everywhere. Professional athletes loved hanging out at *Penthouse* parties, and while I wasn't into the jock look, particularly, the other girls certainly enjoyed having them around.

The party in Chicago, where *Penthouse* had a corporate office, became a two-day celebration that included long hours of media interviews. Practically every day I'd fly to a new city in time to make the network morning news show: "Good Morning Detroit!" "Good Morning Memphis!" "Good Morning Toronto!" During the day, I'd do radio interviews or a daytime talk show, then I'd be back again for the evening news: "Good Night Detroit," "Good Night Memphis," "Good Night Toronto." Cities across the country woke up with me and went to bed with me.

Like the parties, the tour for me became a cloud of continuous activity. All these years later I have to depend on my journals, appointment books, and photographs to serve as reminders. Luckily,

I also have friends with good memories.

My friend Dottie reminded me, "At one promotion, Vicki put a coffee cup in the trash. It had her lipstick on it, and a fan picked it up to save as a memento. Now, it might be on Craig's List or E-bay."

Photo Ops Galore

In every major city a circulation representative from the distribution company, Curtis Circulation, met me and my chaperone at the airport, drove us to the hotel, and got us checked in. The next morning a driver appeared like magic to take us wherever we needed to be. From my friend Jeff I learned that the tour agenda was based on circulation.

"Whichever ten to fifteen cities needed a circulation boost," he said, "that's where we sent the Pet of the Year. The three hooks were Chicago, New York, and LA, and from there the tour map grew according to whatever events were going on, *Penthouse* and Curtis pooling resources to make it all come together. With other girls, *Penthouse* at times became so desperate, because a girl couldn't articulate well or because the press hated *Penthouse* and therefore censored us in that city, we had to set up our own promotions. Magazine signings at airports, at drugstore chains."

Some tours, Jeff said, might consist of merely traveling around each city with the driver who distributed the magazine and signing copies at Walden Books, newsstands, and other distribution points. Fortunately, I had to do none of these things. I stayed much too busy.

Penthouse was a shooting star, going from big in 1976 to huge in 1978, so we suddenly had a desirable bargaining position. Instead of begging for promotion opportunities, businesses were begging us. My tour was amazing. It included primarily newspaper interviews, radio and television shows and other media happenings, plus the occasional Curtis cocktail event. Press was available everywhere I went, and the media liked working with me.

And since we had prominent gift contributors, I was also hired and paid separately to do special promotions for such companies as Lotus Cars, Minolta, Oleg Cassini swimwear, Kawasaki, Panasonic, and Yamaha. Instead of fifteen locations, I flew to twenty-five cities in two months, and returned to Chicago, LA, and Atlanta at least twice.

Being from the huge Southern market of Atlanta, and having had a career there in both modeling and acting, opened quite a number of doors. I appeared with sports teams and sports celebrities, including the Atlanta Flames hockey team.

Before the tour was over I also appeared with the New York Apples tennis team, at another tennis match with Ilie Nastase and Vitas Gerulaitis, and I made the opening of the California Club in Miami with Bobby Riggs. At a Studio 54 fundraiser, I danced again with New York Giants' quarterback, Joe Pisarcik. I appeared at charity events: the Jerry Lewis Telethon, the Heart Fund Association, and the March of Dimes. In Atlanta, I joined Hank Aaron in the 1977 Celebrity Parade for Cerebral Palsy, and standing under a *Penthouse* umbrella with Mayor Ed Koch, I emceed a fundraising benefit for the New York Police Department.

In Buffalo, I appeared on the game show *Dialing for Dollars*. In LA, where *Penthouse* maintained an office, I was on the *Redd Foxx Show*, *Invitation to Dance*, and *Hollywood Connections*. Wonderful shows, wonderful events, and I relished every minute.

Many of these appearances were not based on my sexual identity but on my mental agility and my ability to present myself well. *Hollywood Connections* was hosted by Jim Lange, who also hosted *The Dating Game*. Contestants attempted to score points by matching celebrities' answers to questions posed by the host. Granted, it wasn't a brainiac's show, like *Jeopardy*, but it was a big leap from modeling bathing suits in a store window. The celebrity guests that day included Pat Carroll, Zsa Zsa Gabor, Milton Berle, Nipsey Russell, Anson Williams, and Jack Carter. The show we taped during my tour aired in January 1978.

Bob was in LA at that time, and we took the opportunity to spend an afternoon together shopping on Rodeo Drive. As we taped the show, I could see Bob waiting in the wings, for once not the celebrity on stage but proud to have me representing his magazine. We had such an easy, uncomplicated relationship; it feels odd to look back and only now see the complications others must have noticed. When the show ended, I walked away with $750 cash, a Bassett dining room set, and an eight-day trip to Hawaii. I was surprised and elated, not because of the prizes but because I was smarter than the guy next to me and I won without my "look" being a deciding factor.

Early in my modeling career I once said I could never do a nine-to-five job, because I hate the sameness of day-to-day routine and I liked having mornings to myself when possible. Now here I was doing a year of nine-to-fives in two months. But there was nothing routine about it. These were two months of glorious insanity.

My first chaperone, a big blonde woman with glasses, couldn't keep up the hectic pace and fell out within a few days. The same thing happened with the next one. Then they paired me up with Phia Romanelli, and the tour became not only less stressful but a lot more fun.

A Sad, Sad Day
Phia Daly Billman, *Penthouse* Reception
and Front Office Director
Somebody suggested I go to Penthouse for a job. This was 1976, and ninety percent of the staff was all women. Great women. Women in advertising, women in the editorial department, I think

there may have been five men, mostly gay. So I got the job and I became a Jill of All Trades.

One day I get called to Irwin Billman's office. He's a mucky-muck, and he said to me, "Are you up to traveling with the Pet of the Year?"

I said, "Wow! Of course."

Because Victoria and I were kind of friendly, this was exciting. I had to take over after another woman got sick or whatever.

Irwin told me to be careful about what I discussed, to be very discreet. I didn't exactly know what not to talk about, although it had to be about Victoria or the magazine, but basically Irwin was telling me to keep my mug shut.

Victoria was talented. Beyond being bright and all that good stuff, she had an amazing sense of design. Really quite fabulous. She should have been on the other side of the camera.

On the tour, Victoria and I roomed together. We sat up late one night in our room, and Victoria told me about Bob. On the tour we'd gotten to be even better friends than before, and I guess she trusted me. I knew then what Irwin must have been hinting about when he said, "Be careful what you discuss."

So from then on I knew about Victoria and Bob. Her relationship with him was unique. And it wasn't as much a secret as she assumed. Everybody in the office thought she was going to replace Kathy. That was also the night I told Victoria about having sort of a crush on Irwin Billman. It was so much fun traveling together.

We were on tour together for several weeks. We did Memphis, Atlanta, Nashville, Dallas, Houston, all in the South.

For the Atlanta part of the tour, we went to Victoria's home in Marietta, Georgia. I met Jim and her family. Her mom and dad were so cute. And it was clear that Victoria had achieved a great deal more at that stage in life than a lot of her female contemporaries. Victoria was very together, very, very together. That house she designed was quite something else.

I called the TV crew, the local CBS affiliate, who were supposed to interview Vicki at her house. The woman who came to do the interview was very cocky. Anyway, the television crew was there, and somebody left the door open, and Victoria's cat got out. She had this adorable, sweet little cat. Maybe it got nervous with so many people on the property. Cars, TV vans — and somebody backed over the cat.

Victoria was hysterical. So I called the Penthouse *office and cancelled all her appointments that day. They'd recently brought in a guy from the* Washington Post *to work in the Promotions department, and this guy's nose was all bent out of shape.*

He said, "How could you do that?"

"I'm sorry," I told him, "but she's too hysterical to work."

"Who are you? Who told you to make that decision?"

I said, "What do you expect? One of their people ran over her cat! The girl is too upset."

Then I called Irwin. I said, "Ohhh, I think I'm in big trouble."

"What did you do?" he asked.

"The news crew killed her cat, and I said she couldn't go on the TV show."

Irwin said, "You're fine, you're fine."

Most of the tour that Victoria and I did together was wonderful, was amazing, but that was a sad, sad day.

A Deciding Moment

Sitting there in my house with Phia and Jim, the television crew finally gone, the house finally quiet, and trying not to think about the horror of what had just happened, I felt as if a huge weight had settled into my body. I did not want to move. The crying had stopped, and the trembling, and what filled my mind was a terrible weariness.

Look what this tour and these people have caused. I'd gotten the young cat in New York, and for me, it represented my life there, so I'd named it Gucci after the fashion magnate but also after the magazine and Bob. Keeping it in my apartment, with no one to care for it when I was gone, had become impractical, so I'd brought Gucci home to a safer environment.

This tour, which Jeff told me usually took four weeks, had started out to be six weeks and now was dragging on to two months. I began to question what I was doing. I loved my home, I loved my family, my husband, so why was I allowing myself to be dragged away from them by what I knew was nothing more than fleeting fame? And a rather shabby fame, at that, regardless of how beautifully I reframed it.

Keeping up the pace was hard. Staying constantly "pretty" was hard. No matter how many hours I traveled from city to city, airport to airport, show to show, I could not arrive at an interview or event with bags under my bloodshot eyes from lack of sleep. I was too professional for that. No matter how weary I was, I had to remember the name of the show and the host. I had to answer even the stupidest questions with intelligence. I had to appear vivacious but not giddy, smile often but not too often, with effervescence but also with modesty, and toss in a bit of humor, when possible. Some nights I was so tired I'd step into the elevator afraid I wouldn't make it up to my room before falling asleep.

For the first time, I felt doubt about the choices I'd made. Whether I wanted to believe it or not, the magazine was changing me and was changing my future. This was November. The tour was scheduled to be over in early December, so I'd be home for Christmas, but if I continued with the magazine, this might be the last Christmas with my family intact, the last year I could count on Jim being a part of my family. This wasn't a change I wanted, but it was a reality I needed to face, and this felt like the deciding moment.

Why not call the magazine and tell them I was done? There were only ten days or so left of my tour, and I was certain I wouldn't be the first Pet of the Year to crumple under the weight of it all. If necessary, I could return all the prizes. How many times did I truly expect to play table-top soccer? Should I place the pinball machine next to my four-poster bed or would it look better nestled among the plants in my atrium? And how many televisions could I actually watch at one time?

I thought about it long and hard. In the end, I knew I wasn't a quitter. The least I could do was finish the tour. After all, my idea from the beginning was that posing for *Penthouse* would be a fabulously grand exit from the modeling world. I could take off the month of December and start the 1978 New Year with a whole new career plan.

CHAPTER 15

Pet of the Decade

After the horrifying incident with my cat, I completed the tour and handled a number of other responsibilities and assignments. Then in late December I returned home for the holidays. My life had changed so much since the summer of 1976; I needed some time to contemplate the impact on the people I loved.It would be so easy give it up and stay in Atlanta with Jim. If I chose to go, this could possibly be my last Christmas with my marriage intact. But with gut-wrenching doubt about my decision, I returned to New York and resumed my career.

In the following months, I continued to return home, even to stay in our new house, until the arrangements for our divorce were final. Then it was too hard for either of us. Jim and I managed to remain amicable throughout the proceedings and have continued to this day to respect and love each other. Those qualities are everlasting.

Lick My Face

Long after my centerfold year, I continued to appear on *Penthouse* covers and to represent the magazine in national and international appearances. You might say my final ten days of the official Pet of the Year tour turned into nearly four years in New York before I moved to LA.

Occasionally, the magazine held parties in New York for the opening of a new international edition of *Penthouse*. For some international editions, Bob celebrated in the country where the new magazine was being launched. One day in 1979, Bob called me and asked if I wanted to go to Spain.

"The Spanish publisher has invited me to come over and help promote the new edition," he said. "I know they would want you to be there, too."

Dottie was Pet of the Year, quite popular, and by all rights, this should have been Dottie going off to Spain. But my photo was on the cover of the inaugural Spanish edition, a sensual shot, rather than sexual, with misty shadows, very little skin showing, all eyes and soft attitude and long wavy red hair. Jeff calls it "iconic," because it's so versatile, often cropped so that no one would know I was naked all the way down.

Anyway, I wasn't about to argue. Wasn't Madrid one of those romantic cities I'd always wanted to visit? The event also gave Bob and me an opportunity to enjoy some private time together. The Spanish publisher and his staff treated us like royalty. Those were the years when *Penthouse* was known, read, and respected around the world.

At that time, Bob's sister, Jeri Winston, directed the merchandising division, including the *Penthouse* catalog, Evelyn Rainbird Ltd. She and her staff had put together a collection of high quality clothing, from jogging suits to T-shirts, sexy lingerie, and Pet-of-the-Month panties, all with the *Penthouse* logo, and only a few of the items were intended strictly for erotic nights in steamy bedrooms.

Another catalogue marketed sex-aid paraphernalia and humorous gift items, such as a wool-knit "cock sock" available only in extra large, and innocuous personal items, such as key chains and Pet-of-the-Month coffee mugs. Since Bob loved my image, he instructed the designers to put my face on virtually everything along with the slogan, "*Penthouse*, more than just a pretty face," coined by copywriter Robin Wolaner, before she went on to launch *Runner's World* magazine and found *Parenting* Magazine. During the initial years of the "… pretty face" campaign, my image appeared on billboards, posters and on point-of-purchase materials used at newsstands and stores.

A cover photo by *Penthouse*'s famous female staff photographer Pat Hill, in which I'm obviously hot, wet, and wearing only a turquoise tank top, tugging it down to cover my pubic area while suggestively pouring Perrier over my cleavage, became one of my most popular campaign images. It was displayed everywhere, including on a 36"x48" convention poster. For another famous poster, part of the "rabbit hunting" series designed to attract advertisers, a makeup artist had painted my face, hair, and naked body gold. I wore a shiny gold cape and held a gold turtle-headed staff, symbolizing that *Penthouse*, like the turtle, may have started slow but was destined to overtake the rabbit. The only color on the otherwise solid gold poster was my fluffy pink-and-white bunny slippers.

To commemorate the 1977 Grand Prix, my photo was printed on the front of a Penthouse-Rizla T-shirt. Two different poses graced a double-deck set of playing cards, and a popular desk thermometer was cleverly designed so that when the temperature went up my clothes came off. Similarly, when drink stirrers bearing my photo were touched to liquid, my clothes dissolved. I was on calendar covers and calendar pages. I think I recall seeing my face on a bottle of soothing sex gel, and candy lovers could purchase a set of four giant lollipops printed with my face.

The Perrier cover shot adorned my favorite item, which was "air freshener on a string." When dangled from a car mirror, it refreshed the vehicle's interior air while also entertaining the driver. One day I slid into the back of a New York taxi, and there I was spinning around below the driver's mirror.

I thought, *Oh, my god, will this man recognize me?* He glanced in the mirror occasionally, but in the photo my hair was wet, and I think he was just looking to be looking. If he should dare ask if that was me, I intended to say, "No. Are you kidding?"

Hanging Out with the Rich and Famous

Around this same time, I became the only Pet of the Year to create and sell her own poster separate from *Penthouse*. My personal manager also represented Marjorie Wallace, the 1973 Miss World. This was 1978, and Ms. Wallace was now co-anchoring *Entertainment Tonight*. My manager called one day to say he'd just gotten a poster deal for Marjorie Wallace, and he had a printer's proof he wanted me to see.

"Bring a copy of everything you've done," he added. "The poster company is interested in creating one for you, too."

Each year this company produced exclusive posters of popular celebrities and marketed them through the poster galleries that had sprung up in shopping malls across the country to serve teens and other fans who papered their walls with favorite stars. So I put together a presentation of portfolio photos, press releases, media clips, and celebrity pictures. Marjorie's poster was fabulous. After seeing it, I told my manager to go for it, and he made the deal.

We used a full-figure pose, in which I'm wearing a white tank top and black bikini briefs against a red background. Later, the company printed a promotional piece depicting all the posters for that year, and I found myself appearing among a long list of notables: John Wayne, Loni Anderson, Erik Estrada, Steve Martin, Miss Piggy — who sold more than any of us — Linda Ronstadt, Kermit, King Tut, Dracula, Blondie, the Village People, the Doobie Brothers, Robin Williams, Ted Nugent and Kiss, *The Rocky Horror Picture Show*, and the Beatles. Not a bad group to be seen hanging with.

My poster sold so well that the company made a second version available, and rumors floated that my numbers might reach as high as Farrah Fawcett's. In addition to a thousand-dollar advance, I started earning royalties within a month of the poster's release.

Over the years, my path often crossed with Marjorie Wallace.

Victoria Johnson

When my Pin Up poster was released,
it became the second most popular that year!

We were close in age, moving in similar circles, and many years after I put modeling behind me and moved to Aspen, Marjorie and I became great friends.

Kicking Dirt

Although I did several sports-related photo shoots, including a memorable stint with the Atlanta Braves, the highlight came through the magazine's fashion director, Ed Emmerling. Most issues included at least one fashion spread, usually menswear modeled by name celebrities, and all of it went through Ed.

"Victoria, we're doing an expanded men's fashion layout in the May issue," Ed told me when I returned his call. "In addition to the regular cover, we're doing a special edition cover, and we want you to pose with Billy Martin."

Billy Martin made the sports pages more often than I made the celebrity columns. Asking a few questions around the office, I learned that he was currently, in 1981, the manager of the Oakland A's but was best known for managing the Yankees when they won the World Series in 1977. Everybody I asked laughed when they heard the name.

Remarks I heard included, "A good second baseman, but he has a temper … fired from six different teams … hell on umpires and young pitchers … always stomping around, kicking dirt … too bad Billy's an alcoholic … he took the Yanks to the World Series two years in a row … probably the most colorful of any baseball manager ever, loved and hated … he makes the game fun to watch."

Everybody I talked to was excited about this cover.

Ed hired his own photographer, Bert Miller. The fashion spread inside the magazine, titled "The Sporting Life of the Lite Beer All-Stars," turned out to be quite a showcase of fine-looking men wearing the latest in casual sportswear, and one of my all-time favorite shoots.

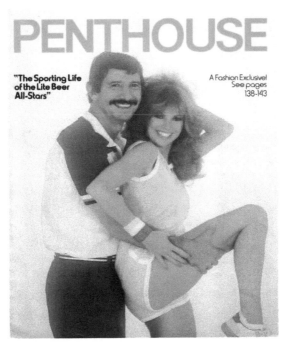

Billy Martin, long time Manager of the New York Yankees, sure was fun to work with

It featured Billy at racquetball and other famous sports figures that had all appeared in popular Miller Lite Beer commercials. A print ad featuring Billy dressed in cowboy clothes kicked off the fashion layout. For the *Penthouse* cover, Billy and I spent an entire day shooting, all fun and games, athletic and playful with no nudity. We talked while we worked, of course, and I learned that Billy had recently opened a Western-wear store on Madison Avenue.

"I'm going to get you a pair of boots," Billy said. "And they're going to match you."

So of course we exchanged numbers. We went out together a few times, which according to the tabloids meant we were "dating." In New York and other cities where I made appearances, I "dated" every night, except for downtime, when I caught up on much needed rest. When I went out on a "date" it would usually be with people I was working with, like Billy, or with my other friends. And it usually made the press. The more dates I had, the more press we got.

Nobody knew for sure who I was really dating, except me. I liked it that way. Relationship or strictly business — that was my call.

The limited-edition *Penthouse* cover that Billy and I posed for made national headline news, and before the magazine hit the newsstands it was already valued at seventy-five dollars, instead of the usual two-fifty cover price.

As much fun as Billy was, he also was a little too wild, dangerous, and "over the edge" for me. Yet it was a privilege to know him. One of the liveliest and most candid people I ever met, when Billy wasn't kicking dirt he was always smiling or laughing.

Not many years later, on Christmas Day of 1989, Billy Martin died in a one-car automobile accident in Johnson City, New York. I still have the boots he gave me thirty years ago, a classic Justin cowboy boot, with stacked wooden heel and pointed toe in a most unusual color, sort of burgundy-rust suede. As Billy promised, they match me. They were special to me, so I wore them only when they stood no chance of being ruined. For most of those years I had the original Billy Martin's Western Wear hang-tag that came with them. I was sad to lose it, because I lost a little bit of Billy.

Billy Martin kicked dirt on the finest of carpets in many bars and hotels. He will always be remembered and thoroughly missed.

CHAPTER 16

Finding Fame in the Most Unusual Places:

An Auction, a Shower Scene, and a Wild Bull Ride

A shining moment of my four New York years of *Penthouse* promotions was the day I appeared on the cover of the *New York Post* with writer-producer Norman Lear. Anyone who watched American television in the 1970s is familiar with at least one of Lear's many sitcoms — *All in the Family, Sanford and Son, One Day at a Time, The Jeffersons, Good Times,* or *Maude.* He also was a supporter of First Amendment rights and, in 1981, founded a civil liberties organization, People for the American Way. But unless you've actually met Norman Lear, you wouldn't know what a fine and quietly amusing gentleman he is.

The Promotions Department of Emerson College in Boston approached *Penthouse* with the idea of offering a date with the Pet of the Year at The Great Celebrity Auction of 1978. Fortunately, that was my year, and as far as I know, it never happened again. At first glance, it sounded a bit sleazy. Then I read the names of other people being auctioned.

Bidders could win a day with actor-director Ron Howard, lunch with actor-director Henry Winkler, a private meeting with Dr. Henry Kissinger or Boston Pops Conductor Arthur Fiedler, or take a dance lesson from Broadway star Ben Vereen. Material-minded bidders might find a thrill in acquiring a signed cartoon original of "Peanuts" by Charles Schulz, tickets to a New York Rangers or Knicks game, or tickets to *Hello, Dolly!*, with a side trip backstage to meet the show's star, Carol Channing. Politically interested bidders might prefer lunch at the White House with top Presidential Assistant Midge Costanza, or lunch with Senator Edward Brooke in the Senate's private dining room, or a day on Capitol Hill with a Washington press photographer. The list went on and on, every name, every item a stellar opportunity.

Or they could bid on a date with me. Wow, what great company to be in fully clothed.

The event was held on Wednesday, May 3, 1978, at Regine's. After agreeing to participate in the auction, my big fear was that I would stand on stage in another gorgeous white designer gown and no one would bid.

Honestly, look at all the items they could choose from. I almost chickened out, because I never like doing anything I can't do well, and in this situation I had no control. I was at the mercy of Emerson College alumni as well as people far more famous than me. But in the end, of course I did it, and fortunately Norman Lear found this to be most amusing.

In competition with commentator Richard Valeriani, Mr. Lear kept raising and raising until he finally won the bid. Then he graciously joined me at the microphone.

"I'm a married man," he told the audience. "Unfortunately, I'm a *happily* married man. I know a lot of you are wondering what I'm going to do with this date. Well, I have a friend who needs a date. He's one of the greatest guys I've ever met. I'm going to donate this incredibly beautiful prize to my friend Stewart Mott."

The room applauded, cameras flashed, film rolled, and the night didn't end until about 2:00 a.m. At 6:00 a.m. I awoke to my phone ringing off the nightstand.

"Did you see the *New York Post* this morning?" said each of the hundred or so callers. "You're on the front page! With Norman Lear!"

TODAY
Cloudy, low 60s
TONIGHT
Chance of rain, 40s
TOMORROW
Rain, mid 50s
Details, page 2

TV: Page 28

NEW YORK POST

THURSDAY, MAY 4, 1978   25 CENTS   © 1978 The New York Post Corporation   Vol. 177, No. 143

WALL ST.
TODAY'S STOCKS

LAST QUARTER'S
DAILY PAID
CIRCULATION   615,690

Levitt bows out after 24 years

By GEORGE ARZT and DAVID SEIFMAN

Arthur Levitt, for 24 years State Controller and the last holdover from the Rockefeller era, has decided to retire and is known to favor former city spending watchdog Stephen Berger as his successor.

Levitt, who will be 78 in June, made a lengthy statement at a press conference today explaining he reached the decision after exhausting "all avenues" including "there have appeared on the scene people who have the same respect for fiduciary responsibility that I do." He is not expected to back Berger publicly, at least for some time.

Democratic sources say Levitt had requested a letter from Berger stating that he would back the Controller's position on not using state employe pension funds to bail out the fiscally strapped city.

In his six terms as the state's chief fiscal officer, Levitt's trademark has been his stance on fiscal austerity in government.

In the last few years, he has engaged in a running battle to keep the $9.3 billion state employe pension funds out of any plans to keep the city from going bankrupt. The State Controller is trustee of those funds.

Secretary of State Mario Cuomo, another of the numerous candidates lining up to enter the race, told The Post last night he has "no desire right now to rush into any race. I have no intention of doing anything right now."

Cuomo is known to be eyeing both Levitt's job and the contest for Attorney General.

Cuomo added that Levitt's retirement represents an incalculable loss to the Democratic ticket. "Probably no one who runs in his stead will bring anything near his strength," he said.

Levitt was one of the most popular vote getters in state history, winning his

Continued on Page 11

WHOLESALE PRICES SOAR

Cost of a date: $2500

TV comedy show wizard Norman Lear studies Lot #93 in a charity auction at Regine's last night. She's Penthouse Pet of the Year Victoria Johnson and Lear bid $2500 for just one date with her. Lear insisted, however, that the date was a gift for millionaire political activist Stewart Mott. The auction was to raise money for Emerson College in Boston.

Post Photo by Richard Lee

WASHINGTON (AP)—Wholesale prices jumped 1.3 per cent in April, the biggest increase in 3½ years, as the inflation outlook worsened sharply, the government reported today.

Wholesale prices of consumer look worsened sharply, the government a four-month surge.

The figures, compiled by the Labor Dept., measure the prices of goods paid by retailers and others just before they reach the consumer. The higher prices usually show up at retail stores shortly afterward.

Before today's wholesale figures were released, the Agriculture Dept. already had bad news for consumers:

Shortages of beef and storm damage to vegetables have forced farm prices up 19.5 per cent since last September. The price of lettuce in the New York area shot up past 90 cents a head this week. In the first three months of this year, retail food prices have risen about 5 per cent.

The April wholesale increase of 1.3 per cent was the biggest since a 1.9 per cent rise in November 1974, also at a time of rising food prices. Wholesale prices of finished goods had risen 0.6 per cent in January, 1.1 per cent in February and 0.6 per cent in March before the latest 1.3 per cent gain.

If the four months of wholesale price increases continued at the same rate all year, they would total about 15 per cent for 1978.

Government economists are counting on volatile food prices

Continued on Page 2

Incredible! I was stunned when Norman Lear bid on a date with me! But I was even more shocked when I learned that he did so for his friend, Stewart Mott! What a once in a lifetime experience.

Celebrity Gossip, Bring It On!

No, the photo didn't appear in the *New York Times* or the *Wall Street Journal*, but the *Post* was read by a hell of a lot more people. The typical New Yorker is addicted to two things: the *New York Post* and coffee from their favorite vendor. Newsstands usually hire an extra person to staff the morning rush. From six a.m. to eight a.m., they do nothing but hand out copies of the *Post* with one hand and take money with the other.

As it happened, I arrived in the city just as this mania of hanging out where celebrities hang out was taking off, and when being in the *Post* was always a good thing. From 1976 through 1982, I appeared frequently in the gossip or entertainment columns, but nothing compared to being front page news with an icon of the television industry — a first for anyone from *Penthouse*.

Looking back, going through my numerous boxes of clippings and memorabilia, I can't help thinking how lucky I was to be there at that moment in time, in the most exciting city in the world and in the golden days of an international bestselling magazine. I never took for granted the limelight that kept finding me during those years. If I'd taken it for granted, I don't believe it would mean so much to me now. As fascinated as others were with me, I was fascinated by what was happening to and all around me: this little girl from the South, seeing every day as a bright new adventure and realizing, *that's me*. At every important turn, I kept thinking, *Oh my, this is just a fluke*.

White Tie on a Moped

Stewart Mott, every bit as gracious a gentleman as Norman Lear, actually arranged our date himself, with a few photo-op suggestions from the *Penthouse* staff. One of Stewart's favorite New York restaurants was a place called Nirvana that served Indian cuisine. We started our evening there with cocktails, then walked across the street to Central Park, where the restaurant's owner personally catered our dinner.

Stewart had packed the picnic utensils, fresh flowers, and a colorful Oriental rug, which he spread on the ground for us to sit on. After a lovely meal of classic Indian fare, we climbed into a horse and buggy. Our leisurely, romantic ride to the clip-clop of horses and the hum of Manhattan traffic ended at the Golden Theater on Broadway.

The Gin Game had only two characters, performed brilliantly by Jessica Tandy and E. G. Marshall. You'd think that living in Manhattan I'd have seen every Broadway play running, but my schedule rarely slowed down enough for a relaxing theater night out. With a handsome, attentive man at my side, I enjoyed every minute and couldn't wait to go backstage and meet two theatrical icons. Too dazzled by it all to remember what everyone said, I do recall that Mr. Marshall, so stern-faced in his performances while exhibiting absolute style and dignity, surprised me.

"I always wanted to meet the *Penthouse* Pet of the Year," he commented.

His smile seemed genuine, so I took him at his word and laughed.

Stewart and Victoria

Sy Presten, the *Penthouse* press agent who arranged for the paparazzi to follow us all night, met Stewart and me at Sardi's for a drink. Looking at one of the many photos that were taken that night, it's obvious we were having fun together. The limo took us to a private party at Studio 54, where we finished the night dancing, as Sy wrote later, "next to tennis star Vitas Gerulaitis."

I believe Stewart enjoyed the media attention, which is fortunate, because it went on for months and months and months. The date did not end after Studio 54 that night. We continued to see

Incredible Experience! Norman Lear bid on a date with ME!
Not for himself. But for his friend, Stewart Mott. And Stewart
eventually became one of my dearest friends.

each other. I found Stewart fascinating and interesting — two of my favorite words. And while many called him eccentric, I found him unique. He was a man ahead of his time, my kind of guy in that nothing he did was ordinary. In addition to orchids, he grew an organic vegetable garden on his rooftop way before organic gardening came into its own. He usually dressed casually and yet always wore a flower, which was different from most men of his age and socioeconomic stratum — but then what man in my life didn't dress differently? He had a terrific, unconventional sense of humor.

A handsome, funny, appealing man whom I sincerely enjoyed being with, and yet we drifted apart. I look back now and think, *What a nice person. Why didn't I take our relationship more seriously?* There's nothing about him I recall not liking. Was I just too busy? Had too many things on my mind? Was I too connected to Bob?

Stewart's being a multi-millionaire might have scared me. I had this stupid habit of thinking, *Aha, you have a lot of money. I'll show you I don't need it.* Stupid, yes, but the attitude stems from the label others attributed to me: "gold digger." People just assumed it, yet I was actually the opposite. Yes, when I needed help with business or personal situations, men came to my aid. Over the years I received many gifts and favors. What I received, someone wanted to give. I didn't make deals. I didn't exchange my body, and I certainly wasn't interested in latching on to a wealthy man, becoming his trophy wife, and taking him for his fortune. That prospect was never a glimmer on my vision of an ideal future. Instead, I developed a habit of possibly closing out someone from fear of being seen as a gold-digger.

For whatever reason, Stewart and I lost contact. Then several years later, I ran into him at the Bermuda airport. He had a home on the island and was leaving as I was arriving. Whoever I was with must not have left an impression, because I can't picture any-one, but I do remember feeling happy to run into Stewart Mott, recalling how much I'd enjoyed his company, noticing that he was alone, and wondering why I'd let such a sweet man get away.

Body Double

Today, when my name is mentioned among people who've actually heard of me, the first thing most will say is, "Victoria Johnson? She was a *Penthouse* Pet of the Year, and … wasn't she in that movie, *Smokey and the Bandit*?" A close second to that response is, "Victoria Johnson — I think she was a famous *Penthouse* centerfold … and she was in a movie with Angie Dickinson and Michael Caine." Or, "Yeah, Vicki Lynn Johnson, Pet of the Year, *Smokey and the Bandit*, and that other movie with the shower scene, *Dressed to Kill*." Usually, they'll remember two out of three, if they remember at all.

The story of being cast in *Dressed to Kill* is one of my favor-ites because it, too, was a media run-away. It kept going and going and going.

Director Brian DePalma was shooting a slasher-thriller starring an interesting mix of characters. Angie Dickinson was a frustrated housewife, Michael Caine was her psychiatrist, and DePalma's wife, Nancy Allen, was a high-priced call girl. The film was mar-keted with the tagline "Brian DePalma, master of the macabre, invites you to a showing of the latest fashion … in murder."

Those two words "latest fashion" seemed to put it solidly in my realm of expertise — though, naturally, that's not what the producers wanted from me. The casting director explained that I'd be a body double for Angie Dickinson, that the scene would require full nudity, and it would be extremely sensual, though not explicitly sexual. Nobody would be in the scene with me.

"Of course, you'll receive film credit," she said.

Body Doubling for Angie Dickinson in Dressed to Kill, which was often referred to as the "immaculate deception" by director Brian DePalma and the media, earned me a Trivial Pursuit, Baby Boomers Edition, card.

I didn't answer right away, but I was thinking, *To do something like this, why would I want credit? It's not a good credit. I'd be just a body double.*

What I said was, "What are you paying?"

"Scale, and it would be a two-day shoot."

Scale at that time was around $500 a day, depending on how long we worked.

"No, I don't think so," I said. "Not for scale." I didn't see a benefit in doing it. I was making great money already, and no matter how big a film this became, no one would ever see my face in it. So where was the gain?

"What would you want?" she asked.

"I'm not sure it's the right fit for me. I'd have to think about it."

"Why don't you come and talk to us? You'd have to meet Mr. DePalma anyway. He's the one who's going to finalize hiring you. So why not come meet with him and talk about it?"

I couldn't help wondering why I was specifically requested. The magazine, or any agency anywhere, could supply dozens of girls eager to be a body double for $500 a day. Since the director needed only an anonymous nude, plenty of actresses and wannabe actresses would jump at the opportunity. Nevertheless, we set up a meeting.

The assistant director and a few other people involved in the film were in the office with Mr. DePalma. They explained what they wanted me to do. DePalma was not at all talkative, and I sensed that he was very much into the film, his art, his work, and not much of a conversationalist.

Finally, he asked if I would mind giving them a quick look at my body. I said I wouldn't mind. I'd expected it, but I was never actually comfortable disrobing for someone, except in front of a camera. By this point in my career, however, it didn't matter whether I was comfortable or not. I'd made every statement there was to make about nudity, so I had to live up to my words. If nothing else, I was meeting a fascinating film director who was noted for telling a story less through dialogue and more through creative and unconventional use of the camera.

So I took off my clothes, put on a robe. Back in the office, I saw that only DePalma and his assistant remained. I slipped the robe off and stood for a moment.

"Thank you," he said. "I appreciate your doing that for us, Victoria." Succinct and strictly business.

Shortly after I returned home, I received a call from the casting director.

"Mr. DePalma would like you to be the body double for Angie Dickinson," she said, her voice full of excitement. "He would need you to, um, to dye your pubic hair blonde."

"You're kidding. How would I even do that?"

"You can go to the best salon, and we'll pay all expenses, of course."

"Let me think about this." At *Penthouse*, much had been made of the fact that I was a natural redhead all the way down. My agent, Gary White, after seeing my centerfold, had even nicknamed me after the Musique hit song, "(Push, Push) In the Bush," and Jeff Zelmanski had once sent me a card naming all the things I was: "Happy birthday to Victoria, Pet of the Year, Miss Posture, Miss Racing Queen, Sex Symbol ..." Twenty titles in all, including, of course, "The Bush."

"About your fee," the casting director said, "would you consider seven hundred and fifty dollars?"

"No."

We finally agreed on $2,500 a day, which was five times scale. But I still had the problem of turning my downstairs blonde.

My gay hairdresser friends thought it would be a hoot. "Sure, we can lighten the carpet so it doesn't match the drapes."

I ended up dyeing it myself, with a non-peroxide lightener. I never got it as blond as they wanted, but I lost all the red tones. I went on the movie set and showed them, knowing this could be a deal breaker.

"This is it," I said. "This is as far as I'm going." I knew it would grow back, but it looked so bizarre.

They went for it. The two-day shoot was relatively easy, with no lines to rehearse. One day was spent setting up the lighting, getting the angles right, with the right amount of steam and suds, so that the audience could see through the shower door but not see too much. We got everything ready for the shoot, a "wet run," so to speak.

The next day I arrived to a closed set, which means only the necessary people were allowed in the room. Brian DePalma, the cameraman, the assistant director, two or three female assistants for makeup and hair. That was it. Not even Angie Dickinson was there.

In directing the scene, Brian DePalma paid meticulous attention to each tiny action, the intricate details of every finger, every hand movement. After a few hours, using several different camera positions, he said, "It's a wrap. Thank you, Victoria. That was well done."

The ladies came with towels and a robe. As I was leaving the set, Angie Dickinson walked on. We were the same size and height, but what caught my attention were her collar bones. We have exactly the same collar bones, unusual because they have deep dips, one on each side of the neck. In the business we call them "caviar and champagne" collar bones. One's for caviar, one's for champagne.

Heavy Edits Get an "R" Rating

Brian DePalma's keen observation, enough to notice the likeness of my bone structure to Dickinson's, was indicative of his meticulous detail in film making. He was determined to have the body double actually appear as if she was the real Angie. When I read what he wrote, using the word immaculate, I thought it was a most interesting way to describe a body and so significant of his way of thinking. He didn't want the most beautiful body or the most perfect body; he wanted the most immaculate body. Only he knows what he meant, but I considered it a compliment. I'd never been described that way before.

The film was released in the US in 1980, with nine minutes cut out to give it an R rating. For me, that was to be the last of it — until the story leaked.

Did it leak from the magazine, perhaps from press agent Sy Presten? From somebody on the set? I had just enough fame and notoriety on my own that the salacious tabloid press proceeded to turn what might have been a totally unremarkable role into a story that's lasted my lifetime.

Angie Dickinson was asked on *The Johnny Carson Show* if that was her body in the shower. She hinted, probably as she'd been instructed by the film's PR department, that she *was* the woman in the shower scene. The press promptly disagreed, and they had proof.

The story ran everywhere. It made *People* magazine again, and all the television entertainment shows. Comedians from *Saturday Night Live* and other late-night shows picked it up. *Hustler* magazine got their hands on some nude photos of Angie Dickinson, and some photos of me, and published them side by side. Angie filed a lawsuit but dropped it, and I could have sued too, but everybody sued *Hustler*, so why bother?

Instead, I considered the whole situation to be one of those ridiculous runaway moments that capture the nation's attention. For the film, it proved a glorious windfall. The controversy drove people to the box office, and thirty years later I still receive residual checks when it runs on cable television. The phrase used by the press most often to describe the movie was "the immaculate deception."

Trivia Happens

In 1983, a few years after the film was released, grossing $29 million, which was an impressive box-office take at that time, I remember being awakened by a phone call from a friend.

"Victoria, you're never going to believe this."

"What I can't believe is that you're calling me at two a.m.," I said. "What's going on?"

"We're playing Trivial Pursuit," he said, "and you're in it! You're one of the questions in the Baby Boomer edition."

Shaking the fog out of my brain, I asked, "What does it say?"

"It was my turn to answer, and I got it right," he said. Then he read it to me:

Question: Who was replaced from the neck down by *Penthouse* Pet Victoria Lynn Johnson for the shower scene of *Dressed to Kill*?

Answer: Angie Dickinson.

"Pretty cool, huh? You're the question, so you get the whole card, and Angie's the answer. She gets just her name in there."

"Works for me," I said, and returned to bed.

My Friend, Jack

Once in the early years of my career I was asked to ride a horse in a commercial. This occurred before *Penthouse* and before I learned to say, "No, I can't do this." By the end of shooting that commercial, I'd been thrown off the horse four times.

Having never signed an exclusive with any agent, I periodically received calls from one or another of those I worked with. The late seventies marked the beginning of the designer jeans era, and one young agent approached me to do a commercial for a company formed by three brothers, Joe, Ralph, and Avi Nakash, that was establishing a new brand. Jordache Jeans was already running an international commercial featuring sexy models romping around outdoors clad only in their Jordaches. All three US networks banned it, and the replacement, while slightly amateurish, was playing nonstop, especially in New York.

With the company still in start-up phase, the Nakash brothers didn't have a fortune yet to invest. They wanted to produce a new and better commercial "under the radar," which meant a non-SAG commercial. The Screen Actors Guild exists to protect actors against being hired for lower-than-scale fees and cheated out of residuals. Technically, actors aren't supposed to participate in non-SAG productions, but they do, and I saw a lot of potential in this commercial. Besides, the description of the model was *me*. I looked the part, and I wanted to do it.

When modeling is your business, money is always a consideration, but so is getting your name attached to a remarkable body of work. I had a hunch that Jordache was going to be a highly successful company and this commercial would be a good credit on my résumé.

There was just one drawback. The contract stated, "She should have riding skills."

Painful memories of falling off a horse came back to me. The producers, however, didn't plan to put me on a real horse.

Disco mania was starting to wane, and following close on its heels was country & western mania, due to the popularity of John Travolta's most recent film *Urban Cowboy*. Every "honky-tonk" and nightclub from New York to Texas to LA had installed a mechanical bull like the one Debra Winger rode at Gilley's in

Pasadena, Texas, in the film. A mechanical bull was what the Jordache crew had in mind.

If any drunken cowboy could do it, how hard could it be? If I got the part, I planned to run over to the Central Park stables and take riding lessons. After meeting with the brothers, I did get the job. They liked the idea of riding lessons and volunteered to pay for them. We established a shoot date two or three weeks away, at a country-western bar in New Jersey.

My riding instructions were held in an enclosed stable filled with stacks of hay, which I appreciated, since it might cushion my landing. I bought all the gear and got through the first lesson but left the stable coughing incessantly. By the time I arrived at Connaught Tower, I was wheezing, my eyes swollen nearly shut. I could barely breathe.

The doorman took one look and reached for the phone to call 911.

"No, I'll be okay," I wheezed.

He didn't look convinced but agreed to hold off. He let me get upstairs to my apartment then checked on me at frequent intervals.

Being allergic to horses and hay meant no more riding lessons. But since I'd managed to hang on to the real horse without a single mishap, I figured I could wing it on the bull.

Butt-Thumping Pain

I arrived in New Jersey for the shoot with my "Jordache Look" nailed: As the camera rolls, I strut through the bar wearing my skin-tight Jordaches with a cream-colored Western shirt. I tip my cream-colored Stetson to the gents lined up along the bar.

The camera focuses on a burly cowboy getting bucked off a mechanical bull. I strut on over and swing into the saddle, all smiles and confidence. So far, so good.

In the practice run, my skinny arms weren't strong enough to

VICTORIA JOHNSON "ON LOCATION FOR JORDACHE"

I had the honor of being the first "Jordache Jeans Girl"

hold on, so the director called "cut" and stopped the bull before I could fall. He told a grip to tape my arms, which would give them more strength. So I rolled up my sleeves to be wrapped in tape, wrist to elbow. We tried again and got through the first take.

But shooting a commercial in one take is rare, and since this was a non-SAG production, we didn't have a savvy SAG crew to smooth out the ride, so to speak. I was bouncing so hard my butt rose a good eight inches off the saddle and *whopped* down again, over and over, and my butt doesn't have much natural padding. My thighs ached with bruises from trying to hold on, yet the assistant director, who looked about twelve years old, wanted to make the bull go faster.

After a few more takes at medium speed, my thighs, waist, and back were taped to make everything stronger. I hurt all over, and I could see the shoot was going to be an all-nighter. For a 60-second commercial, I'd never done so many hours of butt-thumping, back-breaking work.

One guy seemed to know what he was doing. During a short break to fix the lighting, the bartender waved me over.

"Honey, you look like you need a friend," he said, setting a jigger of whiskey on the bar in front of me. "Let me introduce you to Jack."

I'd never tasted Jack Daniels, and I can't say I particularly liked it, but I definitely liked the effect. After a few more shots, the pain of riding that mechanical beast wasn't nearly so bad.

In the end, Jordache Jeans created a hugely successful commercial that night, which played for a good two years. If it had been a SAG production, I'd probably have made $50,000 in residuals. Instead, I walked away with a couple thousand for a painful all-night ride, but it was worth it. The magazine got a ton of publicity even before the commercial started running, and thanks to my bartender buddy, Jack and I became really good friends that night.

CHAPTER 17

Playing Against Type

Fellini and the Seven-Year Itch

Looking at interoffice memos from the years that I was most active with *Penthouse*, I see that scripts were constantly going back and forth with my name attached in some way. Meanwhile, I enjoyed the roles I played on various television programs. A favorite was the first installment in a series starring Andy Griffith. My part had only a couple of lines, but I loved it because Andy was one of my favorite actors.

The series was called *Honeymoon Hotel*. It took place in a legendary honeymoon resort of the Poconos. I was the lotion lady in a scene with Andy, and though the series never took off, I enjoyed rubbing lotion on the hands of one of my all-time favorite actors.

Another of my favorites is Ed Asner, who starred in a series that spun off from *The Mary Tyler Moore Show* and spun its way into thirteen Emmy Awards. Again, I played in only one episode, called "Stroke," which aired on May 4, 1981, but it was an honor to have even a small part in *The Lou Grant Show*.

The episode had two story lines. The second was about a college girl who poses nude for a national men's magazine to make extra money while she's going to college, which causes the college to deny her scholarship. As the girl, I'm interviewed by staff reporter Billie Newman, played by Linda Kelsey.

This may have been the only show I ever did in which casting didn't know I was a *Penthouse* centerfold. I was relatively new to LA, pursuing acting, and I wasn't using *Penthouse* in conversations unless asked. After the first casting interview, I received a call-back. Then William Morris phoned to say I'd gotten the part. No one ever mentioned *Penthouse*.

I laughed when I read the script, thinking they'd asked for me, or my agent had sent me, because they knew who I was. But the play on reality never came up. If anyone had ever put it together, the set would have buzzed with the irony of it. Possibly the most serious acting role I ever had on TV, and I played the role of a centerfold.

I had many glorious moments and opportunities in my career, with and without *Penthouse*. One of those was when Harvey Weinstein of Miramax fame cast me in a small role in *Playing for Keeps,* and I had the privilege of attending my first Cannes Film Festival with Harvey to promote the film.

At *Penthouse*, the Fellini project never materialized. I didn't mind, because as much as I appreciated my time with the magazine, I was feeling a seven-year-itch and ready to move on.

PART 2

DISILLUSIONS

CHAPTER 18

Skyway to Hell

A butterfly, in ancient lore, symbolizes the human soul, or in Egyptian culture, the *immortality* of the soul. The Irish consider butterflies a blessing: *May the wings of the butterfly kiss the sun, find your shoulder to light on, and bring you luck, happiness and riches today, tomorrow and beyond.*

Paging back through my calendar day by day, year by year, I can clearly recognize my "butterfly years," those times when my soul grew restless and I didn't know quite where to land. The choices I made concerning *Penthouse* and my relationship with Bob are choices I'd make again. Despite the anguish of what I gave up, I'm comfortable with those decisions and with where they eventually took me. But I've made a few choices that compromised my own moral values. Dealing honestly with those choices in this book is a challenge.

Oddly, the years surrounding that period were some of my best — productive, focused, comfortable, rewarding. True to my nature, though, when I'm most comfortable is when that mischievous imp living inside pokes me with an elbow and says, *Let's go DO something.*

A Taste of Hollywood

All of 1979 and until the pivotal midsummer of 1980, my life was filled with two very different types of drama. In my career, I usually took center stage, modeling for *Penthouse* covers or fashion layouts, shooting *Dressed to Kill*, the Jordache commercial, and another spot for Paladine Jeans, an editorial layout for *Cosmopolitan* magazine, auditioning for and securing commercials for Lever Brothers and QT Tanning Lotion. At the magazine's request, I was still being "seen" around New York at night and seeing my name in print the next day. At the beginning of the music video craze, I appeared in an Atlantic Records video for the rock band Foreigner.

For one photo shoot, I had to corral my voluminous tresses into a bun. The result was a demure, softly feminine headshot for Betadine Douche. The product, featuring my photo on the box, sold in drugstores for twenty-five years before they finally changed the package design. As recently as three years ago, I saw it in Aspen's only drugstore.

Auditions for film roles continued to occur, and I appeared in several soap operas. A most memorable audition was with Woody Allen. I arrived wearing my best Annie Hall outfit, calm and prepared, and Woody was as dry, witty, and adorably goofy in person as he appeared in his films. I didn't get the part, but merely having the chance to audition was worth the effort.

Socially, life was more comfortable than dramatic. My new family — Bob and the magazine — plus a continuing array of new friends gave my life balance. I received the education of a lifetime from those around me and soaked up a little more of the magic that was New York theater or Hollywood film production. One evening I was invited to a small dinner party at the home of Oscar-winning composer Marvin Hamlisch. He asked me to join him at the piano while he played, and later we continued to see each other casually. With his background in music, Marvin was like fine wine to my thirst for knowledge. I was also still spending time with Stewart Mott. Nothing romantic, just good friends. These were genuine friendships with truly inspiring people I considered to be mentors.

Stage Struck

As if I didn't have enough work-related and social drama in my life, I reached out for theatrical drama in my insatiable need to know and experience new things. Along with my classes at the New York Academy of Theatrical Arts, I had roles in two theatrical productions that year: Amiri Baraka's dark one-act play, *The Dutchman*, shocking when it was first presented in 1964, and Neil Simon's comedy-drama, *Chapter Two*.

For Bob and me, the year of 1979 was one of our best, not only on a personal level but also professionally. Existing in a tornado of constant media attention, television interviews, and continued success with the magazine, we brought out the best in each other. Bob supported my ever-evolving interests, even attending my *Chapter Two* performance. As the opening lights were going down, he quietly entered through the back door. When the play was over, he came to the stage, congratulated me with a hug, and shook hands with Professor Nolan. Philip Nolan, one of Bob's biggest fans, was beside himself with joy.

That was a year of accomplishments and exploration of knowledge, with less focus on being Pet of the Year, more on personal pursuits. Always aware that my *Penthouse* success had opened these doors, I felt privileged and a little proud to have taken that bold turn with the magazine. My next turn, in the summer of 1980, opened equally engaging but far more dangerous doors.

"Trust Me, You're Gonna Be a Star"

Pet of the Year was not a lifetime job, and I wasn't yet ready for corporate *Penthouse*. Pursuing acting seemed the obvious next move to everyone around me, so I felt pressured to at least give Hollywood a try.

About that time, Jeffrey Allen Toffler, Madison Avenue advertising agent and salesman extraordinaire, breezed into my life, all dazzling personality and fast-talking wit. The advertising agency, Tilley, Marlieb and Allen, in which he was a partner, had an auxiliary office at *Penthouse* and handled much of the magazine's advertising, and by coincidence Jeffrey leased an apartment in the Connaught Tower, so we gradually began talking. Six feet tall, thin, a smart dresser with salt and pepper hair and all the right moves, clicking with the right people at the right time, Jeffrey was not extraordinarily handsome but was nice looking. He had a captivating personality. Always "on," he made people laugh. Everyone liked him, liked being around him. Jeffrey could talk anybody, including himself, into just about anything.

At first, I was friendly with him without quite being friends. He wanted to date, and I didn't. When the dating didn't work, Jeffrey decided on his own that he should represent me as a personal manager.

"Next step for you, Hollywood," he told me one day.

"You think so?"

"You're beautiful, talented. What's Farrah Fawcett got that you don't?"

"Hmmm." That didn't take much thought. "Fame? *Charlie's Angels*? The all-powerful William Morris Agency?"

"Yeah? We can do that."

Jeffrey and I talked about my moving to Los Angeles.

"Jeffrey, I'm not doing the struggling actress bit. Been there, done that, got my picture plastered on the T-shirt."

"So where's the struggle? We get you a house, car, the right contacts. Besides, I have a partner in LA, and I need a crash pad." He waved a finger, got the immediate attention of a flight attendant, thanks to his dazzling charm, and ordered another drink. "When we stop off in LA, let's get it done."

Once again, he wasn't kidding. Three months later, I was installed in my own house off Sunset Boulevard in Hollywood, driving a Mercedes 450 SL convertible in a fashionable shade of brown, with $50,000 of Jeffrey's personal investment deposited in my bank account to pay for a year's living expenses. And the astounding, deciding factor? I was signed with the renowned William Morris Agency.

Pretty Girl, Pretty Girl

An older, multi-level home, typical LA style, with outdoor patios and fountains, my house was tucked away on Kings Road among two other residences, all of them leases. The three houses shared a common driveway, parking area, and swimming pool. The smallest belonged to Sherri Spillane, nightclub singer and ex-wife of author Mickey Spillane. I saw Sherri come and go and chatted with her at times. A polite, pleasant woman, but our paths didn't often cross.

The third house was a two-story leased to actor-comedian Chevy Chase.

October in LA is still summertime. Shortly after moving in, I was lying out by the swimming pool, which was directly in front of Chevy's house, when I heard a voice coming from the balcony above me.

"Pretty girl. Pretty girl."

Craning to look up and back, I spied a brilliantly colored parrot sitting on the balcony railing.

"Pretty girl. Pretty girl."

A second later, a man looked down.

"Hello," he said. "I'm Chevy Chase."

"I know."

"Who are you?"

"Victoria Johnson. Just moved in."

"Welcome to the neighborhood."

"Thank you."

"See you around."

"Okay."

At this time in 1980, Chevy had already left *Saturday Night Live* and starred in several films, including *Foul Play*, with Goldie Hawn, and a more recent blockbuster, *Caddyshack*. So, yes, I knew who he was. But I'd never been smitten by movie stars, and while I felt pretty darn lucky to be living next door, where I might cull his brain for acting advice, perhaps get some insider info for negotiating with shifty Hollywood studio types, I had no problem playing it cool with my new neighbor.

My calendar filled up quickly. With Jeffrey Toffler backing me, I'd agreed to give Hollywood one ferocious year, and I meant to make it count. He not only had fulfilled his promise to sign me with William Morris, somehow Jeffrey managed to get me signed with Fred Westheimer, the executive vice president responsible for building a career for numerous stars who went from "never-heard-of" to household names. With Fred as my primary agent, I acquired several additional agents for film and commercials. So I was signed with the premier LA agency and at the top of the struggling-actress pyramid.

The Hollywood Reporter published my name in their ongoing list of who had signed with which agency. My entire portfolio had to be redone, of course, imprinted with the William Morris logo, which I was proud to display on my new résumés, photos, and composites. I learned it was a big deal merely to be listed in the William Morris directory.

As additional backing, I still had my contract with *Penthouse*. The magazine's LA office, headed by Bob's oldest daughter, Tonina, sent me on go-sees that frequently turned into talk-show interviews or small acting parts. That fall, I was far too busy to spend much time lying by the pool.

In early December, I came home to find a Christmas tree

propped beside my door. Florie, my sweet, considerate landlady, had bought one for each of her tenants. Wow. Christmas in LA. I'd just climbed out of a convertible with the top down. Never mind snow, how about sweater weather, at least? And decorations? I hadn't made Christmas travel plans, but I also hadn't considered an LA holiday. What was I going to do with this tree?

That night, about seven-thirty, home by myself, I heard a knock on my door.

One thing about LA, it's open and sunny and carefree. You look out at a beautiful sunset, or down at the circus of lights on Sunset Boulevard, and there are no obvious shadows where monsters might hide. But all that openness didn't exactly make me feel safe. Living in New York, a more difficult environment in many ways, I was tucked away in a secure building with people all around me and doormen I could trust to ward off any unwanted individuals. The magazine offices and security guards were just around the corner. Bob and Kathy's big house was a taxi ride away. I was always in close proximity to people, yet with barriers and protection. I also had credentials there. I was known. If I had a problem, one phone call would bring someone to take care of me.

Here in this lovely 3,000-square-foot house in LA, I felt vulnerable. Exposed. After peeking out to find Chevy Chase standing on my doorstep, I opened the door.

"Hi," he said. His arms were loaded down with a number of unusual items.

"Hello, Chevy."

"I brought you some things."

"So I see." Looking at the items he brought, I was reluctant to let him in.

Another thing I'd learned about LA was that people played games here I didn't know how to play. Everybody wanted to be in the movie business. Every conversation was about who you are, who you know, who you're seen with, what you're in or not in. LA was all about who's who. Okay, New York was like that, too, but in a more meaningful way. Here, it was just posturing, with no purpose and no concrete results expected. And I was the new girl in town, not yet established, totally out of my element. I had no one at hand to show me the ropes.

I was not so new, however, that I hadn't met a few important movie executives. "Victoria, I have this part. I think it's right for you … why don't you come over later and we'll read the lines?" You never knew when it was legit. I'd found myself with one key executive on a project who simply laid it out there. "This is a nothing role. Any pretty girl can play it. You'd be good, Victoria, you've got the right look. Here's what it takes to get the part. I like you. Sleep with me." And, of course, he was married. But at least he was honest.

In Hollywood, I felt disposable. An actress has to really want it badly — the recognition, the parts, the whole package — and has to compromise. If I hadn't looked the way I looked, with *Penthouse* attached to my name, or if I'd done some serious off-Broadway acting, maybe it would have been different. But beautiful women in LA are like seashells on the beach. You can't walk without stumbling over a few, most of them willing to do a whole lot more than I was to enter the sacred club of Hollywood insiders. It was going to be a tough road.

Now here I was, opening my door to this very famous person, whom I believed to be a nice guy, standing with his arms full of things that made no sense to me whatsoever.

I said, "What's all that for?"

"For you."

Hmmm. "What's the ax for?"

"To cut off the bottom of the tree."

"Oh! Okay. Got it. What's the camera for?"

"To take a picture of the tree."

"And the turkey?"

"To cook. Eat."

"And of course the stand is to put the tree in." By now I knew I was asking stupid questions. "The book? The jacket?"

"Oh, those are about me. Just wanted to give you something."

The Party Before the Party

In many ways, that night marked the beginning of one long party for me in LA. Not with Chevy, although we did become friendly neighbors. With his handy ax, he chopped off the bottom of the tree. Together, we wrestled it into the stand, and eventually we took a photo with his Polaroid.

Chevy and I talked half the night, then he took his shiny ax and went home. Over the next months, we'd chat from time to time. Or he'd drop by without notice, wandering in through the downstairs game room rather than climbing the steps to the front door, rather like a cat stopping by when he felt like it. Friendly neighbors.

He never told me what went on when the old black hearse came to his house. This huge limousine with blacked-out windows would occasionally appear in our small parking area, and for two or three days there'd be loud music booming from behind Chevy's doors and windows. Not identifiable tunes, particularly, but like several musicians jamming together, playing wild riffs for hours and hours. After two or three days, the car would leave. The rumor, of course, was that the Blues Brothers — John Belushi, Dan Aykroyd, and the gang — had come to visit their friend.

Life is Fickle and So Am I

As I was adjusting to LA, Jeffrey Toffler swung back through town, which he did from time to time, checking on his investment, and said, "Guess who's opening a new restaurant here."

"I haven't a clue."

"Robáire Pascal! Let's go have dinner with him."

Even though we'd crossed paths in New York, I'd never had an interest in Robert (pronounced Robáire) Pascal. When I dined at his New York restaurant, Chez Pascal — wonderful French food, high-end clientele — I was always with someone. I knew Robáire only as a brilliant restaurateur.

Robáire knew food, but he also knew how to make his guests feel special. He was charismatic and had a devilish twinkle in his eye, everything a good restaurateur needed. Women adored him, and men weren't terribly threatened by him: a perfect combination. No surprise that he was friends with Jeffrey Toffler. Jeffrey had a knack for befriending exactly the right people to connect him with other important people. So when Jeffrey came back to LA in February, maybe it wasn't entirely coincidental that he arrived just as Robáire was there to open his first LA restaurant. At that time in LA, restaurateurs were like celebrities in their own right.

La Cage aux Folles would not open, though, until April, so what better place to meet than at Hollywood's legendary Ma Maison? And who better than Robáire Pascal, good friend of Ma Maison's owner Patrick Terrail, to get us a table where *no one* is guaranteed a table?

My Own Hot New Impresario

A woman can lose her head when surrounded by three passionate men, each enchantingly attractive in his own way and with the ability to delight an audience. Place them at the best table in the most extraordinary restaurant — so exclusive that the telephone number is unlisted — amid Hollywood's most entitled celebrities — Steven Spielberg, Orson Welles, Joan Collins, to name only a few Ma Maison regulars — serve delectable cuisine with good wine, and what woman wouldn't melt in her shoes from the sheer intensity of it all?

Jeffrey, in his usual fast-talking, animated manner, kept everybody laughing. Patrick Terrail, owner of Ma Maison, was the epitome of condescension and arrogance. His haughty façade made a guest feel even more flattered when treated as special, as we were.

And Robáire? It was like meeting him for the first time. He was Moroccan born but raised in France, and you couldn't miss that deep-throated French accent, couldn't help noticing that he spoke somewhat like a frog, the deprecating nickname we Americans sometimes use in referring to a Frenchman. A bout of throat cancer had left his voice strangely husky, but it only added to his appeal, made him even more delightfully unique. It worked for him because of his dynamic personality. It made him "Robáire."

Back in New York, I'd never noticed how truly attractive he was. Energetic. Impulsive. Theatrical. He had that adorable smile and the French way of charming the boots off everybody, including me. And now that he was so close, I picked up on the pheromones, that seductive scent I find irresistible. We had chemistry.

I was intrigued, fascinated, excited — all the emotions I use to describe being smitten. Robáire Pascal swooped into my life and swept me up in a cyclone of madness. He had his own press agent, and as the opening of his new supper club drew nearer, we frequently made all the papers. Ostentatious, dramatic, impetuous — he leased an Excalibur "neoclassic" roadster in white with lots of gold trim — and he just as quickly absorbed my life into his.

With Robáire came an enormous amount of press and friends and celebrity. Whenever he was in LA, he lived at my house, turning my world upside down. And typical of his spontaneous mindset, the first thing he decided we should do is to throw a big party.

"Do You All Want Some Breakfast?"

La Cage aux Folles, a farcical and hugely popular French play, had been made as a film in 1978, which ran for over a year at an art house in New York before winning a Golden Globe for Best Foreign Film and being nominated for three Oscars. In 1996, it was remade as *The Birdcage*, starring Robin Williams and Nathan Lane.

The storyline about two gay men, humorously shocking to middle America, was exactly right for this period of sexual rebellion. It had charmed the nation. Robáire's New York version of La Cage aux Folles was designed with the same theme as its namesake in the stage play and movie. With the LA version of La Cage finished down to creating the menu, testing the food, and staffing, Robáire and I found ourselves in a world of female impersonators. Fascinating, frivolous, ridiculous, these guys would come in, audition, get the part, rehearse, and entertain us all the while. They were consummate performers, friendly and outgoing. Of all the female impersonators available, we got the best. Sitting in the dressing room, watching them put on their Liza Minnelli persona, or Streisand or Judy Garland or Bette Midler, was like living in the film.

And La Cage in LA would upstage its New York sister in one important detail: Benny Luke, the screen actor who played Jacob, the maid, would be the master of ceremonies for the show every night. Anyone who loved the film loved the unforgettable Benny Luke above all.

Robáire had so much energy. Keeping watch on the other four restaurants while getting this one open, you'd think he'd be exhausted, but for him one idea spun nimbly into another, and he wanted to act on all of them. For our spontaneous party, Robáire decided that his La Cage chefs would help prepare the food and his "showgirls" would serve as waitstaff.

No official invitations were sent. We simply told a hundred or so people we were getting together at my house to celebrate our March birthdays. If I'd known how unwieldy the party would get, I certainly wouldn't have acted on my next bright idea.

"I know someone who would adore being here for this," I told Robáire, and I flew my mother in from Georgia.

The showgirls loved my mom. They began arriving early on the afternoon of the party to change into their costumes, and Mom was right in there, helping them. They set up in the bedrooms and bathrooms, turned the pool table into one big makeup counter, wigs all over the place. The house was huge and open, with everyone bantering between rooms and levels, shrieking over whose bra padding was too big and who had the most daring cleavage.

Just a few steps up, big pots of food were going, with ten people cooking and Robáire in the middle, giving orders in his energetic, playfully dramatic but very intense manner.

"Hilda! Hilda!" Absolutely hysterical, one of the guys getting dressed shouted, "Hilda, I need help! I need you!"

Mom went running.

"Oh my," she said in her soft, soothing, Southern way, "what's wrong, dear?"

"I've got a run in my fishnets!" he wailed, standing there in full makeup, no hair, a generously endowed lace bra, the torn fishnet stockings, and a snug triangular patch tucking in his private male parts.

"Oh, honey!" Mom examined the tear. "Oh, I can fix that. Just let me get a needle and thread."

Minutes later she's sewing the fishnets back together on this six-foot-long leg, and I'm thinking, *This is hilarious.* Even in my teen years, Mom could calmly adjust to any scenario I threw at her, no matter how bizarre. That day she might have been dressing female impersonators all her life. Amazingly, and regrettably, nobody took photos during this frivolity.

Since there was no convenient parking for that many vehicles, we hired a valet service to handle the cars. Guests arrived, tossed their keys at anybody in a coat, and the valets parked cars up and down Kings Road. Arriving so fast and in such numbers, the turnout was overwhelming. A hundred invited guests turned into two hundred. The valet service called another service to help out.

The drinks started flowing. Then the food followed in luscious, aromatic waves, one scrumptious presentation after another. Sonny Bono sat down at the piano. Other musicians joined in, mostly just plinking and joking around, having fun. Two hundred people become three hundred, my house busting at the corners and nobody wanting to leave because they were having so much fun enjoying copious amounts of champagne and white powder.

About one o'clock in the morning, Mom decided she'd had enough merriment and went down to her bedroom, intending to call it a night. She found her bed piled high with coats and purses. Typically, she just closed the door, climbed on the bed pushing the coats aside, burrowed in, and went to sleep.

A short while later, the door opened and someone entered her room. Assuming it was a guest coming to retrieve a coat or purse, Mom kept still so as not to startle anyone and waited for the visitor to finish. After a while, hearing one purse after another click open and closed, she realized the intruder was rifling them and stealing money. Keeping still, she didn't say a word.

After the rustling stopped, the door opened and closed. Mom waited a few more minutes then came upstairs and told me what happened. Of course I'd no idea who it might've been. Except for the obvious celebrities and my close friends, I knew very few of the people who'd invaded my house that night. Many had come and gone, but there were scores of guests still partying everywhere I looked.

We moved the coats and purses out of Mom's room. Before she went back downstairs, Sonny Bono moved the piano so that it blocked the staircase and no one else could go down. I don't remember whether any of our guests mentioned missing money from their purses or coat pockets, but everyone was so coked up it hardly mattered.

I do remember Mom saying the next day, "They moved that piano to protect me. *Sonny Bono* moved that piano for me."

As it turned out, purses weren't the only items under attack that night. When Robáire's partner, Lou, and other guests asked to have their cars brought around, the valets couldn't find them. They'd vanished.

Hollywood police are unflappable when dealing with their city's celebrity behavioral quirks. When they arrived, an officer said, "Ma'am, we're not looking for contraband. We're just looking for missing Mercedes."

A professional theft ring, they said, had recently infiltrated the best parties in the area by showing up in the uniform of whichever valet service was working the event.

"And they came *here*," Robáire commented, clearly delighted by the fact. "We hosted one of the best parties in Beverly Hills!"

The next day twenty or thirty people remained draped over various pieces of furniture, sleeping it off. One of our good friends — actually, everybody's friend — actor-socialite Frank Calcagnini, was in the bed with me and Robáire. Not because we were doing anything kinky. Frank just needed a place to crash, so he'd wandered in, told Robáire to move over, and fell in beside him.

That's how Mom found us when she knocked on the door that afternoon, opened it and stuck her head in.

"Do you all want some breakfast? It's about three p.m.," she said, her Southern hospitality fully engaged. Along with her ability to adjust to a situation, Mom also had a knack for seeing only what she wanted to see. She wouldn't have noticed the drugs flowing the night before as copiously as the conversation.

Knowing she often lived vicariously through me, I said, "Mom, take a picture of this scene," and handed her the Polaroid. That's the only photo I have of our fabulous birthday bash: me, Robáire, and Frank Calcagnini waking up in the same bed.

Glittering Distractions

Robáire Pascal was the dangerously attractive sort of man I was drawn to as far back as high school, when Jim Arnold and his burgundy Corvette struck me as dangerous. Robáire lived life bigger than life, in a state of craziness and exuberance and celebrity, and he was a rising star in a land where I was as yet an unknown.

I'd come to LA many times in the past, always as a New Yorker with a specific purpose and with a safe haven awaiting me back home. This time I was here to absorb the lifestyle and mark my territory; about to be tested by a world notorious for chewing up ingénues and spitting them into the streets. Being with Robáire felt like familiar ground. He was a social celebrity, but he was from my Manhattan world. It felt smart to be with someone who was bringing his New York success to LA.

And the more cocaine nights we shared, the smarter I felt.

La Cage aux Folles was the "happening" of the moment. From our party in March until the nightclub's opening in April, Robáire and I appeared in the columns almost daily.

A Grand Hollywood Romp

Less than six months into my LA life, I'd made inroads into the industry. I was beginning to get callbacks. Casting people were telling William Morris to "send Victoria Johnson" to audition for this or that TV show. Most auditions were for guest appearances on weekly TV sitcoms or light drama such as *The Lou Grant Show* and *Charlie's Angels*, which dominated prime-time air in those years.

It's easy to make friends when you already have friends. I'd met Robin Leach in New York at one of the *Penthouse* parties, and we'd become great pals. In LA, he was a regular at Ma Maison. So in addition to having impresario Robáire as my man-about-town, I also had Hollywood reporter Robin Leach as my ambassador. Thus Ma Maison became my place to be seen.

Owner Patrick Terrail had come to America from France, product of a Parisian family acclaimed for culinary brilliance. After studying at Cornell University and apprenticing at several esteemed New York hotels, Patrick had burst onto the Hollywood scene in 1973 to open Ma Maison in a small house on Melrose Avenue.

Patrick presented a magical combination of exquisite cuisine and casual dining to LA's jaded palates, and a love story began on the spot. A serious restaurant, with serious food and accomplished chefs — Wolfgang Puck and Susan Feniger started there — Ma Maison became so famous so fast that by 1981 it was famous simply for existing.

Getting ready for the opening of La Cage, Robáire and I dined at one of the important Hollywood restaurants or supper clubs every night and lunched at Ma Maison several times a week. *Always* on Fridays. If you could get in on Friday, you were somebody special.

This was a superficial world in many ways, a society that existed merely to celebrate and perpetuate its own acclaim. In New York, I called them actors or people of accomplishment — Norman Lear, Jessica Tandy, Mayor Koch. Many of the LA people I met were equally accomplished, yet I thought of them merely as "celebrities." And indeed, many Hollywood names were known mostly for showing up at the best parties and hot spots.

Nevertheless, I was in celebrity heaven.

Everywhere we went the press was there. In *Beverly Hills People*, or the *Los Angeles Daily News,* or the *Hollywood Reporter*, a mention inevitably appeared that "Robáire and Victoria…" were seen at this place or that, did this or did that. Juggling my social life with my attempts to build an LA career, I'd often get up in the morning, leaving Robáire in the bed, and go to an audition or a booking. When auditions resulted in a job, I'd be off to a television shoot at five a.m. I was definitely living two lives.

Sadly, I don't think every part of my heart, body, and soul was into acting. And as time progressed, I became more impressed with my social life and my Rolodex than with my career.

One would think, because of the choices I'd made in modeling and acting, that LA would prove the perfect environment for me. But I found it not very rewarding or fulfilling. Showing up in shorts, bathing suit, or miniskirt so that a producer, director, or casting agent could ogle me one more time for a role that required about as much talent as I had in my middle finger.

Could I have taken my Hollywood career more seriously? Of course. Would I have had as much fun? Probably not. I do know that my hidden fears and insecurities, fear that I wouldn't be good enough to get the best parts or that I'd land an impressive role only to screw it up, made it easy for me to be distracted. I knew what I was doing, that I was probably blowing my opportunities in LA and with William Morris.

If I'd sincerely craved a meaningful movie career, more of my time would have been spent perfecting my craft, learning what casting directors wanted in a professional actress and how to make them look past the "pretty, sexy girl" to the potential talent. Yet I convinced myself that "being seen" was as important as being respected. Now I wonder how I could so thoroughly have deceived myself. A studio executive noticing me at Ma Maison every other day would never have mistaken me for a genuine actress. They would see me as a party girl.

On the whole, however, I can't say that hanging out at Ma Maison with Robáire and my friends was a huge mistake. I experienced a piece of 1980s Hollywood that others never glimpsed.

In April, Robáire and I arrived at the gala opening of La Cage aux Folles. Like on a movie set, cameras, lights, and superstars appeared everywhere I looked. All of Hollywood came, not just the personalities of the moment looking to be seen again, but also the revered actors, politicians, studio heads, people at every level of the industry, because it was a fabulous show. At that time in America, there was nothing else like it.

Every night for weeks on end, I was surrounded by a different set of Hollywood luminaries and persons of prominence. One night I had the privilege of sitting at the table with my good friend Sir Gordon White and his date for the evening, Elizabeth Taylor.

The "C" Generation

In my group, and in many Hollywood circles, decadent excess — overindulgence in life's pleasures — was the norm. The most fashionable restaurants, where nouvelle cuisine drained your wallet without padding your hips, were followed by the choicest clubs, the finest cognac, and the ever-present, pre-eminent head rush: cocaine.

Tiny silver-spoon pendants proclaimed your enchantment with the drug of choice, much as roach clips did in the sixties, and we repeated the same excuses our hippie predecessors had used for indulging in marijuana and LSD.

"Cocaine is not addictive."

"It's certainly no more dangerous than a few drinks."

"Instead of dulling the brain, like alcohol, cocaine gives clarity and focus."

Cocaine became our common bond, and at two in the morning we became profound, prolific, intellectuals. After a night making the Hollywood scenes, we'd end up sitting around the house, designer shoes kicked aside, having another glass of wine, another line of coke, which would turn into many more.

One morning in late June, a couple of months after the opening of La Cage, I awoke feeling horribly sick. Robáire waved me away when I tried to wake him, so I made my way out of bed and to the bathroom. My face looked pale. My chest felt tight. My mouth felt strange inside. I opened it wide, and all I could see at first was darkness. Cocking my head toward the light, I found an angle where I could see better, and it was still dark. In fact, the interior of my mouth was completely black.

Robáire still didn't want to be bothered. He was hung over, had to go to work, and didn't want to hear about my mouth. So I phoned my landlady, Florie.

"I know the best ear, nose, and throat doctor in Beverly Hills," Florie said. She called back to say I had an appointment in an hour with Dr. Joe Sugarman. "Would you like me to come and get you?"

"No, I think Robáire will take me. Thanks, Florie."

I felt so sick and miserable I didn't want to move, but I had to, and I managed to get him up. Grudgingly, he drove me to Dr. Sugarman's office in Beverly Hills, where he let me out and told me he'd wait outside.

The doctor said I had a fungal infection in my mouth and a bronchial infection bordering on pneumonia. He sent me home with a prescription for strong antibiotics and a severe warning to behave. I spent a week in bed, recovering, which was no fun for Robáire, so he vanished to his LA apartment whenever he wasn't back in New York. I never quite knew where he was, because the love affair ended for us after that. I knew only what I heard from friends or read in the columns, that Robáire was seen at this club or that, always with other women, while I lay in bed sick.

Was I surprised? No. To Robáire, life was about having fun. And I wasn't looking for a permanent relationship any more than he was. But I did feel sadness and pain. We had such a strong sexual attraction and chemistry, and I'm sure that's what I missed most, yet I also missed his personality. I missed the exciting times we had together. But his behavior? And the fact that he could do drugs all night then work all day? I didn't miss that.

Getting sick was a wakeup call for me. How ridiculously "Hollywood" to be driving to the doctor with a cocaine-related infection. Obviously, cocaine affected me differently than it did Robáire and my friends. My tolerance level, even for alcohol, was about two compared to their ten, and I'd learned much earlier in my life not to over-drink. Now I knew that my tolerance for cocaine was also low, and I had no desire to push that envelope again. Today, having seen how continued cocaine use damaged many of my friends and my Hollywood acquaintances, I believe my low tolerance was a saving grace.

With my lease still in effect until November, I had time to figure out what to do. Robáire and I remained friendly, though I saw him less and less often. I still lunched regularly at Ma Maison, where I could pretend I was furthering my fledgling movie career by chatting with directors, producers, actors, and other acquaintances attached to the film industry. No longer having Robáire or his celebrity friends to guarantee I'd get a table, I had to make my own reservations at Ma Maison. Being denied admittance would have seemed the ultimate setback. The first time I called, hoping Patrick would remember me and uncertain whether he would acknowledge me as "worthy" of a table, he surprised me with a warm welcome. Still, I was never absolutely certain of getting in until Patrick actually nodded me through the door.

Cornflakes and Cartier

Jeff Zelmanski

Victoria and I always kept in touch. After she moved to California, I went to see her. She picked me up in a car, in itself astounding to my New Yorker mentality, and I knew wherever she took me would be special. She never thought it was special. To her it was like, "This is a nice place."

We drove to Ma Maison. No phone number, you had to know somebody to get in. Every chair in the entire room is facing forward except for one table and two chairs facing the other way. Those were our chairs.

Everybody's looking at us. There was Jack Lemmon, Ernest Borgnine, all these famous people looking at us.

Vicki was so cool about it. I'm aghast — she'd been there all of two months, and already she knew *people.*

Later, when Victoria started writing this book, we were at a luncheon she gave in New York and I said to someone, "I hope Vicki realizes how special she's been to people without ever making a big deal of it."

Like once when I fixed Vicki up with an Armenian photographer at Penthouse. *Very handsome. Really young. They fell in love for about three weeks. They were both a little too good-looking for each other. But one day during those three weeks I walk into my office and find a box of cornflakes on my desk. Inside, on top of the cereal, is a card from Vicki and her Armenian friend. It says, "Maybe if you're hungry there's a gift in here for you."*

At the bottom of the box I find a watch. A Cartier. I'd never owned a Cartier. All these years later, I still have it. Even back then it was valued in the thousands, and she just left it on my desk — in a box of cornflakes.

One Wrong Turn After Another

Patricia Marque came into my life like a cool breeze during the hottest weeks of summer in 1981, so I didn't suspect at first that she was pure evil. Clever and socially extroverted, she was introduced to me as a "producer," a title that in Hollywood could mean almost anything. She traveled in a tight group of women, all young, attractive, with that "Hollywood Hungry" look that comes from being the brightest light in your hometown before arriving in a city crammed with bright, sparkly lights rivaling tirelessly to outshine the others. I joined this little group for dinner a few times. Then Patricia called and asked me to have lunch with her alone.

"I have someone I want to introduce you to," she said, after we were seated.

In LA, when you hear those magic words, "I want to introduce you …" your immediate hope is *producer, director, studio mogul ....*

"Who is it?" I asked.

"A very private, special man. A very unusual man."

During earlier conversations, I'd mentioned that I was on my own, not dating anyone seriously, and would be giving up my lease soon, not sure where to go next. From that, she might have assumed that I needed money. In actuality, I still had my *Penthouse* retainer, along with other income from modeling and acting. Yet I would soon learn that in Patricia 's world any talk of money started at a level much higher than where I was accustomed to living.

"Do you know who Adnan Khashoggi is?"

"I've heard the name," I said vaguely, racking my brain to put a picture with it.

"He's a Saudi businessman, educated in the United States. He owns estates in various countries all over the world and also owns a magnificent yacht."

I didn't know much about Saudi-Arabian lifestyles, but you couldn't live in LA for fifteen minutes without knowing that Saudi

oil money was pouring in to fund many of the major films currently being made. Arabs loved the movie business. They arrived with
huge sums of cash to spend, and although they were not personally
into drugs, their currency provided the means for acquiring cocaine and for attracting women and power. In return, Hollywood
loved Arabs. At that time, half of Hollywood was a whore to Arab
money.

"Mr. Khashoggi is married to a lovely woman. In the Arab culture, attractive women are a symbol of status, and he loves having
beautiful women traveling with him. He doesn't expect anything
from you except what you want to do. Meanwhile, he's generous,
kind, and every person involved in his circle enjoys his fabulous
lifestyle."

Looking back now, it seems so obvious that she'd set her
sights on me the moment we met. Even then I realized that when
she said, "anything," she meant "anything sexual," but she painted
a tantalizing scenario. The one constant in my life was a desire to
experience different cultures, and the Saudi-Arabian culture was
new to all of us.

"Adnan is a good friend of mine," Patricia said. "Several of us
are going to Las Vegas this weekend. Would you like to go with
me and meet him?"

I couldn't help being intrigued by this new experience she was
offering, which was how I'd gotten into most situations in my life,
always keen to sample every opportunity that captured my interest. Patricia was offering me a sample of a mysterious world I'd
heard about but never had come close to experiencing. I hadn't
anything pressing on my calendar for the coming weekend, and I
felt entirely capable of handling myself with this famous Arabian
tycoon.

In Las Vegas, we checked into one of the best hotels. I had
my own suite, large and luxurious. After I unpacked, there came a

knock at my door. Patricia had brought a couple of the girls from the LA group and two more girls I hadn't yet encountered. She ordered wine and hors d'oeuvres, and we sat around chatting like we'd known one another forever.

The only topic was Adnan! Adnan! Adnan! Each of them had an Adnan story. To hear these girls talk, Adnan Khashoggi was Prince Charming in each of their private fairy tales.

I listened, mildly amused but also captivated. When they left, Patricia stayed behind.

"Adnan would like to meet you later," she said.

"Ohhhkay ..." I was still processing the anecdotes I'd heard during this gathering, which included plenty of gushing admiration without much substance. I'd listened to their stories, but had I heard the *real* story? "Is there something I should know, Patricia? Right now I'm comfortable, but am I about to become someone's sex slave?"

She laughed. "Oh, heavens no. Adnan just likes to entertain. And he has so much money he can afford to entertain his every whim. Some men invest in beautiful art, Adnan invests in beautiful women."

"Okay, then. Yes, I'd like to meet him." In fact, I was rather intrigued to meet this man the girls had spoken of with such adoration and longing, almost with the reverent hysteria of Elvis fans grabbing for the King's sweaty discarded scarf.

On the Footstool of Opulence

Around five that afternoon, he came to my door. He was short, not particularly handsome, but with an attractively mischievous twinkle in his infinite black eyes.

"Victoria, how do you do? I am Adnan Khashoggi."

I replied appropriately and invited him into my sitting area.

"I want to welcome you," he said. "Patricia thinks very highly of you. She wanted me to meet you, and now I can see why she is impressed."

So we sat in the living area of my suite and simply talked. A charismatic man with an obvious zest for life, although he'd studied in America and was socially Americanized, he had an appealing international flair. In his presence I couldn't help imagining a strange and glamorous world that only a select few ever come close enough to touch.

"I am having a birthday party in a few weeks," he said. "In Monte Carlo. I would like you to come."

"That sounds wonderful," I admitted. "If possible, I'd love to be there."

"The party will be on my yacht, the *Nabila*. I will have the Loews Monte Carlo reserved for many of my guests, and also the Palace Hotel." He didn't mention where he would be staying, and I learned later that Khashoggi was as security conscious as a US president. No one, except his closest family and advisors, knew precisely where he was at any time. "I will see that you receive a proper invitation. In the meantime, I would like you girls to enjoy Las Vegas as my guests. And I have this present for you."

He gave me a box with what at first looked like a white cotton shirt inside. It had a standup collar lightly stitched with white embroidery. When I lifted it out, I saw that it was ankle-length, more like a robe than a shirt. The initials AK emblazoned the single breast pocket in gold. Also in the box was a simple strand of pearls with tiny gold beads. Not extravagant, but nice.

When I met up later with Patricia and the other girls, she informed me that the garment was a *thobe,* which she pronounced "tob."

"Adnan gives one to all his guests," she explained.

As we sat around in these Arab *thobes*, I began to feel special, part of an elite little club.

That night, we all had dinner together, Adnan and five pretty girls. He obviously enjoyed spending his money on an American lifestyle, although he could fit effortlessly into many different worlds. We talked, laughed. All the other girls knew him. These were LA girls, but it became clear that he cultivated similar groups of women around the world, entertained them, and paid their expenses. To what extent, I wasn't sure, but I was invited to become one of his entourage.

On departure, I received an envelope from the concierge. Inside was an invitation to the party, a personal note from Mr. Khashoggi saying he enjoyed meeting me, and a thousand dollars in cash.

I kept it. But back in LA, I called Patricia .

"Adnan's world sounds fascinating," I said. "But what's the thousand dollars for, exactly?"

"Nothing," she said. "It's taxi fare home. It's thank you for coming. It's nothing to him. It's insignificant."

Adnan's idea of booking a flight turned out to be the entire top section of a 747 airliner. A lounge that would easily accommodate fifty people provided luxurious seating for our six-woman troupe.

During the flight, individual personalities began to surface, and I became engrossed in learning about these women with whom I'd be spending the next couple of weeks. Imogen, originally from England, was tough and independent, with a balls-to-the-wall, bring-it-on attitude. Imogen would come out okay no matter what situation she found herself in. There was a Jewish girl I couldn't quite figure out. She seemed to have money and to view this escapade much as I did, as an alluring experience. Patricia 's cousin, Linda, was so obviously the self-defeated flunky of the group, along only to do Patricia 's bidding, that I wanted to pull her aside and straighten out her backbone. Seeing Patricia 's influence on each of these girls, I began to grasp the shrewd, scheming, manipulative side of her that scarcely had surfaced before now. She was clearly a queen bee in Adnan Khashoggi's opulent fiefdom, and we were the handmaidens at the foot of her throne.

Never Say Never Again

The Loews Monte Carlo asked me to provide them with my passport. I'd traveled enough to know this practice was not unheard-of abroad, so I didn't think much about it. Upstairs in another luxurious suite, I found that I had a roommate, an attractive blonde girl who seemed nice and was totally mad about Adnan. She "so hoped to be a permanent part of Adnan's world."

The party was five days away. With so many people coming in from all over the globe, I had no concerns about anything happening that I didn't want to happen or couldn't handle. Meanwhile, there was plenty to see and do in Monte Carlo. We were invited to enjoy the hotel and shopping, with a car available to take us wherever we wanted to go. The five days passed in a leisurely frenzy of bustle and commotion. One of our stops was to Christian Dior to buy gowns for the party. I was beginning to feel connected to this elite coterie of well-kept women, and shopping at Dior was enough to seal the deal. Why not enjoy the nectar of this particularly luscious flower for a while longer before I fluttered away?

Designed and built specifically for Adnan Khashoggi in 1980 at a cost of $100 million (equivalent to over $260 million in 2011), the *Nabila*, named for Adnan's daughter, was at that time one of the largest private vessels in the world. In 1983, it would feature in the James Bond movie *Never Say Never Again* as the villain's super-yacht headquarters.

But on that magical night in July 1981, the glorious *Nabila* was a floating birthday party for one of the world's richest men.

The Scent of Money

To say the *Nabila* was a huge yacht was like saying the QE2 was a nice-sized ocean liner. The first thing I noticed on entering was the aroma. I'd never smelled anything quite so sensual and at the same time, woodsy and refreshing.

Walls throughout the ship were covered in exquisite chamois leather divided into a Mondrian tapestry by strips of smoked crystal. Although I'd worn Italian leather of the sort authors describe as "buttery soft," these walls felt even softer. Pushbutton telephones were new at the time, as was satellite communication, yet the *Nabila* had both, plus state-of-the art music systems and custom-designed Edward Fields carpeting.

Intended for entertainment as much as for deep-sea voyages, the yacht contained a dazzling discotheque, with mirrored ceiling, gleaming bronze flooring, and special lighting effects. When guests weren't swimming in the pool, sunning on the decks, or relaxing in one of the guest suites fitted with every amenity and luxury possible, they could enjoy a movie in the *Nabila*'s theater. For the health conscious, there was a fitness center, saunas, steam rooms, and a cold-plunge pool. There was also a beauty salon and massage room, a temperature- and humidity-controlled wine cellar, a medical suite with a medical team on staff, and a morgue, in the unfortunate event that medical facilities didn't suffice.

The *Nabila* pulled slowly out to sea, and the party started. As the evening progressed, I saw different levels of women assembled around Adnan and his beautiful wife, Lamia. Seated closest were the European girls, a small group that seemed to know Adnan better than the others. Next were up-and-coming American girls, and finally the new girls like me. At around three in the morning, after other guests had gone, I found myself sitting in the discotheque with Adnan, Lamia, Patricia , and the European clique. Adnan had wanted all of us to remain — his closest friends, he said.

Wow, I thought, *what a strange and fascinating lifestyle. And nothing inappropriate has happened yet.*

I never forgot the aroma that permeated the air. Starting at four a.m., the shuttle boats took the remaining guests back to shore, and before we left, I asked one of the stewards, "What *is* that wonderful smell."

"Rigaud candles," he told me.

When I returned to LA, I asked at stores until I found them, $65 each for the smallest, purchased them rarely, and discovered that only one color, the original Cypres green, smells so fantastic. There must have been 150 Rigaud candles in the *Nabila*'s Main Salon, and that haunting aroma is my best memory from my two-week encounter with Adnan Khashoggi.

The Party's Over

The next day, out by the pool, I met up with several of the girls. Among the buzz about fashions and food and celebrity-spotting at Adnan's party, I heard the word "peedubbleyeu," eventually working out that they were saying the initials PW.

"PW?" I asked Imogen. "What does that stand for?"

"Really, Victoria, don't you know? That's what you are. What I am."

I shook my head, still puzzled.

"You're a Pleasure Wife."

Like hell I am. But I didn't say it; I only stared, knowing I'd just heard the other shoe drop and wondering what to do about it.

"You *are* going to stay with us, aren't you?" one of the other girls asked.

I sort of shrugged and smiled, my brain so mesmerized by the luxurious warmth of the Monte Carlo sun on my skin and the sounds of high-dollar luxury living tittering from the pool, tinkling from the poolside bar, where my tab was endlessly open, shuffling past on the heels of the hotel crew ready to fulfill my every whim. Enveloped in such lavish comforts, a person can be ever so gradually seduced.

Swimming, shopping, and lunches filled our days, with dinner parties aboard the Nabila almost every night. About five days into the trip, I noticed that attendance at dinner was shrinking. Instead of the usual thirty or so guests, there were only twenty, and I was seated closer to Adnan and Lamia than ever before. This time I actually had a conversation with Adnan's business partner, Bob Shaheen. Another business partner also sat nearby, Victor Dananza, with his wife Anna, along with Adnan's nephew, Dodi Fayed. No longer in the newbie seats, I was surrounded by Prince Charming's royal family.

I couldn't help comparing Adnan and Lamia to Bob and Kathy back in New York. Lamia was much younger than Kathy, about my age actually, with a much warmer nature than Kathy's. Nineteen when she and Adnan married, shortly after his divorce from Saria, the mother of his two sons, Lamia had changed her Italian name from Laura Biancolini to Lamia Khashoggi. Like Bob, Adnan was in his mid-forties, and like Bob, he surrounded himself with beautiful women. The dinner guests were a mixture of gorgeous young women and notable social, political, or business personalities, much as I had often encountered at Bob and Kathy's. *Déjà vu* with an Arabian twist.

Sitting there, listening to Adnan and Lamia converse, I drifted into a haze of a different kind. Maybe it was the luscious aroma of the Rigaud candles, or the hypnotizing murmur of voices, or the lavish surroundings of handmade silk and butter-soft chamois leather. I began to wonder what it might be like to drift through life swaddled in such opulence, never a care beyond what to wear for dinner. The sound of my name brought me back.

"Victoria, tell us about yourself." Lamia was leaning slightly toward me, her intense Italian eyes filled with genuine interest. "How are you enjoying Monte Carlo?"

Just like a normal dinner party, only this one was at the prince's palace, and the princess had just invited me to join the inner circle of conversation. I stammered through it.

The next day, a phone call from Patricia awoke me.

"We're having lunch on the *Nabila*. Bring your swimsuit. Lots of people are coming."

So I boarded the speed launch with my new girlfriends, motored out to the yacht, and spent a leisurely day lying in the sun beside the swimming pool on the upper deck. Two of my poolside companions were Adnan's son, Mohammed Khashoggi, and his nephew, Dodi Fayed. Mohammed and Dodi, friends as well as cousins, seemed to be fairly normal guys, around my age—amusing, enjoyable company. There was no hint that many years later, film producer Dodi Fayed would become the lover of Diana, Princess of Wales, and thought by many to be the cause of her death.

My Passport, Please

Dinner that night was a smaller affair than usual. I was becoming one of the inner circle of Adnan's girls. After several days of exploring Monte Carlo and shuttling across to the *Nabila* when summoned, I'd grown accustomed to phone calls from Patricia telling me where to meet for whatever excursion or event was on the schedule. A call the next day, however, came from Bob Shaheen.

"Please be in the hotel lobby at ten o'clock," he said. "Patricia will meet you there."

Downstairs, I asked Patricia , "Where are we going today?"

"Just outside Monte Carlo," she said, "to the next town over."

"Beausoleil?" I'd heard there was a wonderful covered market there.

"You girls need to see Doctor —"

After the word "doctor," I ignored the name she uttered. *Why were we seeing a doctor?*

"Why?" There were four of us in the car, including Imogen and the Jewish girl whose name I can't recall, although I remember hearing that she later married the owner of a major Hollywood studio.

"Why?" I repeated.

"To get checked out." Patricia 's tone had turned abrupt, terse, a side of her I'd glimpsed on the flight from LA.

"Checked out for what?" I persisted.

"You know. To make sure you're clean."

"Clean of what? Where?"

"Gynecological diseases, Victoria. Stop being dense." Her words were clipped, as if she were biting them off with her tiny, even, white teeth. Except for a streak of meanness, I sensed no feelings for me or for any of us girls. We'd ceased being her friends and were now simply product. *Wow. What a switch.*

"I have no diseases," I said calmly, feeling anything but calm inside.

"Then you'll check out all right, won't you?"

After a moment, I said, "So you assume I'm going to have sex with Adnan."

She didn't bother to glance at me, much less respond. The other girls hadn't uttered a word, and truly, I didn't need an answer. I finally took off my rose-colored blinders. At the parties and dinners, no one had mentioned sex, and now I knew why: I hadn't yet been deemed "clean" by their doctor.

It was time for me to leave Monte Carlo, to opt out of Adnan's seductive aura. *In the meantime,* I reasoned, *Adnan Khashoggi is a highly visible businessman.* He was well known and, at that time, respected worldwide. Until now, nobody had suggested I do anything strange or had taken me anywhere beyond my comfort zone.

This trip to the doctor was unusual, and while it didn't strike me as imminently dangerous, my imagination ran wild: I was trapped. They had my passport. If they could pick me up and take me to a doctor without asking my consent, they could just as easily take me aboard the *Nabila*, or Khashoggi's private jet, and whisk me away to any country in the world, chain me up in some obscure Arabian harem. I had no control.

I'd never been in such a position before. Patricia had changed as swiftly as a chameleon, from friendly and reassuring to cold and commanding. Her voice made the hair rise on the back of my neck.

By the next morning, I was packed. I intended to leave on my own and quietly. Fortunately, my airplane ticket to Monte Carlo included the return flight.

In the hotel lobby, I asked for my passport.

"I'm sorry," the desk attendant said, "Mr. Khashoggi has it, because you're his guest. You'll have to ask him."

I called Bob Shaheen from the lobby phone.

"Where is my passport?" I asked.

"Mr. Khashoggi has it."

"I'd like to have it back, please." I tried to keep my rapidly pumping adrenaline from making my voice shake.

"Are you leaving us?" His tone was friendly and concerned.

"Yes, I have to go back," I said, keeping my own manner friendly, as well, with a hint of regret — my acting skills kicking in. "The trip has been wonderful. Thank you so much for your hospitality, and I want to thank Mr. Khashoggi and Lamia, as well, but I have to go back to LA."

"Adnan will be sad to lose you, Victoria, but we will take care of the details."

Back in my suite, the next call I got was from Khashoggi.

"I understand you want to leave."

"Yes, Adnan, I do."

"At least come and visit with me before you go."

He opened the door and invited me in, as gracious and respectful as ever. Walking into his suite was like entering a house, no bed in sight. I saw a tray with cups and a coffee carafe, and I was glad he didn't offer me a cup. I might worry what would be in it besides coffee. We sat down—acquaintances, not quite friends, and talked.

"I respect your world," I told him, "but I don't feel I would benefit, or that you would benefit, from my being part of it."

"You don't actually know my world."

"True, but I do know it involves having a great many women. I respect that your culture encourages men of your stature to have many women in their lives. The girls I've met are lovely, and they seem to enjoy very much being a part of your world, but I don't believe it's what I want to do. This is your culture, not mine. If I'm not happy, I would not make you happy."

"If that is your decision, Victoria, so be it. Nevertheless, I am disappointed."

"I appreciate your saying that."

"I would like to give you a going-away present."

I hoped it was my passport, which he did give me a few minutes later. What he gave me now was a jewelry box. Inside I found an intricate and fascinating ring of yellow, white, and pink gold in the form of a coiled snake. Emerald eyes sparkled in the serpent's head, which rose high, capped by a huge sapphire and encircled by a crown of gold filigree filled with tiny diamonds.

Was there some significance to the choice of a snake? Snake in the grass? Snake shedding its skin? Snake eyes? In years since, I've shown the ring to jewelers. They suggest that it's one of a kind and definitely Egyptian.

After leaving Monte Carlo, my butterfly wings took me to England, my safe place, where I visited with friends in London before driving up the English countryside to clear my head. In going with Patricia in the first place, no matter how I tried to justify my decision, I'd crossed my own moral boundaries. Allowing myself to become enthralled by Adnan's world, without knowing it was safe, was an indication to me that I was losing control of my judgment.

It had started with Robáire, and I no sooner shook my addiction to him than I jumped into a situation even more volatile. With a few more steps, I would have found myself in a foreign and untenable situation, where women have no control over their sexual choices, at a man's beck and call for sex, and in his world, whatever goes along with it. Wash that fact with as many kinds of scented soaps as you can find, but in the end I would have been merely a high-class call girl.

CHAPTER 19

What Am I Doing Here?

Safely home from Monaco, I recognized that the risky thrill of playing in Adnan Khashoggi's sandbox was like my dalliance with cocaine in one respect: it took me away. It separated me from the everyday drudgery of making my mark in Hollywood. It takes more than talent. And although I seemed to have the right look at the right moment, you also need incredibly good luck. Talent, timing, and luck have to come together at once. I was smart enough to know that even with the illustrious William Morris Agency working in my behalf, there was no guarantee.

Movie sets typically close down in the summer. Around the end of August, one of my agents, Allen Iseman, asked me to attend a party with him at Chasen's, another popular hangout for Hollywood luminaries. Allen was the agent at William Morris who worked with me more than any of the others, and I liked him, so it wasn't unusual for us to attend events together. While we were on the dance floor, an odd feeling of calm and completion came over me.

"Allen, I've made a decision," I said. "I'm going to tell you now instead of in the office on Monday. I'm resigning from William Morris."

He stopped dancing and stepped back to look at me.

"Victoria, you're joking, right?"

"No, I'm entirely serious." I smiled to show I wasn't upset, certainly not upset about anything the agency had done.

"My god. Nobody resigns from William Morris." He stared at me, his brow wrinkled as if he was trying to solve a complicated puzzle.

I kept smiling.

And he continued looking totally bewildered. "Victoria, I've never had *any* client fire me, certainly not *on a dance floor.*"

One More Trip Down Aisle C

Although my spontaneous resignation from the agency made sense to me at the time, I had no clear vision of what I intended to do next. It did, however, remove some of the pressure I felt to succeed as an actress. Now, whether I decided to go for it or fold my tent and go home, I'd be disappointing no one but myself.

My life in LA slowed down to a murmur of its previous energetic abundance. Jeffrey Toffler's investment money was fast running out, and he'd disappeared, probably doing too many drugs, so I didn't want him around, anyway. I wanted no one in my life who was part of the cocaine world.

I considered returning to New York. *Penthouse* still booked me as Pet of the Year for important events. On the other hand, with my *Penthouse* contract paying the essentials, I could give LA another six months, but I would not become one of the pitiful "almosts" that hang around film studios picking up crumbs, refusing to believe their moment has come and gone.

One day *Penthouse* called, needing me back in New York for an assignment, which typically would mean a quick flight out and back. Instead, I decided that a short stay in New York would work wonders for my psyche.

My tiny peach and silver-gray apartment proved a refreshing haven. My friends in the building welcomed me back with smiles and hugs. I visited the *Penthouse* offices, chatted with Jeff Zelmanski and Irwin and Phia. I had dinner at The House with Bob and Kathy.

New York was exactly as it should be, but I felt a bit alienated from it. A year is a long time away, and I'd changed. One night, at loose ends for dinner and feeling out of place in my formerly comfortable niche, I visited Chez Pascal.

And there was Robáire, with his charm and his energy, and I fell in lust all over again. We closed up the restaurant together then spent the rest of the night in a cocaine cloud.

For the first time in my life, I awoke unable to remember coming home. It was morning, yet I was wearing the same black glittery outfit I'd worn to dinner. My face was greasy and smeared from not washing it before I fell into bed. That had never happened before, not even on my wildest nights out. My stockings were torn. I was a mess, and in shock that I'd let myself get in this condition.

Even when I was dating Robáire, doing cocaine almost daily, and woke up with a mouth fungus, nothing this bad had ever happened. It scared me.

Pulling myself together, I suddenly couldn't breathe. Shaking inside and frightened that I might be having a heart attack, I'd never felt so horrible, so helpless, so unable to move. I couldn't *breathe*.

I remembered nothing of the evening before, other than having dinner with Robáire and doing that first line of coke. Today was Sunday. I was alone in my apartment, surrounded by people I knew but not people I trusted to see me like this, to help me, to keep me from dying. Bob would help, but to get through his security and speak to him on a Sunday would require more effort than I was physically capable of at the moment. And part of me would rather die than have him see me this way.

I should call 911!

As I reached for the phone, I saw tomorrow's headline above a photo of me the way I looked in my mirror, horribly disheveled, pitifully and obviously coming off a drug overdose: *Penthouse* Pet Cokes Out.

If I could still worry about newspaper headlines, maybe I wasn't dying. But I couldn't breathe, and I was shaking, dizzy, and frightened, my heart pounding furiously. My hands felt like they were being stabbed by pins. When I tried to see the numbers on the phone, they blurred. Thirsty, parched, I tried to drink water, had trouble swallowing, and that frightened me even more. I called the one person I trusted to help.

Thank God Shaun Henderson was home and answered right away. I told him how I was feeling, that I must be having a heart attack.

"I'm coming right down."

He had a paper bag with him. He seemed to know immediately what to do.

"Here," he said, "breathe into this."

I'll never forget how amazed I was that he would know not to panic, to reassure me, and to bring a paper bag so I could stop hyperventilating. At that time, I'd never heard the words "anxiety attack" or "panic attack." It was one of the scariest situations I'd ever experienced, and I learned later that they can be quite serious.

The Reclusive Road Home

Before leaving for New York, I'd rented a smaller, more affordable house in Benedict Canyon. When I returned from New York to my new house, I shut myself inside with the intention of turning my life around. The top of Benedict Canyon is a retreat from all the lights, bustle, pressures, and celebrity that is Hollywood. Except for my walking excursions up the hill, I rarely went out for several weeks, afraid of having another attack.

My doctor put me in touch with a brilliant female psychiatrist. Unlike those I knew socially or had seen in films, who tend to answer every question with another question--"Why do you think you did that?"--this woman actually communicated with me. She understood me, helped me to understand myself and to examine my worries objectively.

"Most people," she said, "have a dominant need that focuses their personality in one direction, or two at the most. You have multiple needs and a more complex focus."

"You're not telling me I have multiple personalities." That scary notion had been floating around Hollywood since a TV miniseries starring Sally Field and Joanne Woodward had made *Sybil* a household name.

"No. You don't have dissociative identity disorder, or anything like that. You simply have multiple dominant interests. Where one person focuses primarily on business or sports or creative pursuits or family, you have an almost equal driving need in many directions."

This woman would make a great friend, I decided, if she wasn't my doctor. Having many dominant sides, she explained, I was always in conflict. When I turn my attention to finances or making real estate deals, my business side is very much in control, and I excel in that direction. But another part craves an active social life, craves attention, sparkle, drama, and it becomes dominant at times. Another side wants to be sequestered in my home, building a lovely life with someone special. My creative side that focuses on cooking, decorating, and other artistic crafts. These different dominant interests accounted for the push-pull I felt right now in respect to acting, she explained, and I could always expect to be tugged in different directions. Years later, after I was diagnosed with cancer and had spent my savings researching and dealing with my disease, I turned my attention to making and selling baskets, throws, and soft furnishings for the home. Because of what the psychiatrist had taught me, I knew this was my creative side coming forward to help me take control of my life.

"You want this, but you want that," she said, "so it's difficult to find a balance. You probably never will."

Merely recognizing that my interests would constantly be tilting me off balance helped me tremendously. Instead of making me feel I was nuts, it made me realize I could take control at any time by allowing whichever of my driving forces most needed to take the lead for a while do so before reining it in.

A lot of people with my background, and diagnosed with cancer, would go crazy if they couldn't continue their social life, had to stay at home instead of going out with friends. For me, it was a blessing. I need to be social, but I also need time alone, and the side of me that enjoyed alone time became a saving grace.

Talking with that psychiatrist, I began to truly understand myself and my behaviors. Dating Robáire was not a bad decision, but doing cocaine was, for me, a *very* bad decision. Going with Patricia Marque, flirting with the idea of becoming part of Adnan Khashoggi's seductive world, was a *terrible* decision. But the psychiatrist helped me balance that against the decision to leave Adnan's world when I did. She couldn't give me all the answers, but she provided the tools and abilities to understand my choices, and how my actions reflected those choices.

Fortunately, I had the support of my most stable New York and LA friends, even without telling them what had happened. Gradually, I improved. I learned that my anxiety attack happened when my brain, already malfunctioning because I'd fed it copious lines of cocaine, had interpreted my anxiety as an actual threat to my wellbeing. It then responded to the symptoms as an actual threat, creating more fear and producing more symptoms in what's known as an anxiety cycle. I learned that if I could get through the first few minutes, the anxiety would lessen, and I would feel better.

It happened once again, but by understanding the problem, I was able to defuse the attack before it fully manifested. Living a simpler life made me feel more in control. Over the next few months, I regained my stability.

One night an NBC special came on TV that I'd filmed earlier in the year, *Women Who Rate a 10*. An exceptional program, hosted by Morgan Fairchild and Erik Estrada, it began with tributes to beautiful Hollywood women of the past, Marilyn Monroe and Sophia Loren, followed by interviews with famous, gorgeous women from the 1970s and '80s. I was privileged to be featured among Victoria Principal, Lynda Carter, Maud Adams, Ann Jillian, and Loni Anderson. The opportunity had come through *Penthouse*. In addition to interviewing both Bob and me, they had asked Bob to choose the *Penthouse* model that to him rated a ten, and to allow them to film a photo shoot of him and that model. It was a watershed moment for us, a show to be proud of, and as I listened to Bob talking about me on the show, I saw the familiar connection between us that was more than photographer and model, more than just lovers, and I felt a little sad that I was in LA, watching it alone, and he was in New York.

During a break between segments, my Jordache commercial appeared. I felt at that moment as if a butterfly collector had caught me in his net.

"Wake up, dummy," he whispered, "it's time to put LA behind you."

Okay, I thought. *I'm out. I'm gone.* This was the end of acting and modeling as I knew it. *Women Who Rate a 10* and Jordache at the same time — if I never did anything else, life had been good.

I'd actually enjoyed my last six months in LA and didn't feel I was leaving anything behind or anything important left undone. I was leaving healthy and whole, and I arrived at my New York home on the day I turned thirty.

CHAPTER 20

Eurotrash Invasion

My fascination with foreign lands and cultures began while I was too young to read, yet already easily captivated by people and events outside my ordinary world. Among the books my parents gave me was the kind we now call "learning books." My favorite transported me to faraway lands I never knew existed. It was like a portal I could step through and explore with my imagination. Every child looked entirely different from me; their clothes different from the clothes I wore. I studied those pages so thoroughly that the ink wore thin in places. This same childhood attraction to the exotic drew me to many of my favorite people — Robáire, Sir Gordon White, Shaun Henderson with his British accent, Phia Daly, who was charmingly Irish, and of course, Bob.

So when I returned to New York and found that Europeans had continued to infiltrate our city much the way Arabs had infiltrated LA, I didn't feel as dismayed as many other New Yorkers. The European influx had started around the same time I arrived in 1976, and I was accustomed to seeing large groups of them hanging out together. Labeled "Eurotrash" by an outspoken journalist, these young aristocrats clinging to their lost legacy of nobility entered New York with attitude and were now taking over our clubs, restaurants, Wall Street, and the banking industry.

Their penniless friends — counts with "no accounts" forced to come to America and get a real job — existed largely by mooching off their friends. It's hard to be a prince if you're a pauper.

Champagne and Vinegar

After the glory days of Studio 54 ended, the favorite Eurotrash haunts were Regine's, located in the Delmonico Hotel on Park Avenue, and Club A, a new nightclub on East 60ᵗʰ Street. Regine herself was a French import, and she greeted the brashest European visitor with open arms. Robert Couturier, the club's French designer, was quoted as saying, "We are Eurotrash. We are obnoxious. We are spoiled. We are brats…. We are the beautiful people of the future." He was absolutely right, except about being "the future."

To be fair, it was the European influx that bolstered New York City's economy during those years, especially at restaurants, nightclubs, and high-end retail clothing stores. For the most part, these visitors were the upper crust of European society, the titled and the wealthy, fleeing political unrest and danger in their own countries, and they were big spenders. But they also brought an appetite for conspicuous consumption that made LA appear frugal in comparison.

My personal friends, well-bred, mannerly, aristocratic Europeans, were as different from Eurotrash as champagne from vinegar. Yet even with their insufferably spoiled attitude, I found our obnoxious new imports fascinating.

A Jewel Among Princes

One entrancing European in particular, Andréas Wolfgang Dreyhaupt, was not the most handsome man I'd ever met, a bit overweight and his nose slightly too big. Introduced to me by a friend of Sir Gordon's, Andréas was German, though I couldn't tell that by looking. From his coloring — dark hair, dark complexion — I would have guessed he came from Italy or South America.

Andréas radiated affluence, importance, and authority, but in a mischievous, playful manner. His presence lit the room, and I saw

The irony is, my relation with Andreus ended at M. D. Anderson.
The same hospital that treated me for 20 years.

immediately that I wasn't the only person who found him appealing. He attracted friends, both male and female, like candy attracts children, and his friends obviously adored him.

What surprised me most was how I felt when his eyes captured mine even as he joked with his associates in a language I didn't understand. We were at Club A, where English was a foreign language. After our introduction, in which he gazed up at me with teasing eyes as his warm lips briefly brushed my hand, Andréas adeptly switched from German to English, and I knew this was for my benefit. That small sign of respect endeared me to him.

He had that twinkle, that sparkle, that raw recklessness that always ignited my physical desire, but this time a much softer intuitive feeling overpowered the physical. I desired to know him intellectually and emotionally, imagined cuddling with him to watch a sunset and chatting with him over morning coffee. Before the evening was over, without ever being alone with this boyishly charismatic gentleman, I had an odd thought that had never come to me before no matter how attracted I felt: *Wow, I could marry this man.*

That he was equally attracted to me was obvious to everyone, and I got my first subliminal impression of a pride of lions protecting their kill. *Andréas is ours,* their manner told me, *so back off.*

These were German counts, countesses, dukes, and barons, flashing their family crests, their Patek Phillipe watches and Bvlgari diamonds and aristocratic condescension, letting me know how important they were and how inferior I was in comparison. Fairly worldly in my own right by now, having been to Europe several times and having worked around celebrities and wealth in both New York and LA, I was somewhat spoiled, so neither fame nor money overly impressed me. Nor was I easily rattled by any social situation I encountered. But the self-centered rudeness that rolled off these young Europeans like stench off a rancid pond was a quality I'd never come upon in my travels.

For them what was ultimately important was where they came from and who they were — class, education, lineage. Some were internationally famous, others not, but they came from countries centuries old, with a feudal system and royalty. They could trace their roots to the Ottoman Empire, or the Austrian Dukes, or the line of King Frederick II, who called himself "the Lord of the World." They might be liars, murderers, thieves, or rapists, but with such lineage they were still considered of higher station than the common folk of their country.

Such deeply rooted history created a reality Americans could not compete with, nor should we have to. We're a new country. Look what America has accomplished in 200-plus years; yet such achievement was to them insignificant. Our forefathers were rebels fleeing the same ancestral system these Eurotrash took pride in, and for that reason alone they considered us forever inferior. Yet their precious Andréas was smitten with an American model. How many blue-blooded feminine veins were sizzling with outrage that night, I wonder?

Dinner and Destiny

The next morning, after our meeting at Club A, I awoke wondering if Andréas would call. Since the day my *Penthouse* centerfold first arrived on Atlanta newsstands, I'd been an irresistible attraction for millions of men, and their buzzing adoration was a familiar sound. But last night, all the buzz was directed toward Andréas. While I found myself the object of *his* attention, I'd sensed only reluctant tolerance from his influential friends, who obviously were very important to him. I'd no idea how much their response might affect his decisions. The uncommon uncertainty I felt was unsettling.

That same day, however, Andréas called and invited me to dinner. We went to Regine's, where we sat on brocade couches surrounded by Art Deco mirrors and lighted by snake-wrapped lamps — an eclectic ambiance she designed for all her clubs. Although people came up constantly to say hello to Andréas or, less often, to me, we enjoyed our meal alone, getting to know each other.

He came from a small town near Stuttgart, Germany, he told me, and maintained an apartment in Frankfurt but also kept an apartment here in the Delmonico Hotel, just upstairs from where we were sitting. He traveled extensively for his business, which was international banking for Citibank, and would be leaving the next day for a three-week trip through Europe.

After dinner, we went to Club A, where we met up with the crowd from last night. I realized then that getting to know Andréas might mean getting to know his offensive friends. I didn't quite understand his attraction to them. He was so charming and gregarious, while his friends were snooty and sneering. I smiled at their jokes but saved my brightest smiles for the man who so quickly had captured my heart.

A few days later, Andréas called. He was back from Europe, and I wanted to see where our mutual paths would lead. After my wicked little tryst, a room full of rude Germans didn't seem so daunting.

A Little Weight

The hiatus I'd planned after returning from LA was meant to be a transition from unofficial "Pet of the Decade" to whatever came next, focusing my life and career in a new direction. This was 1982, six years after my centerfold issue, five years since my Pet of the Year tour, yet I was still modeling for *Penthouse* covers and fashion layouts.

I hadn't abandoned my film career entirely after leaving LA, and the *Penthouse* limelight never stopped swinging in my direction — which didn't make the other Pets very happy. From the beginning, Kathy Keeton had wanted me to participate in the business side of the magazine, so when I suggested this might be a good time to make it happen, she was delighted. Did she genuinely believe I'd be an asset to the executive staff, or was she just happy that I seemed to be moving out of Bob's life? Or maybe she believed in keeping her friends close and her enemies closer. In any case, I had a few ideas, which we discussed and Kathy seemed to like.

Meanwhile, I still found myself often in front of the camera. Until I figured out precisely what I wanted to do next, modeling was easy and familiar.

One day Bob came to me with a suggestion I didn't find

quite so agreeable. Looking back, I believe he was going through his own transition at this time. He'd conquered *Playboy*, made *Penthouse* an international success, and he was searching for new mountains to climb.

"Vicki," he said, "you and I should make a video."

My initial reaction was not the positive response I knew he wanted to hear. The video business was reputed to be a cash cow, yet Bob never chased an idea simply for the money. He wanted to stretch his artistic horizon, and video was an exciting new medium for him.

For me, video pushed the adult entertainment envelope further than I wanted to take it. Inwardly, I squirmed.

"A video of what, exactly?"

"People want to know what it's like for me to photograph a centerfold," he said. "This will be similar to the mock photo shoots we've done for so many TV interviews."

"But video isn't television. I assume it will be more sexually explicit." I was long past being modest with Bob, and I'd seen some of his more recent, more risqué centerfolds.

"We'll do only what you're comfortable with."

I was comfortable not doing it at all. When I didn't answer immediately, he added, "Remember the day you saw your first cover? You were shocked at first. This is no different, except that it's film instead of print."

"Print leaves a lot more to the imagination."

"Our video won't go further that what has appeared in the magazine."

Bob always kept his word in that respect, so I had no reason to doubt him now. Yet this side of the video business teemed with so-called producers making cheap X-rated skin-flicks, and while Bob might want to lift it to more artistic levels, I wasn't convinced it was possible. His first film, *Caligula,* remained a stunning example.

When I again didn't respond, he said, "Vicki, you're a natural for this. The camera loves you and so will your audience. You'll be gorgeous."

"How many gorgeous models has the magazine published? Hundreds, maybe thousands, in addition to the centerfolds. You have so many to choose from."

"None of them can bring to the project what you can. You understand how to move naturally, how to create a sensual connection. I need you for this."

We discussed what he wanted, a ten-minute segment on "How to Photograph a Centerfold." As he said, we'd done such clips for TV interviews in the past, but I knew the video would take it beyond what can be shown on network television.

The magazine had been extremely tolerant, however, of my desire to test different waters. Even when I did nothing substantial to earn my retainer for weeks, the paycheck always came. True, my stint in LA was mutually beneficial, since every time my name appeared in print, "*Penthouse* Pet of the Year" usually followed in the same sentence.

In the end, I agreed.

During a preliminary discussion of the shoot, Bob commented casually, and not unkindly, "You've gained a little weight."

"I have," I agreed. "I won't look my best. You should choose a girl who's in better shape."

We were talking about three pounds, perhaps, which in "model" weight can seem disastrous. The camera exaggerates every extra ounce.

Bob shook his head and smiled at me, seeing right through my attempt to escape.

"On you, even 'out of shape' will look great."

As always, Bob and I worked well together. Although our relationship was different now, the connection between us remained.

We shared a unique bond that didn't exist in any of my other relationships, and I believe it was the same for him. Bob gave me the space I needed to explore where I wanted to go next with my life, the way he had explored in his thirties. A really good friendship was a comfortable place for us to be at this point. We cared too much for the entirety of this rather extraordinary relationship to risk it all for sex.

To this day I've never stopped loving Bob, never stopped caring what was happening in his life, whether he was happy and well. Thinking about it now, I realize that on some level, we both knew the love would always be there, in case circumstances ever changed in such a way that he and I were both free to pursue a life together. In that respect, our personal relationship never ended, it simply evolved and lingered, even as the emotional family connection became more important.

My segment, "How to Photograph a Centerfold" on the video titled *Girls of Penthouse*, was as tasteful as Bob promised.

I Never Tell Her How Great She Really Is
Bob Guccione, from the video, *The Girls of Penthouse*,
Penthouse Productions
Victoria is one of the most successful centerfolds, if not the most successful centerfold, we've ever had. She was Pet of the Year like that! (Snaps his fingers.) There was a constant demand to see more and more of her. She's been enormously successful for the readership. She's beautiful to look at. The issues that carry her on the cover sell better, normally, than the issues that don't have her on the cover. I tell her it's the time of the year, state of the economy, the weather. I never tell her how great she really is (laughing). Vicki represents a lot of what Penthouse stands for. She's educated, a very ambitious young lady, a very bright girl,

very representative of what the best of feminism has brought about in this new era.

A Magnetism of Opposites

Women tell me, "I hate dating. I just want to be in a relationship." And I have to confess, I loved dating. I'm one of those few people who enjoy the first, second and third date, the getting-to-know-you period when a man is still going all out to impress and entertain and court me. Until they get boring.

Andréas existed comfortably in a jet-setting world I'd never experienced. Unlike his many associates, he was neither titled nor wealthy, yet he had a charm and presence they appreciated as much as they valued his ability to handle their money efficiently. He traveled constantly, mostly in Europe, primarily for business but also because jet-setting suited him. His apartment in New York was little more than a rest stop, a place to hang his clothes and sleep before boarding the next jet.

Over dinner, Andréas often talked about "our" life, his impish eyes dazzling me as his words painted tantalizing pictures of lands I'd longed to explore since I was a child. I couldn't help wanting to know the Europe he knew. But that's not what attracted me. I honestly can't say what made my heart leap ecstatically every time I saw Andréas across a room or heard his voice on the phone or felt his essence envelop me.

In so many ways we were direct opposites. He was spoiled in one way, I in another. Where I was neat, he was sloppy. Where I needed a harmonious environment, he never noticed his apartment was a complete mess. Where I put great effort into planning, he operated spontaneously. Yet every happy couple I knew was like opposite sides of a coin, alike in some ways, different in others, and these differences we could work out.

"Come to Europe with me," he said one day.

This was my first clue that traveling between New York and anywhere in Europe took no more thought for Andréas than for me to take the seaplane to the Hamptons. Nevertheless, in twenty-four hours, my Louis Vuitton was packed with my best designer clothes and we were off.

After a quick stop at his Frankfurt apartment, which showed as much disarray as the one in New York, we flew to the most romantic place in the world: the Hotel Danieli in Venice, Italy. Like honeymooners, we took the gondola along the Grand Canal and its many interconnecting waterways. We visited the Isle of Murano, where we watched artists at the glass factory create delicate hand-blown masterpieces. In the evenings, we walked the pathway from Rialto Bridge to St. Mark's Square, usually stopping for dinner at one of the many charming restaurants, where I discovered gelato — Italian ice cream.

While I was absorbed in the uniqueness of being encircled on all sides by Byzantine architecture, and at the same time by water in every direction, Andréas seemed interested only in me. It was like living the storyline of a five-star romantic movie, Andréas an enchantingly mischievous imp one moment, a vividly attentive lover the next. Perhaps it was the absence of motor vehicles that soothed away all tension, all thoughts of work, and any worries of where this romance was going. Exploring that richly historic city, by gondola or by cobbled path, I felt completely at ease with this man I'd known for little more than a month. With every marble palace we explored, every traditional Veneto meal we shared, and every serene moment we spent together, our arms, our hands seemed to automatically entwine. I couldn't get enough of touching him. Sex between us was easy and sweet at times, playful at others, always passionate, never demanding. Venice was a joy, and by the end of our five days there, I was so deeply in love that I could not imagine a future without Andréas as part of it.

Classless Asses

From Venice we flew to the town of Lugano, Switzerland, only a short drive from where we would stay next, the Villa d' Este on Lake Como. At this remarkably elegant resort, I relived yet another piece of history as I walked the corridors and viewed the magnificent 15th and 16th century artworks. After two precious weeks in Italy and Switzerland, Andréas and I rarely went anywhere alone. His European friends, some twenty-five or so from the larger party group, often traveled together or met at some prearranged location. Wherever one decided to go, at least ten or twelve others would go as well.

Andréas's friends included the famous and the infamous. Claus von Bulow, a British socialite with German and Danish ancestry, was both. When Andréas and I met, Claus was on trial for the attempted murder of his American wife, Sunny, who previously was married to Prince Alfred of Auersperg and now lay in an irreversible coma in a New York hospital. Claus was convicted and sentenced to thirty years in prison. The criminal appellate lawyer, Alan Dershowitz, who successfully argued an appeal and got the decision reversed, later wrote a book, *Reversal of Fortune: Inside the von Bülow Case,* and the book eventually spawned a movie starring Jeremy Irons as Claus and Glenn Close as Sunny.

I personally found Claus to be a cold, politely charming man, and I couldn't help staring when he wasn't aware, or catching his eye at an odd moment, hoping to discern the truth. Though not really one of the invading newcomers, Claus had connections within that group, and in Andréas's crowd, each of us harbored separate opinions as to his guilt.

Possibly Andréas's closest friend was Mick Flick. Formally known as Friedrich Christian Flick, Mick was the grandson of Friedrich Flick, who was convicted of war crimes in the Nuremberg Trials and served three years of a seven-year sentence.

After his release from prison, he built a business empire in coal and steel. He eventually became a minority holder in Daimler AG, the German manufacturing company that builds Mercedes automobiles, among others, and before his death in 1972 was named among the richest men in the world. His heirs, including Mick and his brother, Muck, inherited the legacy, both good and bad. So during those days of 1982 through 1985, when we weren't reading about Claus's murder trial, we could tune in to the ongoing affairs of the Flick family.

On one of our early trips to Europe, visiting the home of yet another of Andréas's friends, in Marbella, Spain, I began to realize the extent to which they considered me an outsider. The constant guttural sounds of German chatter grated on me as we lounged by the pool, everyone conversing in a language they knew I didn't understand. I refused to ask them to speak English, because I knew they were intentionally shutting me out. Instead, I laughed when they laughed, as if I knew what they were saying. One evening when Andréas and I were finally alone, however, I asked why his friends insisted on speaking German, even when I was in the room.

"They all speak English," I said. "So it would be easy for them to include me in the conversation. Yet I'm sitting there among them, clearly interested, trying to be polite, and they act like I don't exist. Why are they so rude?"

"They are not rude, Victoria. You exaggerate." His tone was not sympathetic.

"You could ask them to speak English. They adore you. They would listen to you."

"Why should they speak English? You are the only American. We are German. You have to get used to it."

As I write this, I've put some thought to why they might have been so small-minded. Even then I knew it was partly because I was an American, but also, the word spread quickly that I was a

Penthouse centerfold and still actively involved with the magazine. My latest cover had come out early that same year. Being photographed nude for a commercial magazine was considered unrefined, a detriment they might use to control Andréas. And little by little I began to understand just how thoroughly they controlled him. They entrusted him with managing their finances, and in return they expected him to run any time they called.

Another reason they shut me out, I realize now, had to do with the way I looked. If I'd been homely, I might have been more acceptable. Most of them were Andréas's age, thirty-seven or so. At thirty, and appearing even younger, I outshone any woman in the group — after all, homely girls don't become centerfolds. Many of the women were looking for a suitable husband, and Andréas was a great catch. They had the title and money, while he had education, charm, presence, and the ability to fit seamlessly into their world. I'm sure it galled them to know that an American stranger had stolen the heart of their precious puppet while they weren't looking.

In the weeks and months that followed our trip to Marbella, Andréas's friends never once paid me the courtesy of speaking English to include me in the group. Individually, some were worse than others. The men, when away from the women, were often polite enough to use my native language, but once together again, forget it. And on those few occasions when someone in the group addressed me in English, it was always as if they were explaining the obvious to an idiot. A putdown.

Never a woman to back down from a challenge, however, I resolved to not let his friends get to me. To bolster my self-confidence, I started taking private classes when I was in New York, because I was damned determined I would learn to speak German.

Dominant Woman

Andréas and I lived busy lives. I had to fight for free time with him. Day by day I slept more often at his apartment than I did at my own. Gradually, my clothes gravitated to his closet, my makeup and personal items to his bureau drawers. I kept my apartment, but we lived at his.

I'd experienced a number of relationships by now, some significant, some not, mostly passionate choices based on mutual physical attraction. I knew this one was different. The passion was there, but so was a deep emotional connection. This was the real thing, and at a time in my life when I was ready for grownup, fully committed love.

The love I'd known with Jim was first love, young, naïve, and filled with discovery. With Bob, there was never an expectation of long-term involvement. The allure of Bob was the clandestine, unexpected nature of our relationship and the anticipation of what might come entwined with the magazine, freedom of expression, and breaking free of my Georgia persona. My romp with Robáire was merely a wild and dangerous liaison.

Andréas was difficult, sloppy, had jet lag half the time, had the rudest friends in the world, but the plain truth was that I loved him. I also loved the exciting world he was introducing me to. Whenever Andréas and I were alone together, away from his friends or family, he was a completely different man. I knew he wanted to be with me, wanted a simpler, more honest relationship. He wanted to be in love and to live a normal life. But he was pulled away to the other side by his heritage and his upbringing.

Regardless of how much we loved each other, his family's prospect for Andréas's future would never include me. Being German, he was allowed a period of time to live with "wild abandon," but in the end was expected to own up to his responsibilities and do what was best for the family. Andréas was thirty-seven. In his mother's opinion, the time to do the right thing was at hand.

Her expectation was that her son would marry into royalty, no matter what it took to make that happen.

Birds of a Feather

In October 1982, while we were still in the honeymoon phase of our romance, I received a call from Andréas in London.

"I had an accident," he said, "fell down the stairs at Harry's Bar."

"Oh, my god! Are you okay?"

"It is nothing, but the doctors tell me to stay in hospital overnight."

A few hours later, he phoned again. This time he was clearly sedated to some extent, on pain pills, no doubt, and he started to ramble, alternating between German and English.

This was so odd for him. I'd never seen Andréas when he was not totally in control. He talked about his blood, and for the first time I heard the whining voice I would come to know quite well. When he was sick or hurt, and being himself, without his friends around to see, he could sound truly pitiful.

"There is something wrong with me, Victoria. The doctors say there is something wrong."

"Yes, you fell down the stairs. Are you hurt badly?"

"No, it is my blood. My blood is bad."

That made no sense. His blood would have nothing to do with his taking a fall, unless it showed heavy alcohol consumption, and he'd sounded completely sober when he called earlier. But I felt there was something more in what he was saying, so I listened.

"What's wrong with your blood, Andréas? What did they say?"

"There is something bad in my blood. It is terrible, they tell me."

Within seconds he was falling asleep, without giving me any additional information, so I filed the conversation in the back of my mind and let it go. When he was released from the hospital and returned to New York, I asked him about it.

"You must be wrong, Victoria. I would never say that."

I found it strange that he was so adamant when clearly he'd been under the influence of pain medication. He didn't merely deny making the call or say he didn't remember the call; he denied he would ever have said anything about his blood or about testing his blood.

Medical records began coming to the apartment after that. They were in German, for the most part, so I couldn't read them. I believe now that a doctor at some point must have told Andréas, "You have the beginning stages of multiple myeloma. If it progresses, you'll have eighteen months to live." But that's only in hindsight. He never would admit having a debilitating, much less a life-threatening, disease. We'd been together about five months, and I don't believe anyone, except possibly his father, knew the seriousness of his illness.

In 1983, we traveled to Acapulco and took a drift boat ride through a mangrove swamp, where the city chaos faded like a summer sunset. Seagulls, vivid tropical birds, and tropical plant life abounded, a serene sight I'd never expected to see in the bustle of activity that was Mexico. The guide oared quietly and spoke softly, so as not to disturb indigenous animals that occasionally scurried from behind a log. An alligator rose silently in the water to peer at us. The scene was so breathtakingly picturesque that even the Germans shut up.

A couple of weeks later, Andréas was admitted to a hospital in New York. His physician suspected he had tuberculosis, so all his friends and I ran to be at his side, suited up in full protective gear. After a day or two, the doctors figured out that it was not TB but histoplasmosis, an infectious disease caused by inhaling microscopic spores of the fungus Histoplasma capsulatum. The disease primarily affects the lungs, is very rare, and is carried by birds.

Thousands of people go through that marsh without contracting this disease. For Andréas to get it, I now suspect his immune system must already have been compromised. Fortunately, he responded well to the antifungal drugs and was soon jetting around the globe again.

By now, we'd spent a year and several months together, and I was thoroughly embedded in his world. We enjoyed a fabulous life, attending the most dazzling parties and events, but for me, they were rarely enjoyable. Finding myself among pompous, obnoxious people was no longer surprising but no less infuriating.

What was most maddening at the time was Andréas's behavior when they were around. Like birds of a feather, he could be as brash as they were. It was clear to me by now that he could never stand up to them. He didn't own his life.

Breaking Away

Eventually, I gravitated to the few people in Andréas's group who were amiable and developed a set of friends of my own among the larger crowd. I was going to pursue this relationship with Andréas on my terms, I decided, or not at all.

I often left him. Then he would call with that whiny little-boy voice.

"You don't understand, Victoria--"

No, I didn't understand.

"Stand up to your friends," I would tell him. "If you don't make them respect me as an important part of your life, I will not be there."

His personality was changing. He became obstinate and as patronizing as his friends, especially in public. On occasion, when we were with them he even behaved rudely to me, his partner. It hurt to know that on some level he disrespected Americans as much as his friends did. Yet when we were alone, he was still unpretentious, undemanding, and loving. I knew Andréas loved me, and I missed him when we were apart. When he called begging me to come back, eventually I would go.

In the fall of 1983, however, I did move out. I left him . . . or thought I did.

CHAPTER 21

Living to Die

In looking back over my relationships, it's still a mystery to me why I couldn't lose my heart to nice guys. With so many fine men in my life, why was I drawn to Andréas? Does anyone know the true essence of love? It isn't definable. It isn't concrete. The feeling is like gossamer, slipping through my fingers every time I try to grab hold of it. I could say it was his effervescent personality. He was playful, mischievous, always laughing, smiling, teasing. That was certainly part of it. I could say it was the lifestyle, traveling to the lands I'd imagined in my youth, traveling not like a tourist but in a style worthy of royalty. Yes, that was part of it, especially in the beginning. In the end, there's no explaining what makes a woman choose one man over another, a troublesome relationship over one that's practical and easy.

The break-up with Andréas hadn't come easy for me but only after many fights, yet he treated our parting as merely a temporary separation.

"Victoria, I don't want to lose you," he would say every time he called. "You know I need you. Please come."

In spring of 1984, I went back. Living with Andréas, I saw more medical records coming in, and I became more alarmed than merely inquisitive. That July, while attending the 1984 Summer Olympics in LA, I finally asked Andréas, "What is really wrong with you? I want the truth."

"Nothing. There is nothing wrong."

"Why do I keep seeing reports from doctors and clinics? What's going on?"

"You should not read my mail, Victoria. That's not right."

"If I could read it, I'd know what was wrong. I want you to tell me. Right now, while we're away from New York, away from your friends, I want the truth about your illness."

For a time he continued to be evasive and defensive, then he broke down, almost crying. Because he was German, he wasn't allowed to show weakness, and I don't believe he could have allowed himself such an emotional collapse with anyone else.

"The doctor tells me I have cancer."

In 1984 the odds against anyone surviving cancer were even more depressing than they are today, but the sadness I saw in Andréas appeared far deeper than sorrow for himself. I could see his misery, but I didn't fully understand it yet.

"Multiple myeloma it is called. For some time it has been dormant, but now it is not."

After all these months, I had my answer and didn't know what to say. I know now that multiple myeloma is a bone cancer, one of the most painful cancers of all, that it was considered "incurable" at that time and is rare in people under thirty-five. If you have myeloma without symptoms, you may not need cancer treatment right away, which might well have been the case for Andréas in the beginning, leading to his belief that it had been "dormant." The progression includes susceptibility to infection, bone fractures, and a tendency to hemorrhage.

At the time, I couldn't bring myself to ask the hard question: *Are you dying?* In any case, the disease apparently was progressing.

"You should get additional opinions —"

"I have done all that, Victoria. I am being treated." Having finally said the dreadful words that revealed his secret, he seemed more at ease than since the earliest days of our relationship.

"Chemotherapy?"

He did that thing with his hand — no more discussion. "We will enjoy the Olympics, and then I have a big surprise for you."

He wouldn't tell me exactly what the surprise was.

Adventures in Living

Andréas asked if I would go with him to Rochester, Minnesota. He was going to have some tests done at the Mayo Clinic, he said, and he wanted me to be with him. Despite the dreadful reason for our stay, our evenings held some of our most treasured moments. When Andréas and I were alone together, he was still the same sweet man with whom I'd fallen so deeply in love. I witnessed the pain of his being torn in one direction by commitment to friends, family, the life he'd built for himself and in another direction by his undeniable love for me. If he could have lived his life the way he wanted, I believe things between us would have played out much differently in the following year.

When the tests were finished, we flew to Johannesburg, South Africa and took a small plane to Mala Mala, South Africa's largest game reserve.

"This," Andréas said, "is your surprise."

Of all the trips I've ever taken anywhere in the world, Mala Mala is by far my favorite. We awoke at the unbelievable hour of four in the morning, left our thatched huts, loaded into two open four-wheel-drive safari vehicles, with tiered seating so that everyone had a clear view, and drove out into the bushveld to watch the animals grazing. Our two guides spoke reverently of the big five — lion, leopard, rhinoceros, buffalo, elephant — and eventually we saw them all, but the first animals we encountered were giraffes.

Our spotter was a Shangaan tracker, an indigenous South African who spoke no English. We drove deep into the bush, no animals in sight. Our spotter made a *clicking* noise with his mouth, and the driver stopped.

All of a sudden, the magnificent animals were there. I'd never seen a giraffe except in the zoo, and here in their own environment were dozens of them, so much taller than I remembered, walking gracefully among the trees. After they passed by, we continued driving, the guide quietly pointing out zebras, impalas, elands, aardvarks, hyenas, and strange little creatures with names I can't recall. An amazing sight, an amazing day, and we were lulled to sleep that night by a nocturnal symphony of sound.

On one of our night safaris we spotted a lion cub that seemed to be abandoned. Even the Germans wanted to get out and save it, but the guide said, "We cannot interfere in the cycle of life. Either the lion cub will lie here and be dead in the morning, or its mother is waiting in the grass for you to get out of this vehicle, and *you* will be dead in the morning."

Except for that rather fearsome warning, we had only one scary incident. During our morning ride, the vehicle stopped near a herd of grazing elephants.

"The African elephant is the largest land mammal," our guide reminded us, as we gazed in awe, cameras busily clicking. "An adult bull elephant can weigh up to 14,000 pounds. His tusks are modified incisor teeth, used as weapons and as an aid in procuring food. There are fifty-five thousand muscles in an elephant's trunk —"

I'm not sure what spooked them, but about that time the elephants began stamping their heavy feet. Their trunks went up, and they started coming our way.Instantly, the guides raised their rifles, the driver backed away and we got out of there.

Of the three and a half years I knew Andréas, our month in Africa was perhaps our most tenderly pleasurable. Between the trips to Italy and Africa, Andréas continued to see doctors, and their reports continued to come to the house. His illness was now fully confirmed. Realizing that Andréas could vanish from my life made me more tolerant of his periodic brashness.

Harsh Facts

As 1984 drew to a close, Andréas was living hard, pushing the envelope. Even with the harsh facts of his cancer finally out in the open, if only to me, he still needed to maintain the appearance that all was well. He also began planning a "Summer Ball" during that winter, mailing out save-the-date invitations as early as January for an extravaganza. He scheduled it to take place in Vienna on June 30, 1985, his birthday.

Early in 1985, I received a call from the *Penthouse* office. They were about to launch a Japanese edition, and Bob asked me to go to Japan to represent the magazine. I questioned his wanting to send me, at thirty-three years old, as Pet of the Year. When he insisted I was the person they wanted, I agreed but decided this would be my last appearance under that title. In fact, I relished the opportunity to be engaged in a project I knew I could do well.

In Japan, the photos taken were some of my best ever, a brilliant spark to mark the end of my New York modeling career and my final appearance as "Pet of the Decade."

Bob and Kathy also wanted me in Japan as an executive knowledgeable about the magazine as a business. Representing *Penthouse*, I knew exactly where I stood and had no problem dealing with Japanese businessmen. The trip was scheduled to take about ten days.

Near the end of my stay in Japan, I received a call from Andréas. He was in a hospital in Germany and asked if I could come. I flew with my escort back to New York and, with barely twenty-four hours to regroup, boarded a flight to Frankfurt feeling certain this was the beginning of the end. I arrived in Germany and stayed in his apartment in Frankfurt from mid-June through early July, which included one miserable week I shared the apartment with his parents. For some reason, Andréas wanted us together despite how much his mother despised me.

From his hospital bed, Andréas continued his life as usual. Always on the phone, when he wasn't doing business, he continued organizing his birthday party. He met with Niko, and I suspected he was finalizing his financial affairs. His closest friends must have known the severity of his illness by now, and his employers at Citibank were likely aware.

Andréas drove the doctors and nurses crazy as they came to examine him, give him injections, check his vitals, or change his IV. He wouldn't get off the telephone. He insisted on smoking. I can still see that ridiculous scene in my mind.

When you're diagnosed with cancer, you make a choice. Either live to get better, doing everything you can to prolong your life, or live like you're dying, which Andréas was doing. I believe if he'd taken better care of himself, he would have lived longer, but he chose not to.

Happy Birthday and Goodbye

Andréas's celebration in Vienna turned out to be a three-day birthday event, with parties and luncheons each day. The guest list of nearly 500 people read like the Who's Who of European aristocracy. He reserved every room in the finest hotel in Vienna. He hired the Vienna Symphony to play and European ballet companies to dance. I don't believe many guests had any idea this was Andréas's farewell, making it even more difficult and sad for those of us who did.

A spectacular circus, the weekend started with cocktails on Friday night and didn't end until Sunday evening. I never arrived at these events with Andréas. Although we stayed in the same hotel, we had separate rooms. He shared a suite with his parents, and he either came to the events with them or with a group in which I wasn't included. The night of the party, his mother strolled around with her son, commanding attention, working the crowd like a pro. His father walked alongside, vacantly, as if wishing he could just leave, knowing the truth that Andréas was dying and refusing to engage in the festivities as absurdly as his wife.

Like Andréas's father, I wandered around also with a false smile on my face, seeking out the few people I knew from New York, or anyone who might speak English. I felt as if everyone around me was moving in slow motion, like the home movies people make for funerals, where a person's life runs in frame-by-frame silence against a score of classical music. That whole evening for me was a slow-motion nightmare.

Andréas sat at a center table orchestrated by his mother. Again, I wasn't included. I was merely one of his many guests, part of the periphery, watching each person come up to him, and Andréas smiling, pretending nothing was wrong, that he was fine. He was trying to be his usual animated self as every female wished him a happy birthday, touched him, hugged him, played kissy face on his cheeks. Men came, too, and if they showed any emotion at all it was false heartiness.

I wondered how many knew this was his farewell party, not merely a celebration of his fortieth birthday. I noticed he rarely left the table. He must have been in terrible pain. In his advanced stage of multiple myeloma, his bones disintegrating, it had to be painful to simply sit in a chair and excruciating to walk.

Toward the end of the party, Andréas rose from his seat. His mother bounced up right behind him, chattering like a magpie, and they started walking the pathway to the hotel proper, Andréas holding to his mother's arm. His father caught up to them and took his son's other arm.

He needed physical support to walk. *He's in a lot of pain,* I realized, and hurried to follow, to find out if Andréas was all right. They spoke German, of course, his mother arguing vociferously with husband and son. Andréas spoke abruptly to her, obviously upset. I caught a few words, enough to know he was definitely hurting.

"Andréas, what is wrong?" I asked.

They ignored me, just kept walking, with me following behind like a worried puppy. After a moment, I asked again, "Andréas, please, what's wrong?"

He turned to me and said quietly, "I am bleeding."

Then his mother *screamed* at me, "He's bleeding inside! Don't you understand? He's bleeding inside!"

His father simply looked worried, lips pressed together in a fierce frown, and I understood then why they had to get Andréas back to the hotel. He'd pushed himself through three days of festivities and had almost made it. His doctors had come with him, and I suspect his hotel suite was set up much like a hospital room. Now another symptom of his cancer had emerged: he was hemorrhaging.

When we reached the hotel, I asked what I could do to help, but they ignored me in their rush to get Andréas back to his room. All evening I'd thought I might have an opportunity later to catch his attention long enough to say "Happy birthday" and "I love you" and "This will get better. *You* will get better." But the evening ended, and all I could see were their backs to me as they shuffled him away to their suite. I'd endured the entire horrible three days without being alone with Andréas for a single instant.

As I stood watching them leave without a word, something died inside me. I'd known for months this time was coming, but now the end clearly was imminent.

Last Call

Andréas phoned as often as possible to update me on his progress.

"I am getting better," he would tell me. "I am going to get over this."

Nevertheless, I was moving on with my life, working, associating with a few close friends, reorganizing my future along with my attitude. In November, I'd acquired my New York State real estate license in anticipation of pursuing a completely new career.

Then one day in December, Andréas called to tell me he was being moved to MD Anderson hospital in Houston, Texas.

"Why are you going there?" I couldn't imagine Texas doctors doing any more for him than was already being done by the best physicians in Europe.

"I believe they will cure me. We are doing what they call a bone marrow transplant."

I'd never heard of the hospital or the procedure, but the possibilities clearly had renewed his hope. His voice sounded stronger than I'd heard it in weeks.

"It is a special cancer hospital," he said. "Citibank has offered the use of their jet to fly me to Houston."

I wanted to fly down to Houston and see him, but I knew I should stay away for my own healing process. I kept him in my private thoughts, though, silently hoping the bone marrow transplant would prove to be our long-awaited miracle.

Meanwhile, I had been invited to a black-tie Christmas party with my girlfriend Iris. As I was getting ready, the phone rang. Instead of Iris, it was Andréas. The relief I felt at hearing his voice, knowing he'd arrived safely, and that MD Anderson might miraculously extend his life was like a shot of high-powered vitamins.

"Merry Christmas!" I said. "How are you?"

"I'm okay." He sounded weaker. The trip must have taken its toll. And there was a new sadness in his voice. "I have to tell you something, Victoria, something very serious."

They've told him he's dying, I thought at once. *He must have only days ... or hours ....*

"I want you to know ...." He mumbled and couldn't quite seem to get the words out. "I do not know how to ... I've ... I've gotten married ... to someone else."

Whatever I expected, it was not this. I had no words. I couldn't talk.

I think all I said was, "Why?"

I couldn't scream, couldn't curse him. I could not even feel my voice coming from my body. I felt nothing, had no emotion, not sorrow, not hatred, I was just numb. My heart and mind were void. *Why? Why would you do something like this?* I think my body went into shock.

"I had to do this, Victoria." He offered no explanation, only, "Someday you'll understand."

He continued talking, but I dropped the phone and stared down at it. *Someday you'll understand?*

I don't know how long I stood there. I remember the buzzer sounding from downstairs. The doorman knew my friend, Iris, and he said, "She's on her way up."

The party.

I couldn't stop her. When the doorbell rang, I managed to open it, still not thinking clearly, not sure what to do or say.

When Iris saw me, her eyes opened very wide.

"Oh, my god, what is wrong with you?"

I told her as best I could, and as I talked, my senses returned, though I still felt numb.

"Okay," she said, "I'm going to call and cancel."

"No. Don't do that." I had enough pride and wherewithal left to know that if I didn't counteract this shock, if I let myself continue to feel the way I was feeling, I would fall apart. Whatever sort of mechanism that keeps you going at such times kicked in. Although it wasn't a German party, there would be a crossover of guests from Andréas's crowd. By now they probably knew or soon would, but I would not allow them to know what this had done to me, would not be seen as a devastated victim. Andréas would not take away my last human dignity.

"Don't cancel," I said. "We'll go."

Still in shock, I went to the Christmas party to make an appearance, go through the necessary motions. On the way, I contrived a pretense for leaving early.

"If I can't pull this off," I told Iris, "I'll just say I'm sick."

At the party, I thought of a better story. "Thank you for inviting me," I told my hosts. "I wanted to come and say Merry Christmas. I can only stay for cocktails, because my family is in town."

That pretense got me out of the room after I made the rounds. I saw the people I wanted to see, said my "hellos" and "thank yous," and I left.

In the taxi ride home and in the elevator, the protective shell I'd erected around my heart began to break, and by the time I opened my door I could hardly control my emotions. Relief that I'd gotten through the evening. Anger that I'd been put in a position once again to feel that I'd never have closure. Sadness that no matter what transpired now with Andréas's health, there was no future for us. He had dropped an ax, cut the cord that had kept me bound to him for our years together — in health but mostly in sickness.

I felt pain I never knew existed, worse than any physical pain I'd experienced. My heart actually hurt. I'd never known before how a broken heart truly felt. I cried uncontrollably until I had to stop long enough to vomit. Then I cried so hard I started hyperventilating. Still, I couldn't stop crying, couldn't stop throwing up, because I was so sick inside. Physically sick. Emotionally sick. My heart just... it just hurt.

Bouts of pain and sadness continued throughout the night, until I fell asleep from sheer exhaustion. The next afternoon, as soon as I could get out of bed and pull myself together, I called Delta airlines and booked a flight to Atlanta. I could have gone a lot of places, but I didn't want to go anywhere else, didn't want to see friends. I could go home to Georgia and hide. My family would never question or judge me, and I could deal with my misery in private.

My mom knew right away something was terribly wrong. She knew Andréas was dying, so I let her think that was the reason I was so sad. The entire reason. I'd never told her how bad the situation was with his friends and family; now I didn't tell her he'd married someone else. I couldn't say the words.

On December 28th, I received a message on my answering service from Andréas's friend Jochem in New York: *Victoria, could you please call me?* When I did, Jochem asked delicately, "Has anyone let you know that Andréas died yesterday?"

While awaiting the transplant procedure, his health had steadily worsened and, unfortunately, the transplant never happened.

"No, this is the first I've heard," I said. "Thank you for calling, Jochem."

It was also the last I heard. No one in his family, nor any of his other friends bothered to phone or send a card. To them, our relationship was never of any importance.

CHAPTER 22

Fresh Mountain Air

Unwilling to linger in the ashes of what my life had become, I shook off those ill-fated Andréas years by concentrating on where to go and what to do next. For the following year I remained with *Penthouse* as a special promotions coordinator, a position I'd created for myself during my travels with Andréas, but my heart and soul were no longer bound to the magazine. Bob was taking the photography and editorials into darker directions, which I found too explicit for me. I didn't want to do anything to taint the flawlessly successful career I'd shaped there. In late 1986, with one of the hardest decisions I've ever had to make, I resigned.

In January 1988, I sold my New York condo, which netted me a nice chunk of money. I decided to take a sabbatical and figure out what I wanted to do with the next stage of my life. Aspen represented to me the American version of European resort living and the part of America I loved most — cowboys, the spirit of the Ute Indians, and remnants of the Wild West. Over the phone, I rented a house for six months in Aspen's west end, just outside of town. After shipping my clothes and eighteen footlockers, I realized I didn't want to arrive there as "Victoria, high-profile *Penthouse* Pet of the Year," so I traded in my high heels for cowboy boots and became an official Aspen local.

Ski resorts are usually just sprawling hotels surrounded by breathtaking slopes. The uniqueness of Aspen is that it's a real town with a colorful historical background, its own police force, courthouse, and a working government of outspoken politicians. Rich, poor, and in between, people arrive in Aspen looking for something — miners in the past looking for silver, ranchers looking for land, individuals looking for peace, solitude, and discovery within themselves. Everyone is unique in some way. Everybody knows one another and eventually learns to at least accept their neighbors' eccentricities.

Moving to Aspen takes a lot of effort. The very different lifestyle requires a special kind of tenacity and a willingness to make sacrifices. But if you're willing and tenacious, there's no environment more rewarding, at least for me at that time in my life. Within ten city blocks, I found everything I was looking for, the beauty and glitz of St. Moritz, the culture of New York but at slower a pace, the star power of LA, plus the tranquility and splendor of living among thousands of acres of mountains, rivers, and forest.

A resident's summer consists of hiking, biking, canoeing, fishing, rafting, camping, or horseback riding. For a less athletic culture there's the Wine Festival, Music Festival, Art Festival, to mention a few. Winter centers on skiing, snowboarding, snowshoeing and, what I enjoyed most at first, a lot of après-skiing — it's like the town giving a big party for everyone, whether skiers or workers, every afternoon at four o'clock.

At the favorite hangouts, The Little Nell or Mezzaluna, you'd find yourself mingling with ski bums and athletes, tourists as well as locals and part-time residents, rich and poor. You might be sitting next to Melanie Griffith and Don Johnson, but nobody cared. Racecar driver Danny Sullivan lived there. The gonzo writer, Hunter Thompson, lived there—and of course, John Denver. Tennis player Martina Navratilova had the same trainer I did for a while. It was a community at that time that accepted everybody and wasn't impressed with anybody.

By the early 1990s I needed to work more, to provide additional income and avoid totally depleting my savings. After identifying a need in the valley I felt was not being provided, I started

*Idyllic times in Aspen. Mostly with
Sandy Iglehart and friends.*

a discount clothing business, a source for local girls to buy great clothes at affordable prices. Aspen has every kind of high-end clothing store imaginable—Prada, Gucci, Burberry, Ralph Lauren, Fendi—but other than the GAP, there was nothing for the less than super wealthy.

By the end of March, department stores were already buying fall merchandise while leftover summer stock hung on racks in New York or LA warehouses. Also by March, Aspen ski season had ended and the locals had their winter income. I learned the business, which was a natural for me, chose LA as my source, and purchased women's clothing at discount prices. Pieces that retailed between $200 and $400 I could sell for $39 to $99. Four times a year, I rented vacant retail spaces and held huge sales that lasted two to four weeks. The business proved financially success-ful and immensely satisfying to my creative-fashion side while also leaving me with time to enjoy Aspen's distinctively laid-back, recreation-oriented lifestyle.

Often taking me to LA, my business grew until I needed a place to work there other than small hotel rooms, so set I up a sec-ond residence. LA life was different for me this time, with no rem-nants of my "Decade of Decadence" past, but one thing that hadn't changed was the importance of lunches. When I wasn't downtown going through warehouses, I often enjoyed lunching with friends. Ma Maison had closed, but The Bistro and several others had filled in the gap. One day I bumped into my friend, Mark Saginore, a well known celebrity MD, an endocrinologist, and Hugh Hefner's personal doctor. I asked what he'd been up to lately.

Mark said he was about to take a course in homeopathic medi-cine, a hot topic at the time.

"I'd love to do something like that," I admitted.

"Then you should join me."

This was a credited college course in homeopathic studies. I knew I wouldn't fit in.

"Come on," he said. "Just sit in on the first class with me."

The class was eight hours on a Saturday, but I did it, and I was captivated. When the day came, I introduced myself to the instructor and asked if it was all right for me to attend that day with Doctor Mark.

"Sure you can," he said, "but why not take the course?"

I had already met a few of the students — doctors, chiropractors, dentists, veterinarians, nurses, physician's assistants.

"Everybody here is connected to the medical world. I have no medical background."

"That's not required," he assured me.

But just the thought of it was intimidating. After all, my favorite classes in high school were Drill Team and Drama Club. Certainly not Science.

"I'll pay for the course," I said. "But I'd like to simply audit the classes."

Before that day ended, I was bitten by the homeopathic bug, engrossed in the subject, and too competitive not to give it my best shot. By the next class, I had enrolled and purchased the textbooks. I kept up with the other students over the course of the following year, not feeling the need to socialize as much as to study. In the end, I took the tests and felt a great sense of accomplishment when I stepped up to the podium to receive my diplomatic degree in homeopathic medicine. I had the privilege of interning under one of Aspen's most revered MDs and finest homeopaths, Dr. Harold Whitcombe. On my business card, should I choose to make one, I can add my credentials, D. Hom. Med. after my name.

As much as I enjoyed my work, new friends, and LA's weather, I hated the commute, the fires that broke out too close to home that year, and the devastating rainstorms that produced mudslides. I had arrived during the Rodney King riots, and the area where my apartment was located was in lockdown. But the event that shattered any loyalty to LA was the massive 6.7 Northridge earthquake that occurred on January 17, 1994, causing at least thirty-three deaths and leaving more than 8,700 injured.

After the earthquake, LA was not quite so comfortable for me. I realized I didn't need a second residence there, after all. I could commute as often as needed for my buying trips, always with a pair of sneakers and a flashlight to place under my bed in an earthquake-proof hotel, for visits with friends, and to take care of any personal business I might have there, then return to Aspen, where I really wanted to be. I loved visiting LA, had enjoyed this two-year stay, but after two attempts, I knew I wasn't meant to live there.

In the spring of 1994, I gave up my California residence, and instead of renewing my lease, I found a perfect apartment behind City Market, Aspen's only in-town grocery store. Aspen had become the place I felt most comfortable as well as most alive and involved with people I cared about. Replacing New York in my heart, Aspen had become my home.

CHAPTER 23

Friends, Families, Heartaches

The acquaintances I made during the ten years of my new life, skiing, hiking, living, loving, and partying in the fresh mountain air, became lifelong friends. The friendships I developed ran deep, perhaps because I felt I had so much in common with the strong women of Aspen. Finding mutual interests was astoundingly easy. Being involved with worthwhile projects and events drew me to individuals who, though I didn't know it at the time, would comfort, support, and reassure me through a most difficult future.

My earliest introduction to the town and many of the people there was through Sandy Goldman, now Sandy Goldman Israel. Like me, Sandy was a former model in the fashion business, and when we met she was managing the cashmere store where I worked a few hours a week. Sandy had recently founded the Aspen Chapter of the Susan G. Komen Foundation, an organization I knew nothing about until one afternoon in 1990, when I ran into her.

"You should come to our meeting tonight," she said, clearly excited. "It includes a class on how to do a breast self-examination."

I was barely thirty-eight at that time, and women didn't start getting annual breast exams or worrying about such things until at least age forty. But I liked Sandy, and this women's group sounded informative. The lecture became much more fascinating and personal than I'd anticipated when I learned that tall, beautiful Sandy Goldman was a breast cancer survivor. Both her breasts had been surgically removed ten years earlier to defeat the cancer.

I thought, *Wow, she couldn't have been much older than me*

when she lost her breasts. Since I knew little about breast cancer, and was keenly interested in any subject concerning health, the lecture fell on my highly receptive ears.

In the Hotel Jerome event room, approximately 100 women were gathered to hear Sandy's talk. Each of us received an artificial breast, soft, malleable, fairly realistic, and we sat holding this perfect pink breast, trying not to giggle.

"Somewhere in that breast is a pea," Sandy told us. "Hard and round, it won't feel like the surrounding tissue." She demonstrated how to gently probe, fingers together, in a circular pattern.

Finding that pea was not easy. Afterward, when Sandy asked me to volunteer for Komen, I said yes immediately and decided I would start early getting regular mammograms and breast exams, never realizing how my decision would eventually impact my life. Scarcely eight years later, I came to truly appreciate what Sandy had done for me.

Pink Flamingo Ball

The best psychics come to Aspen and set up business for a month, usually as someone's house guest. Aspen clientele, eager to hear a new clairvoyant version of the future, flock in for readings. When Sandy insisted I see the new psychic she'd found, I sat down one day to learn what my future held.

"Do you ever go to Texas?" she asked.

"Other than a wedding in Dallas a couple of years ago, no."

"Do you see Texas in your future?"

"Not at all."

"Do you have any illnesses? Or is someone close to you ill?"

"No." This was getting boring. I was ready for her to move on.

"You're going to meet somebody new," she said. "You've already come close, but you don't realize it. He's tall, and he'll be wearing one of those Aspen shirts. Plaid flannel. His name might be Biggly? … Brumbly?"

She kept burbling b's, and I kept saying, "No. That name doesn't ring a bell."

Another friend, Billie Pierce, in her role as a socially active real estate agent, had been shepherding a new man around to all the events. He planned to buy a house in town, and Billie wanted me to meet him.

"Bob noticed you right away," Billie told me. "He asked who you were. He's tall, handsome, and set on meeting you, Victoria."

In early January of 1998, I called Billie. "Who's that guy you want me to meet?"

"Bob Bradley," she said.

Instantly, I recalled the psychic burbling b's as she described a man I would soon encounter. Laughing, I told Billie about it. She believed psychics had a direct line to divine knowledge.

"You've *got* to meet Bob. I'll call him and we'll have lunch together."

When I arrived at the restaurant, Bob was wearing a blue plaid shirt — exactly as the psychic predicted. I'd never mentioned to Billie this aspect of the prediction. In more ways than just looks, Bob Bradley was my kind of guy. During that lunch meeting, we explored some of our mutual interests. As it turned out, Bob and I were perfectly compatible. We moved at the same pace. We both loved to travel, loved mountains as well as the beach. We liked skiing. I was from Georgia, he was from nearby Virginia. Our friends were the same. We were invited to the same events. He was tall, I liked tall. I was me, he liked me. Bob was the whole package, and our life together was easy. For the first time in many years, I felt completely relaxed in a relationship. I began to feel that Bob and I might go the distance.

CHAPTER 24

An Unexpected Biopsy

Those ten years in Aspen, breathing fresh mountain air, I was enjoying the healthiest time of my life. At forty-six, I felt better in many ways than I had at thirty. In summer, I went hiking or biking. When fall approached I worked out at the gym, strength training to get my ski legs; then winter came with intense exercise on the slopes.

In July 1998 my dad flew in with his best friend, David Howser, to move furniture from my storage unit to their house in Georgia. This was also the first year I hadn't gone to my doctor in LA for my annual checkup and breast exam, which was my routine ever since Sandy Goldman's "find the pea in the breast" class eight years earlier. Usually, I flew to LA in late June, combining my work with a medical checkup and a visit with friends. This year I had no time to go, so I'd scheduled the breast exam to be done in Aspen. Today was the day.

We planned to pick up the U-Haul truck later that day, too, and load it with furniture. I knew my doctor's appointment wouldn't take long, since everything happens on time and fast in that small town — in, out, done. I dropped off Dad and David at the Hickory House for lunch.

"Have fun. I'll be back in an hour or so," I told them. The hospital was right up the road.

When the mammogram took longer than I expected, I looked at my watch and decided to go.

The nurse stopped me. "Don't you want to do your ultrasound?"

"I need to pick up my dad," I said. "I do the ultrasound every year, and I doubt anything has changed."

"You've been consistent with your breast examinations for eight years," she said, looking at my patient information sheet. "Why stop now? The ultrasound won't take long."

I agreed. While they were setting up the machine, I phoned the Hickory House. After we finished the ultrasound, the nurse stopped me again before I could leave.

"The radiologist wants to do one more scan."

This was unusual, but the clinic had never done my breast exams before, didn't have my past eight years of images, didn't know I had fibrocystic breasts. They were just being cautious, I decided. We did the scan. Then the radiologist had questions.

He wasn't the sort of doctor who gives you a warm fuzzy feeling. The stern skepticism on his face told me he didn't like what he saw on my scan.

"There's a spot that looks suspicious," he said. Blunt, matter of fact. "I want to do a needle aspiration."

I'd had those before. Because I have dense breast tissue and fibrocystic breasts, which make mammograms and ultrasounds more difficult to read, "a suspicious spot" wasn't uncommon, and even when a doctor assured me it was fibrocystic tissue, I'd always say to stick it anyway. A needle prick is a lot easier than the worry that comes from not doing it.

The radiologist completed the needle aspiration, and I waited for his verdict, a bit agitated about the delays but still not overly concerned. When he returned, his expression was as sternly ambiguous as before.

"I think we should do a biopsy."

Now I knew something was wrong.

"Okay," I said, "but I have my father waiting for me at the Hickory House. Let me take him home and I'll come back."

"If you don't do it now, I may not get the results tomorrow."

There was no lab in Aspen, so the biopsy would be sent to

Glenwood Springs, and since this was Thursday, it could be after the weekend before we'd know.

"I'm going to be out all-day Monday in a conference," he added. "This is probably nothing to worry about, but I won't be able to call with the results until five in the afternoon."

His terse tone was not sympathetic: *Just get it done.* But by now, Dad and David had been waiting too long and would be worried.

"I'll come right back." I rushed to the Hickory House, picked up the guys, and dropped them at my apartment.

"The doctor didn't finish my tests," I told them. "We'll load the furniture tomorrow."

With the biopsy taking until close to four o'clock, the doctor was certain the results wouldn't come back on Friday but said he would call if they did. All day Friday we loaded the U-Haul from the storage unit, and I checked my cell phone constantly for messages. Load a chair, check for messages. Load a hutch, check for messages. Load a bench, call 611 to make sure the phone is working. Load a lamp, a cushion, a rug, bang the phone against the couch in frustration. The doctor never called.

At the end of the day, my nerves stretched as thin as the varnish on the antique table we shoved into the truck last, we drove down valley, and this time I decided to stay at the ranch. Bob was still in Virginia, and I wanted to spend time with Dad before he left town Tuesday morning. Besides, waiting for those test results was going to make for a long, tense weekend. I didn't want to spend it alone.

CHAPTER 25

Combat Zone

Monday, July 13th. When the phone rang shortly after lunch, I snatched it up and was surprised to hear not the voice of the radiologist, but the voice of my general practitioner, Dr. Morris Cohen.

"Victoria, I see that you had some tests done at the hospital on Thursday," he said.

"A biopsy." I was thinking how nice to live in a small town, where your doctor cares enough to call before you have to call him. "I don't have the results yet. The radiologist said he would phone after five o'clock."

"Why don't you come in now," he said. "I'll see if they're available."

Dr. Cohen had a nice face. He looked and acted more like a real doctor than some of the more recent arrivals in Aspen, who came to experience the lifestyle, ski, and practice medicine at the same time. He welcomed me softly that day, holding my hand with both of his a little longer than usual.

"Have a seat, Victoria."

He was silent for a moment and I could see everything he needed to tell me written on his kind face.

"I didn't want you to have to wait until five p.m. and hear this over the phone." His eyes held mine, not glancing down or away, as he waited for me to prepare myself for what he was about to say. He knew I knew. "It's cancer, Victoria."

In his gentle voice, he read the findings. I watched his mouth moving in slow motion. I couldn't hear him. My flight-or-fight instinct was urging me to run out of there, and I knew I had to hold it together, to not panic. *Dr. Cohen isn't a cancer doctor*, I reminded myself. At that time, the clinic had only a visiting oncologist from Denver once a month. I needed to talk with someone, anyone, who was available and had specific knowledge of cancer.

Dr. Cohen understood completely.

"You can talk to our surgeon," he said. "He's familiar with breast cancer and the necessary treatment."

I knew this surgeon had done a number of mastectomies at Aspen Valley Hospital. I was eager to hear what he had to say.

"It's definitely breast cancer," he confirmed. "I can schedule you into the hospital on Thursday for surgery."

"You want to operate this Thursday?" My mind was racing, trying to take it all in, to process this sudden news. Unwilling to let my emotions take me to the floor with inconsolable crying, although I'm sure the surgeon had witnessed such loss of control before, I went numb. "You could remove the cancer from my breast?"

"I would be removing your breast."

Just like that. One day I'm perfectly healthy, a few days later I'm loading furniture with Dad and feeling perfectly fine when I'm told I should check into the hospital and have a breast chopped off.

All in a day's work for this surgeon.

Before our conversation, I knew instinctively that I'd never choose Aspen Valley Hospital or Glenwood Springs Hospital — forty miles away in a town large enough to boast a Wal-Mart and —to have such an important surgery. Ski-knees, yes. Cancer, no! And this surgeon, who was ready to cut at the drop of a knife, would never be my surgeon of choice. All I wanted from him was information.

"Together, the two tumors form quite a large area," he said, more delicately, "so we would need to do a mastectomy."

"What happens after the mastectomy?" So much more technical

than "remove your breast," the word "mastectomy" instilled another degree of panic. Although I kept my voice and manner calm, I wanted to leave, to get out of this office where I could breathe and push down the panic, but not until I knew everything this doctor had to say.

"After surgery, you would need chemotherapy and radiation."

"What if I do nothing?"

He frowned. "In my opinion, that's a bad scenario. The cancer would probably increase rapidly. If it breaks through the skin, you'd suffer severe pain. You don't want to do that."

"And if I do what you say?"

"If you respond to treatment, you'll have possibly a year and a half. If you don't respond to treatment, or if you do nothing, you'll have about six months."

How Do I Tell Dad?

Outside, the day was still bright and warm, people walking along the sidewalk smiling, chattering amiably. Someone waved and I think I waved back.

Oh, god. Dad and David would be leaving the next morning. How would I tell them? Always in the past, when I had shocking or disturbing news, I told Mom first and let her tell Dad. But *cancer*? I couldn't let Dad leave without knowing and then have to tell him later over the phone, when he was back in Georgia. Somehow, I had to tell him. This was no time to be shy about discussing my breasts, with the possibility of losing one to cancer. I always shared the good news as well as the bad, often using my parents as a sounding board or a trial run before finalizing my decisions. Dad was stronger than Mom, who was a sensitive, terribly emotional person. Dad and I, even at sixteen, had been the ones to hold Mom together when she lost her mom. I knew what she'd gone through and could only imagine what she'd do now. I was the first daughter, the one she'd wrapped so many of her own dreams around. Mom and Dad lived so much of their lives through me, and until now, they'd never had to deal with this sort of news.

Oh god, how will I tell Mom?

Calling All Troops

After recovering from my shock, I called Bob in Virginia and went through the devastating scenario with him. I then explained the situation to Dad without going into detail, not that I had much detail. He seemed to sense that I needed his strength now more than his consolation. I was glad David would be driving back to Georgia with him. My parents loved David, a kind, compassionate man who would keep Dad from worrying so much on the drive.

"When you get home tomorrow," I said, "don't tell Mom right away."

"No, we need to do that together," Dad agreed. The tears in his eyes told me that maybe this was one of those times when I needed to be the strong one.

"Unfortunately, I'm going to have to do it over the phone," I said. "I want you on the other line. We're going to need you. I don't know how this will affect Mom, or how telling her will affect *me*."

I honestly didn't know if I could say the words to my mom, *I have cancer.* Having to admit it to someone so close meant admitting it to myself.

Dad and David wouldn't arrive home until Wednesday night. Before then, I wanted to fly to Cedars-Sinai in LA, where my doctor had my records from the past eight years to compare with these new ones and make certain the Aspen doctors knew what they were talking about. They hadn't completely convinced me I had cancer.

In Virginia, Bob was in combat mode, moving things along

from that end, making our plane reservations, hotel reservations, and calling doctors he knew. I worked from my apartment, making the medical appointments in LA. By now I'd come to grips with the fact that I might lose a breast, but I didn't plan to let that happen until I knew exactly what to expect next.

Leaving Aspen - Journal entry, July 1998
I knew I had to leave, not only because of treatment resources, but because I didn't want to be a side show for the curiosity seekers waiting to see how I handled this. That bizarre habit we have as humans to look at a car wreck as we pass by, to constantly be entertained by tragedy and death — I didn't want to be Aspen's next car wreck.

I was well known in Aspen, where everybody is known for something. I was known for my past, which people assessed along with my body image, breasts, legs, ass, and of course, my hair. I was about to lose all of my external attributes in one shot. Life was never going to be the same. I knew the one resource that would get me through this was practically untapped and had nothing to do with looks: the three pounds of gray matter that rested between my ears.

CHAPTER 26

Occam's Razor

Cedars-Sinai Medical Center is known for providing the highest quality patient care that modern medicine has to offer. It says so on the front of their brochure. When I lived in LA, I'd parroted the typical California attitude, *we have the best of everything,* and the familiarity of my personal physician's offices at Cedars-Sinai gave me comfort.

Yet as I walked the hallways, I also was seeing it for the first time. In years past, healthy, happy, I merely showed up for my annual exams. Today, I had a "suspicious spot." In my dreams, that spot grew, distorted like a mutant parasite, sprouted claws, and tore its way through my breast, where it sat ripping at my body, grinning its evil grin.

After making the difficult call to Mom, and with little time left before my flight, I'd phoned my best friend, Sandy Iglehart, to give her the news personally. Then I called Billie Pierce, more emotionally drained each time I repeated the story. Billie and I had drawn closer since she introduced me to Bob, and I entrusted her with the task of delivering the news without fanfare to our other friends.

From Aspen, I hand-carried my scans, lab reports, and the surgeon's daunting prognosis. My gynecologist had sent over my file of eight years to the oncologist.

"I see nothing suspicious on these previous films," he said, studying them on the lighted display. "And yet you always followed up with ultrasound."

Despite his shrugging it off as "no big deal," this actually made me feel better. It meant I'd done everything I could to detect the disease in its earliest stage.

"So, in one year you're saying that I went from a healthy body to having breast cancer?" This fact seemed to have everyone a bit baffled.

"It appears so from what we can see on this imaging. Now, let's listen to what your body tells me."

He began the breast exam, deciding fairly quickly that the lump might be larger than it appeared in the initial findings. That prompted him to start feeling under my arm, moving down and along with his fingers. What I didn't know then and have since learned is that everything is okay as long as they keep moving, but when the doctor's fingers stop, or the ultrasound stops, or the mammography has to be redone five times on the same breast at the same angle, you know they've found a problem.

"This lymph node doesn't feel right to me," he said. "I think we should do more imaging."

I progressed from one huge, impersonal machine to the next as we did more breast scans, my first computed tomography (CT) scan of my abdomen, an x-ray of my lungs, then a positron emission tomography (PET) scan of my body. After viewing the preliminary findings, the doctor decided to do a liver biopsy. I didn't realize at the time the significance of a liver biopsy.

Friendly Support

Two days later, I arrived for my scheduled appointments at Sloan-Kettering Hospital, which I was familiar with from living in New York. As one of the world's premier cancer centers, Memorial Sloan-Kettering is committed to exceptional patient care, leading-edge research, and superb educational programs. It says so on their brochure.

Moving Forward

After my day of being inundated with doctors, tests, and new information, Bob provided the perfect sounding board. We didn't always agree, but he helped me sort through the multitude of details, and I truly appreciated having him in my life.

Loving him and knowing he loved me was only part of it. Many men just go away emotionally when trauma strikes, but throughout the process, Bob was compassionate and never distant. At each unexpected turn, he helped me choose the right direction and guided me through it as best he could. He impressed upon me that we would do everything possible to put cancer behind us.

The Sloan-Kettering physicians mapped out a program of surgery, chemotherapy, and radiation, beginning with the removal of my breast. I especially liked the oncologist, Dr. Patrick Borgen, who made me feel more confident about the potential success of the treatment regimen than anyone I'd talked with so far.

Little more than a week had passed since I received my first diagnosis in Aspen. My mind was reeling, my heart and my entire body were filled with dread for what lay ahead, but I was beginning to feel in control of my life again. I felt certain now that the Aspen surgeon was wrong — there was no way I had only a year and a half to live — and while I couldn't undo the fact that I had breast cancer, I could go forward knowing I was in the best hands. The prospect of being treated at Sloan-Kettering and moving back to New York for the period of time it would take, felt like the best decision possible.

Bob, however, didn't share my certainty.

Opinions and Alternatives

"I know you're the one who has to deal with this, Victoria, and ultimately it's your decision. I'm just telling you what I believe is best."

Bob was insisting we go to MD Anderson in Texas for yet another opinion. I thought I'd made my feelings clear, yet while we were still at Sloan-Kettering, Bob asked Dr. Borgen his opinion.

"I want Victoria to consider MD Anderson," Bob told him. "What would you say to that?"

"He's not speaking on my behalf," I said quickly. "I want to stay in New York."

Dr. Borgen didn't seem at all put off by the question.

"Both hospitals are excellent," he said. "MD Anderson is a top-class cancer institute. It's just a matter of choice. If you want to go to MDA, I'll make the calls for you."

That really impressed me, although I was comfortable with Dr. Borgen. I'd made my choice. Still, it couldn't hurt to get more information, and Bob was adamant that we should go. My first appointment there was with Dr. Singletary, a warm, friendly woman with a gentle face and light brown hair who stood when I entered and greeted me with both hands. I loved this woman quickly and completely.

"I will perform your breast surgery," she said, "if that's what's required, but I want you to meet with an oncologist. We have many. I believe Doctor Theriault would be best for prescribing your treatment of chemotherapy and radiation."

I couldn't place her slight accent. She had a way of saying "kim-mo-therapy" that made it sound not quite so detestable. The other thing she'd said, however, grabbed my attention: *IF surgery is required.*

Of course it's required. Every doctor I'd spoken with during this ten-day whirlwind of appointments from Aspen to Cedars-Sinai to Sloan-Kettering had begun their diagnosis with the presumption that my breast would be removed. I was finally conditioned for losing my breast.

"Is there a question about the breast surgery?" I asked.

"The percutaneous liver biopsy that was done at Cedars-Sinai indicates a possible liver metastasis," she said, "which changes the treatment procedure considerably."

The first time my LA doctors had mentioned "liver biopsy," the words hadn't meant a great deal, but preparation for the procedure had instilled only fear. The doctor applied a local anesthetic to my abdomen. His needle appeared, from my horizontal position on the table, to be as long as a small sword, even more frightening than it was painful. I'd never before considered my liver. In fact, I wonder if we ever notice an organ until it becomes painful or a foreign object invades it. He made a small incision just below my rib cage, then asked me to exhale and hold my breath. He inserted the needle, watching its image on the ultrasound. Once the needle passed through the anesthetized area, I felt every centimeter as it found its way to my liver, punctured it, and searched for the lesion suspected to be cancer. I felt my liver being tugged, the needle moving in and out. Just as we left New York, the biopsy results had arrived, but only now did I learn they were inconclusive.

"Naturally, we will conduct our own biopsy," Dr. Singletary added. "If the cancer has indeed metastasized to the liver, our prognosis would need to include this new information."

Before we finished talking, I learned that once breast cancer leaves the primary area and is present in the lymph nodes, it usually goes first to the lungs and bones, and then to the liver. Except for the brain, the liver is the worst possible place for the cancer to go.

More Information

"Sloan-Kettering didn't seem to have a problem accepting my test results from Cedars-Sinai," I told Dr. Richard Theriault. I'd taken an instant dislike to this oncologist who would be treating me if I stayed at MDA. A nice-looking man with a neatly groomed beard and short dark hair, he'd begun by explaining the tests that would have to be conducted, duplicates to those I'd already experienced. "Cedars is a highly respected hospital with a qualified lab."

"Nevertheless, we prefer to rely on our own technicians and our own equipment. These tests are necessary, and it never hurts to take a second look."

Reluctantly, I agreed, and they proceeded with the tests and scans. Surprisingly, the liver biopsy proceeded faster and easier this time. The needle went quickly to the suspicious area, one snip and out, and produced conclusive results: the cancer was in my liver.

Dr. Theriault laid out two options.

One: I could take the standard set of chemotherapies, FAC, which had a proven long-term history. Hard on the body, difficult to undergo, but FAC had a predictable success rate. If I chose that regimen, I had to continue with it.

Or two: I could choose the relatively newer, possibly less difficult option, a combination of docetaxel and cyclophosphamide, which also was a frontline chemotherapy for metastatic breast cancer. This drug combo might prove as effective, but it hadn't acquired a long documented history.

The choice was up to me.

"If I take the less difficult option," I said, "and it doesn't work, then I cannot go back and take the FAC."

"That's correct."

"But if I take the FAC, and it isn't completely successful, then I can continue with the docetaxel therapy, if necessary?"

I asked Dr. Theriault the same question I'd asked at the Aspen clinic.

"What if I do nothing?"

"The cancer will advance rapidly and painfully. You don't

want that, Victoria."

No, I didn't. My fact-finding mission, from the first diagnosis in Aspen to Doctor Theriault's prognosis, had taken two weeks. Between doctor visits, I'd read every pamphlet and article I could find on breast cancer. I had too much information spinning around in my head.

"I want to go back to Aspen," I said. "I'll decide there."

Tough Love

Deep down, I still wanted to go to Sloan-Kettering. They'd seemed so much more reasonable and clearly focused: surgery, chemotherapy, radiation — only they weren't basing their prognosis on a conclusive liver biopsy.

MD Anderson had laid the options in my lap. Take this or take that. How could I decide until I understood precisely what each procedure would entail and the expected results? I'd listened to the various explanations, but I needed time to absorb and process.

Once in Aspen, I planned another trip to Cedars-Sinai, where doctors I knew well and felt comfortable with could help me understand. I was still reading, still assimilating as much information as I could gather.

"Why do you want to go back to LA?" Bob asked.

"I'd feel better being treated there than in Texas. I know the doctors there. Chemotherapy treatment won't be easy, and I have friends in LA, just as I have in New York, who can help me when you have to go back East. The physicians at Cedars have been doing cancer surgeries successfully, so there's no reason to believe they can't be successful with mine. Where do all the Hollywood celebrities go who have cancer? Cedars-Sinai. So it must be a good hospital."

"I'm sure it is." Bob looked as stubborn as I'd ever seen him. "But you need the best. Go to MD Anderson."

Despite Bob's feeling that I was wasting time, I took the trip to LA without him. My mind was now set on being treated either at Cedars-Sinai or Sloan-Kettering. For me, MD Anderson was completely out.

The LA oncologist, after reviewing my reports and prognoses from the other two hospitals, still planned to do a mastectomy followed by the harshest chemotherapy and radiation, which he didn't describe as gently as Dr. Theriault had. In my hotel room that night, I reread the material and test reports I'd gathered from each doctor, plus other literature I'd compiled. Somewhere, I'd picked up a copy of *Dr. Susan Love's Breast Book*. Sitting alone in my hotel room, I read almost all 600 pages. It explained each stage of cancer, from Stage 1, the most likely to be cured, to Stage 4. I read about metastases to the bones, lungs, and other organs, including the liver, and I realized I was going to die.

Excluding All Peripheral Realities

This time when I returned home to Aspen, I was less cocky and self-assured. The LA oncologist was so unemotionally cavalier about my case that he'd left me feeling cold, so I'd given up on LA and was more determined than ever to go to Sloan-Kettering. To appease Bob, though, I agreed to give MDA another chance. But not Dr. Theriault. When I phoned for an appointment, I asked Dr. Singletary to refer me to someone else. It turned out to be the head of the Oncology Department, Dr. Gabriel Hortobagyi. No longer taking new patients of his own, he'd agreed to see me out of respect for Dr. Singletary.

I still found it hard to believe that a year ago I was physically healthy, yet within three weeks I'd gone from "it's probably nothing" to the reality of losing a breast to Stage 4 Cancer with metastasis to the liver. Dr. Hortobagyi explained to me in great detail why we would *not* be doing a mastectomy.

"If the cancer had remained in the breast area, we would have removed it there with a good possibility of preventing any involvement with other organs. Once it left the breast, the entire picture changed. Removing the breast will not make the cancer go away."

"But it would remove it from one area," I said. "And then, couldn't you do another surgery to remove it from the liver?"

"That's not the way it works. You would need time to recover from the mastectomy. Meanwhile, the cancer continues to grow. Victoria, you have very late-stage cancer. We have to do everything possible to get the disease under control. You need to start chemotherapy as soon as possible."

He went over again everything Dr. Theriault had told me about the two options, but this time more explicitly explaining each drug.

"The usual course requires six cycles three weeks apart," he said, "providing you recover quickly enough, and your blood counts go back up. If not, you may need a few more days between cycles. Dr. Theriault believes you should have eight cycles, which is a more aggressive approach, but ultimately could be in your best interest."

I appreciated Dr. Hortobagyi's ability to clarify the treatment. On this trip, I spent more time getting a tour of MDA, which at that time was one huge hospital connected to a housing facility called the Jesse H. Jones Rotary House.

Having read extensively about the side effects of FAC, the chemotherapy I felt had the best chance of success, I knew that I wouldn't be spending much time visiting friends during the months I was in treatment. Would I even want my friends to see me under the conditions described?

Fluorouracil, which was frequently referred to as 5-FU, could be expected to lower my white blood cell count, which would increase my chance of getting an infection. It also might lower my platelet count, increasing my risk of bleeding, and my red blood cell count, causing anemia, which might result in shortness of breath and tiredness. I might also have nausea and vomiting, mouth and lip sores, severe diarrhea and stomach pain, sensitivity to sunlight, and allergic reactions that could cause dizziness, itching, hives, rapid heartbeat, coughing, wheezing, and swelling of the face, tongue or throat. A condition known as hand-foot syndrome, in which a patient experiences pain, numbness, tingling, reddening, or swelling in the hands and feet, along with peeling, blistering, or sores on the skin, was also possible.

Adriamycin was nicknamed "red death," and would likely cause nausea, vomiting, and heart arrhythmias, along with a decrease in white blood cells and complete hair loss. It increased the risk of cardiac side effects, such as dilated cardiomyopathy and cardiotoxicity, and death. It might cause skin eruptions on the palms of my hands or soles of my feet, accompanied by swelling, pain, and redness. The "red death," I soon learned, would have me crawling on the floor by the end of the seventy-two hours that it took for the entire dosage to be administered.

As if that weren't enough, I could count on Cytoxan, the third drug in the FAC cocktail, to cause absence of menstrual periods, a change in skin color, diarrhea, a general "unwell" feeling, hair loss, nausea, skin rash, stomach discomfort or pain, vomiting, and weakness. Those were only the common side effects. More brutal effects could include severe allergic reactions, hallucinations, pneumonia, blistered skin, and yellowing of the skin or eyes.

Learning what I was in for once I started chemotherapy, and learning more about the Rotary House, were the two factors that finally nudged aside every other consideration.

The Heuristic of Cancer

Rotary House is a residential hotel for cancer patients and their families. Rooms have kitchenettes, so a patient, or their family members, can stay a week, a month, even a year, if necessary. I could live and be treated in a place completely confined to a world of cancer. Some of my friends I mentioned this to thought that was the worst scenario possible. For me it was the best scenario, the one that convinced me of what Bob had said from the beginning: MD Anderson was the best place for me.

Downstairs was a patient library, video room, social room, quiet room, reading room, gym, swimming pool, computer room, with life alert buttons everywhere. Patients could have blood drawn at the nurse's station at night. Drawing blood, I'd learned, was a frequent necessity of chemotherapy. Everything a cancer patient might need was under one roof. Then you could walk across an enclosed bridge and be at the hospital.

Not only did I not want my friends to see me gaunt, bald, and crawling on the floor in misery, I didn't see how I could manage getting into a New York taxi and going in for my chemotherapy treatments. Sloan-Kettering didn't have a housing facility such as the Rotary House. I'd have to rent an apartment. This was mid-August, so I would be receiving treatment during the hottest and coldest months. Such weather, combined with the smells and noise of New York City streets, would be unbearable under the conditions I could expect from chemotherapy side effects. Even if I rented a place across from the hospital, many of the doctors' offices were located elsewhere. For the first time I began to appreciate the sprawling Texas Medical Center, where most buildings were connected and where I would have only to cross a single enclosed bridge to travel from my apartment at Rotary House to all the facilities I would need at MDA.

There's a scientific heuristic, or general guideline, called Occam's Razor, which suggests, in general terms, that, all other issues being equal, the simplest answer is usually the best. I'd come to believe that all three hospitals were excellent choices, but when it came down to not only surviving the cancer but also to enduring and surviving the treatment, there was only one choice.

For the third time, I flew home to Aspen, but this time I left Houston with the intention of returning there for treatment. Nowhere else had I received the options Dr. Theriault had presented, and I realized now that, for me, having options was a good thing. I've never been comfortable with others dictating what I should do with my body; certainly not with my life.

I packed my suitcases with necessary clothing and personal items and moved to the Rotary House. That was the beginning.

PART 3

BREAKTHROUGHS

CHAPTER 27

Hair

The volunteer stylists at MD Anderson's beauty salon might shape your hair if you asked nicely, but that's not their purpose. The salon is on the premises to either cut your hair short for chemotherapy or shave it off, help you maintain a healthy scalp during treatment, and shave your head again if it itches too much. They will also help fit you for wigs or provide one for you.

Walking the halls of the Rotary House and hospital, I still looked like *me,* with my massive mane of red hair, designer clothes, and high heels, being more *me* than ever, perhaps, because I would soon lose it all. With tall-and-handsome Bob walking alongside, I drew an enormous amount of attention. In a somewhat frantic mood of time closing in, we also ventured around Houston a bit, enjoying our time together despite my daily tests or our concerns for the future, and knowing these might be the last romantic moments we'd have for quite some time.

This adjustment period brought me to terms with reality, but I hadn't fully accepted what was about to happen. Knowledge isn't the same as acceptance. Whether I liked the fact or not, my physical image was how people judged me, and much of my life revolved around my appearance. Yet I knew I had a deeper soul and more inner strength and intelligence than people assumed, simply because they never saw beyond my looks. I'd come to rely on my external attributes to get what I needed in life, even when it left a bitter taste. Usually, it was just the easiest thing to do.

But now, I had to rely on my inner strength. My hair and my body image were useless here, and they'd be gone or changed in a matter of days. My forty-six years as gorgeous, glamorous Victoria Johnson were ending. Not only did I face the probability of an early death, I was losing everything I depended on to authenticate me. However long I lived, how well I did or didn't do on chemotherapy, Victoria the model was the past. I was now Victoria the cancer patient.

It came to me then that I needed to be more appropriate and respectful to the patients I saw around me. These people were suffering. I didn't want to add to their discomfort by trying to hold on to my superficial assets. I was about to become one of them.

So I put on my jeans and casual clothes. When handsome Bob had to leave for a while, and I brought my mom out to be with me, I felt I'd finally made my home at Rotary House.

Telling Mom of my diagnosis had been so hard, but she'd taken it better than I or anyone expected. About to leave for my first appointment with the LA oncologist, I'd phoned knowing Dad and David would have arrived home.

"Does she know?" I asked when Dad answered.

"No. I'm having a hard time with this. I'm so worried about you, and I need to tell her."

"Okay." I dreaded this more than the LA appointment. "Put her on the phone."

She didn't become hysterical, didn't break down, as I expected. Instead, she seemed quietly shocked then went immediately into her Southern Mom caretaker mode.

"What do you need me to do?" she asked. "Is Bob with you?"

They hadn't met Bob yet, but they knew about him. I said yes, and that I would keep her posted every step of the way. And now that I needed her, Mom made her plans to come to Houston, despite her aversion to flying, and to stay throughout the treatment.

Buying Time

One thing I learned quickly about MD Anderson: they never give you an expiration date. They're in the business of treating cancer, curing it if possible, and unlike the Aspen surgeon who'd given me only eighteen months, the doctors at MDA never directly answered my question, "How long will I live?"

"You have to be honest with me," I told Dr. Theriault. "No rose-colored glasses. What can I expect?" By now, I'd come to like him and trust him. Neither of us has ever quite determined what put me off at that first session, other than my bad attitude.

"This is what we'll try to accomplish," he said, his hands out flat, palms down, and one hand about twelve inches higher than the other. "Imagine this is a ladder. You're down here." He indicated the lower of his two hands. "You're never going to get up here, to the top again, but we want to bring you somewhere into the middle. If we can move you to the middle with treatment, and you can stay there, that's a great thing."

So far, nothing I'd heard about chemotherapy equated to "a great thing." I knew I'd be living on nausea medication, and that the chemotherapy alone wasn't going to cure me.

"I've chosen FAC, and I've read all the side effects," I said, "but what can I actually expect during treatment?"

"Let's put it this way: I have a patient on this drug therapy who still walks, and sometimes runs, almost every day. Another patient on this drug arrives here in an ambulance every three weeks. I suspect you'll be somewhere in the middle."

Scheduled to start chemotherapy the third week of August, for eight cycles of three weeks each, which added up to six months, I'd finish treatment in late February of 1999, providing I could endure it that long.

"All we're doing," he added, "is buying time. We hope it's going to make a substantial difference. We hope it will stop the cancer for a while. With metastasis to the liver, we hope for miracles, but we'll do this chemotherapy, and re-evaluate, then go to the next one, if need be, pursuing all the options."

"Buying time" thus became my mantra. One goal I set for myself during our discussion was to never use a wheelchair to cross the bridge to the hospital treatment room. I was determined to be stronger than that.

And So It Begins

Of all the people in my life at that time, Mom was the person I wanted with me during the toughest times of my treatment, and I soon learned that was a good decision. The day before treatment, a catheter was implanted in my chest. This small tube, a permanent fixture during chemotherapy, would allow me to receive drugs too strong to be administered through a vein.

The next day, Mom and I went to the treatment room together. Before chemotherapy there's "pre-chemo," treatment, which includes infused fluids, anti-nausea medication, and liquid Ativan. Most patients, I learned, took liquid Ativan throughout the weeks of treatment, not only to control anxiety but because Ativan also calms the physical body, enabling it to better handle the drugs and to suffer less nausea.

After pre-chemo, I received the first of the three drugs, 5-FU, which long-term patients called "5 Feet Under," by IV drip, followed immediately by the second drug. We were there for four hours or more, counting wait time. The third drug, Adriamycin, was contained in a small pouch along with a monitoring device that would slowly release the bright red liquid over the next seventy-two hours through a tube attached to my catheter. I walked out of the treatment room wearing the pouch over my shoulder like a purse and attached to a strap around my waist to keep it in place.

Except for a "drugged up" giddiness, I actually felt fine,

without the wave of nausea I'd anticipated.

"This isn't bad at all," I told Mom.

All's Well ...

The evening of the day following my first treatment, I still thought, *Wow, this isn't bad at all.* Mom and I ordered dinner in our room. Mine was steak and a baked potato. About halfway through the meal, the nausea hit, and I started throwing up.

Ceaseless vomiting followed by strenuous dry heaves continued long after my stomach had nothing left to give. I took another dose of the prescribed anti-nausea drug, Compazine, which almost everyone took and was extremely reliable, but from the moment I started vomiting, my side effects worsened by the hour as Adriamycin dripped into my system. Long before my seventy-two hours were up, I was ready to rip the tube out of my catheter. Even with the anti-nausea medicine, the sickness was so bad that I was literally crawling on the floor in the hours before I returned to the hospital to have the empty pouch disconnected.

Distortion

Monday night, I was weary of being sick, eating nothing but crackers and Ensure to stay nourished between bouts of nausea. I decided I felt well enough to venture downstairs to the restaurant. Passing a desk with a big bowl of complimentary peppermints, I smiled, grabbed one, and asked Mom if she'd noticed them.

"Now that you mention it," she said, "I've seen bowls of peppermint candies everywhere we go."

"A day or so after I arrived, I asked a patient, 'Why all the peppermints?' She said everyone here is constantly fighting nausea, and these help a little. Now I understand."

Sitting at our table waiting for our food to arrive, I felt a strange sensation on the left side of my face and neck. I touched my jaw, didn't feel any swelling, but the sensation was odd and my jaw was starting to hurt.

"Are you all right?" Mom asked, frowning.

"I — oh!" My face and neck muscles contracted so painfully I couldn't talk.

"Victoria!" Mom screamed. "Something's happening to your face!"

She called out to someone who quickly brought a wheelchair and ran across the bridge with me to the ER. Seeing my face, they started me on muscle relaxers, in case I was having a stroke, and other medications, in case it was an allergic reaction.

No one knew what was wrong. In unbelievable pain and recalling words from the list of FAC side effects, *dilated cardiomyopathy, cardiotoxicity, death,* I knew it was not uncommon to code blue while taking chemotherapy. This felt like the end. It passed through my mind that I was not even going to have my one and a half years promised by the Aspen surgeon, that I needed to give Mom my last words. But I couldn't move the left side of my horribly distorted face. The words came out slurred, inaudible, indecipherable, and Mom was sobbing so hard she couldn't understand.

After hours of medication, with doctors trying one thing after another, I was finally stabilized. In the early morning, a nurse told me what they believed had happened.

"We think you had a reaction to the Compazine, which is incredibly rare."

I recalled seeing warnings, big letters, small letters, for all the drugs I was taking, and virtually nobody reacts negatively to Compazine, but one person out of God knows how many might develop a symptom similar to lockjaw. That's what had happened.

Crying and trying to be strong, Mom told me later it was the worst thing she'd ever witnessed. "Your face was all twisted. It was awful."

Of all the ER visits I would have over the next months, that one was the most serious. A doctor's report stated, "… severe dystonic reaction to the Compazine … received intravenous Cogentin …" Unfortunately, the Cogentin caused dizziness, disorientation, and persistent blurred vision. Needless to say, I was never prescribed Compazine again.

There was another choice, Zofran, about $50 a tablet now, even more back then. On the next round of chemotherapy they gave me the Zofran, hoping it wouldn't also trigger an allergic reaction. It worked.

CHAPTER 28

Twelve Good Days

During the first week of chemotherapy, my week in Hell, I experienced so many of the potential side effects that I lost count. After the Compazine horror, I lay on my back in misery, waiting for my blood counts to improve and replenish my energy. When the counts were low, I was monitored to ensure they didn't drop so far that I'd need a transfusion.

After the first seven to ten days of each cycle, as my blood counts rose, and with nausea and other symptoms abated, I'd want to go out, move around, be anywhere except in that sickbed. Mom, a resolute trooper, stayed with me well into the second treatment. Then she swapped visits with Bob, one or the other always there during the first three months. Mom would fly home briefly to check on Dad and her house and other responsibilities.I'd say, "Mom, I'm starting a new drug" or "They want to do a new test," and she was there. Every surgery, every new diagnosis, every tough moment, she was there.

Rose-Incarnation

Many of my friends came to visit during those first months. Cards and flowers, mostly roses, began arriving almost daily, until my room was filled with three or four arrangements at all times. The Rotary House staff loved my room and would laugh when they phoned to tell me another bouquet had arrived.

"Ms. Johnson, you have another lovely delivery. If you're out of space, I'm sure we can find a place for it at the front desk." Or when I'd get a bunch of cards in one mail batch. "Ms. Johnson, your mail's here. Would you like to come down or should we load up a cart?" Always teasing me.

When each arrangement started to die, I felt I was losing the special thought behind it and wanted to somehow preserve that memory. I dried as many as possible to make potpourri. Then I discovered that within the medical center was a wholesale flower district where I could buy a dozen roses for eight dollars. During the days between treatments, when I felt well enough, I'd visit the outdoor markets and buy more flowers, which I dried along with my arrangements, scented with essential oils, and tucked into little satin pouches. I sent them as thank-you gifts. I learned the colors that dried best, which didn't include red. Making potpourri during my up time, and planning what to make next during my down-time, created a distraction that bolstered me through the horrors of chemotherapy.

During my last months at the Rotary House and after I moved into my townhome in late January of 1999, I turned my rose-drying obsession into a basket business, calling it Rose-Incarnation. You'd be surprised how many people didn't get the word play, even in a hospital where people are dying, and a lot of them want to believe in second lives and reincarnation. But Houston's PBS channel came to my house and produced a segment about my business for their program, *WeekDay*. "Rose-Incarnation — Victoria is giving flowers a second chance."

Believe it or not, people started sending me their dead roses. I'd open a UPS delivery and find it full of dead flowers, sent in the spirit of helping. I also made cards and gift boxes decorated with dried petals, and when I eventually grew jaded with roses, I expanded my business to sell handmade pillows and throws.

Throughout my years of cancer, my friends have supported all my endeavors, but my "Rose-Incarnation" period stands out as significant because it gave me something to concentrate on be-sides agony during the seven Hell Days of each cycle. I survived it, one wretched hour at a time, to get to the precious ten to twelve good days when I was functional, when I could leave the hospital for a quiet dinner or a walk in the park, or could rearrange and sort and dry the armfuls of fresh flowers that flooded in.

Angel Alice

There's no other time in our lives when spiritual help is needed more than when terminal illness strikes, and when it comes to religion, I've tried on a lot of shoes. I was born Southern Baptist, but that never quite fit. It frightened me as a child. Years later, as an adult in New York, I found a quiet Presbyterian church. In California, I tried several, all with odd-sounding names — Agape Church, Church for All Mankind, and a name that had something to do with "Love." Then my friend Jeanine asked me to go to Catholic Mass with her. When it was over I told her I liked the structure and ritual. Although her priest had better clothing, my church had better music. The only thing I didn't like was that my knees hurt for days afterward.

At MD Anderson, I was reintroduced to religion by the Chaplaincy Department. Their spiritual counseling, unexpected visits, and their affirmation of hope were invaluable. In the days before I started chemotherapy, the gentleman who was in charge of patient services invited me to join one of the support groups. Usually led by an MDA chaplain, even though group interaction wasn't based on religion, the groups met weeknights at the Rotary House. I was quite open to the idea, determined to do everything I could to stay positive and active, and to avoid being depressed by my future or by the severe therapy I was about to undertake.

For the first time in my life, I had no responsibilities except to stay alive. Living in a hotel, I had no need to shop, even for clothes, since I had nowhere to wear them, nowhere to go, no one to take care of, and no job except for taking care of myself. Being part of a support group seemed an excellent way to stay positive.

The group met on Thursday nights. I walked in to find a short, round, chubby-faced, high-spirited, bouncy, amazingly friendly and effervescent older woman radiating warmth and love.

"Hi!" she said to the group. "I'm Sister Alice."

"*Sister* Alice?" I whispered to the patient services director. "That means she's a Catholic nun."

"Yes, but the group is nondenominational, and she's not like any other nun you've met."

My knowledge of nuns came from movies, where they dressed in black and white habits and were terribly strict with boarding school students. Sister Alice wore a bright fuchsia blouse coordinated with a pretty print skirt and sensible shoes. Her short white hair waved neatly around her face. A touch of color brightened her cheeks and lips. She wore out her sensible shoes frequently, I discovered, by walking the halls of MD Anderson twelve to fourteen hours a day. Most of the patients called her Angel Alice.

Wine and Wigs

At the time I joined her support group, Sister Alice was in her early seventies. She filled the room with light and hope. People told her stories as she sat with them and empathized, and they felt better afterward. She was a shining star at MDA, to the point that news crews came to focus on her and her ability to change patient's lives. She appeared on *Good Morning America,* in the *Wall Street Journal*, and countless other venues. Among dozens of awards she received over the years, one was given at the Loving Hearts Caring Hands awards dinner in 2000. I had the honor of standing beside two exemplary physicians, Dr. John Mendelsohn and Dr. Andrew von Eschenbach, as I presented Sister Alice with that award.

"I don't sympathize with my patients," she often said during interviews. "I empathize. I can't cure them, but I can help them."

She had a brilliant philosophy along with a tremendous strength and power of healing. Everybody wanted to be around Sister Alice, including me. She became much more to me than merely the leader of my support group. She must have felt similarly about me, because we became the best of friends. Without asking, she had an uncanny way of showing up at just the right time. Wherever I was in the hospital, she would find me. She helped me survive.

"Let's go to dinner," she said soon after we met. "You decide where, and we'll go."

I thought, *Where do you take a nun to dinner? Every place serves alcohol. What do you say to a nun at dinner? What could we have in common besides my cancer?* I'd no idea what was appropriate.

"I don't know the restaurants nearby," I said, to put it back in her lap. "Where do you suggest?"

"Anywhere's fine with me, hon." She called everybody *hon*. "That restaurant in the Village called Benjy's is nice. Let's go there."

Benjy's turned out to be rather upscale compared to what I expected. I was dying for a glass of wine, not only to calm my "dinner-with-a-nun" nerves but also because it was my last chance before starting chemotherapy.

"Would you mind if I have a glass of wine?" I asked.

Once again, Sister Alice surprised me. "Not at all. I think I'll have one with you."

I hadn't realized nuns drank. I didn't associate nuns with priests in that respect.

A day or so later, she said, "You've got to meet my friend Kathy. She's been a patient here for thirteen years, and she'll be in the hospital today. You're going to love her."

Kathy, who lived in the Houston suburbs with her family, came to MDA for chemotherapy. The first time we met, Kathy was climbing into bed, about to be hooked up to IVs. After stretching out and leaning against the headboard, she pulled off her wig and threw it on a chair. At the time, I still had my hair, and I suddenly felt odd, thick red tresses falling down around my shoulders while Kathy sat there bald.

"Does it make you feel more comfortable to wear the wig?" I asked, naturally curious, knowing I'd soon be equally bald.

"I hate it," Kathy said. "It's horrible. Hot and itchy. I don't wear it for me, I wear the dumb thing because it makes other people more comfortable."

How right she was. I'd felt much more at ease when she was wearing the wig.

Kathy was a social worker, so she dealt with people daily who might or might not know about her illness.

"I only wear it," she added, "when I have a meeting. The people I work with are suffering, and they don't need to see me suffering when they're looking to me for help."

Shortly after that day, my chemotherapy started and I understood all too well what Kathy meant. My hair fell out, then after the initial loss it attempted to grow back every three weeks. Each time my scalp was itchy, stubbly, and a little more irritated. I tried hats, but my head was too tender, so I learned the art of the perfect scarf.

For those times when I wanted the real thing, I decided to have a custom wig made of human hair that looked just like my own. It was actually made from long black Asian hair, as are most human-hair wigs. Mine was dyed red, and it really did look like my hair, but it was the most uncomfortable thing I ever wore. The synthetic wigs were better, but Kathy was right: I wore them for other people, not for myself.

As it turned out in years to come, Kathy was the patient with a story closest to mine. Her cancer had come back a second time and a third. When we met, she was at Stage 4, as was I. A thirteen-year cancer patient, she'd taken the FAC cocktail many times and was now going through brain radiation. I learned a lot from Kathy about treatments I'd be dealing with soon.

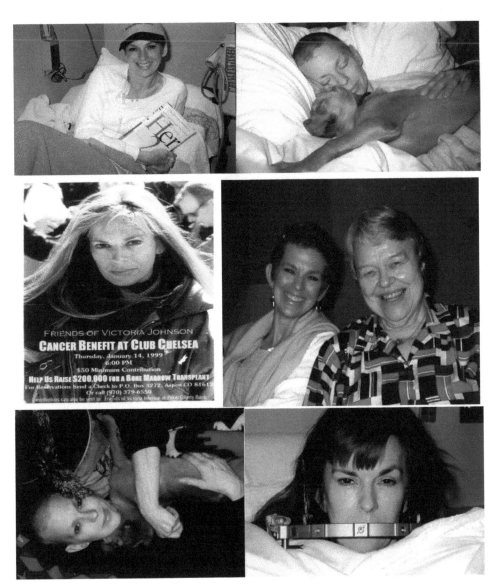

The faces of treatment: good and bad

Celebrating occassions even during treatment is a must

CHAPTER 29

Beyond Rotary House

It was quickly becoming apparent to me that Houston was not a temporary relocation but my permanent residence for the remainder of what might be a short-term existence. The Rotary House was a comfort to patients who, like me, were in the early days of their new diagnosis and treatment. It wasn't depressing or sad. It was comforting to be with other people experiencing the same awfulness as I, and to be surrounded by staff and support help who understood. It was consoling to have a lifeline to the ER. If I could have stayed, I think I would still live at the Rotary House.

The routine we settled into, without ever voicing it or making a conscious decision, was for Mom to stay with me during chemotherapy and the toughest seven days following treatment, plus a few more days so we could enjoy the "good" part of the cycle together. Then Bob would come, and she'd visit a day with both of us, then fly home to update Dad on my progress and carry on with her life until time approached for my next treatment.

Bob was usually there for my best days. We'd go out and about Houston, trying to enjoy some semblance of a normal life. Ours was no longer a "relationship." We couldn't make plans for a life together, because even though my MDA doctors never gave me an expiration date, we knew the prognosis for Stage 4 Cancer: not curable, and few people live with it longer than a couple of years. Bob, in his mid-fifties, still had a lot of living ahead, and we didn't have years of history to remember fondly, having been together only six months before cancer struck. This wasn't his battle, even though he tried very hard to fight it right alongside me.

A Friend Indeed

I felt much brighter about my future at my regular appointment with Dr. Theriault three cycles into the process. My cancer was responding to the chemotherapy!

My particular cancer, it seemed, was unique, unpredictable, and aggressive. It wasn't estrogen receptive or progesterone receptive, which meant I couldn't be treated with hormonal therapies. The liver was the worst organ, besides the brain, for metastases, also the least treatable, yet it was responding to the FAC. For that I could be thankful.

I wanted to celebrate, of course, so Bob and I went to dinner. I could tell he was exhausted. We all were. My cancer was grueling on everyone. Flying back and forth took its toll, and I'd noticed our moments together were becoming tedious.

Not that Bob did or said anything wrong, but any energy I had left was focused on surviving, not on maintaining the ghost of a relationship. Bob was a good friend and a good caretaker, but I couldn't consider a future with him, or with anyone. The only way I could survive was to not look too far ahead, to live each day as it came; and living with me and cancer was not easy. He never complained, yet I came to the realization that Bob needed to be out of this.

Wanting a normal night out, we went to dinner at Ruth's Chris Steak House. With my wig and my Victoria Johnson clothes, I was desperately trying not to be a cancer patient. If you declaw a cat, it still scratches the furniture, and like a cat, I couldn't help wanting to run my fingers through my hair or flip it back with a toss of my head. It was there, but it wasn't mine, and it itched. At times it was hard to remember what it was like to have real hair.

Neither of us was up to the charade that night. I would say something, and Bob seemed agitated, then he'd say something that upset me. We weren't fighting, we just weren't connecting.

Watching him, I knew what he was feeling. So I calmly approached the subject that was on both our minds.

"Bob, you need out, and I think that would be best for both of us." When he opened his mouth to speak, I raised my hand to stop him. "You need out, but first I need your help."

"That's not true, I'm just tired," he argued, as if not hearing what I'd said last.

"You know it's true," I said. "You can't go through this disease with me. We haven't been together long enough. We can't look back on years of history together, the love and devotion, the ups and downs of a long-term relationship. We had six months. All the things that made ours a perfect relationship — travel, excitement, sex, socializing — none of those things exist for us anymore. I wouldn't have made it without you, but you don't have to do this. As much as you've done for me, I need to move forward with those that I've known longer and am closer to."

He continued to deny it, but later, as we communicated further, he denied it less. And we laid out a plan.

"What do you want me to do?" he said.

"I would like to find a place to live in Houston. The first three cycles of chemotherapy have made a significant decrease in the cancer. MDA hasn't given me a drop-dead date, but I believe I have at least two years. I can't stay at the Rotary House—it's too expensive—yet I'll need to live close to the hospital to continue whatever therapy lies ahead." Bob agreed to help me find a new home. We found a street within the medical center, where one row of townhomes was completed and others were being built. It was close to Herman Park, with a hospice across the street, which I knew would be my next residence, now that I was thinking ahead. The location was perfect, with the sort of atmosphere any cancer patient dealing with reality would want.

The townhomes were being presold. Empty ground with construction surrounded all sides of a sales office, where we made a fabulous deal on one of the unfinished shells already standing. After walking through them all, I found one I liked next to the corner, since no corner lots were available, and Bob bought it at a reasonable price compared to what it would be finished. It had a small backyard patio with a large shade tree, and since it was merely a shell, I'd be able to finish it out. My agreement with Bob was that I could live in the townhome for two years or more, then he'd sell it. At that moment, two years seemed like an eternity.

House-hunting together was good for us. We remained extremely close during that time. After putting up a strong front, saying, "No I don't feel that way," I think it was a great relief for him. I know it was a relief for me, because I couldn't keep up the façade of being a normal, healthy woman without cancer. And by releasing him from what he perceived as a commitment, I felt okay about asking for his help. I was learning not to be embarrassed to ask, and I would say to any cancer patient: Never be embarrassed to ask for help. There'll never be a time in your life when you'll need it more. And never underestimate the power of people, or the possibilities of what they will do for you if you're in a true crisis, a state from which you won't survive if you don't get help.

But pay your dues forward. The world is round, and what goes around comes around.

I never believed that I'd done enough in that respect, didn't feel I'd had the opportunity, or felt I'd overlooked opportunities to help people. Too shy and deep-down insecure to put myself out there, to be vulnerable, I'd often been hurt by women, and men, with preconceived opinions about me, which intimidated me further, and I was reluctant to be hurt again. Victoria Johnson was disliked and misunderstood, I thought, a woman who inspired only jealousy.

When cancer struck, people came forward to remind me of the many times I'd shown respect and appreciation. I didn't realize I'd done so many good things for other people. But had I paid forward enough for the help I now so desperately needed?

Success Breeds a New Plan

The FAC therapy gave my cancer a jolt, and that success set my doctors to looking ahead for our next big step. No one expected the chemotherapy alone to cure the cancer. We were only buying time, stalling the disease long enough to determine our next round of attack.

In October, at Dr. Theriault's recommendation, I met with Dr. James Gajewski, who was in charge of the bone marrow transplant unit. Somewhat hopeful, yet knowing little about this procedure other than the term, I went to the meeting prepared with a list of questions.

"If you were close to complete remission," Dr. Gajewski explained, "we would consider autologous stem cell transplant, in which a patient's stem cells are harvested from the blood or bone marrow, cleaned, and replaced. It happens that our team is conducting a trial study on the use of allogeneic transplants, in which the cells are harvested from a donor, to treat late-stage breast cancer patients. Whichever is appropriate for you when your chemotherapy is complete, our goal is that the transplanted cells would rebuild your immune system and cure the underlying cancer."

"If you took cells from a donor, who would that be?"

"The best match would be a sibling in good health. I understand that you have a brother and sister. If you choose this option, we would certainly want to have them tested first."

As usual, I supplemented the information I obtained from Dr. Gajewski with every piece of written material I could find in the MDA patient library. The trial Dr. Gajewski mentioned would include fifty women and was in the beginning of stage two of the study. I learned that stage one of a trial establishes the dosage and mortality, and stage two is still too early to form any conclusions as to success. The best trials to be a part of are in stage three. Even then, you wouldn't know the success of the trial until it was over. People often think, "A trial, a new drug, that's what I want." I preferred to go with what was proven, yet sometimes there's no choice other than a new trial.

So this was a big step. I liked Dr. Gajewski, and if I decided to have a transplant, I felt comfortable with his team doing it.

My decision needn't be made until my eighth cycle of chemo-therapy, of which I'd only completed the third, but in preparation for the possibility of a transplant, I agreed to have my bone mar-row tested. It was many times worse than the liver biopsy. To find a match, I was put into the donor bank, while at the same time I contacted my brother, Stacey, and my sister, Carla.

They both asked, "What do you need me to do?"

"It's only a blood test to start with," I said. "MD Anderson will send a kit, and a location for having your blood drawn. The results will be sent back to MDA. The possibility of your being a match is only twenty-five percent. If you are, then I'll tell you what's next."

I'd learned that the donor half of the procedure was minimal. The bone marrow would be harvested in the hospital under gen-eral anesthesia.

"At most, you'd spend about twenty-four hours in a hospi-tal bed," I added, trying to make it sound not nearly as bad as it could be. I believe this was the first time they both realized how seriously ill I was. For them to agree to do this was a big deal, because Stacey and Carla both feared hospitals and doctors. They didn't hesitate to commit, however, proving they loved their big sister more than they feared the procedure. As it turned out, Stacey, who not only hates hospitals but absolutely won't fly, was a ninety-eight percent match. After he recovered from the initial shock, my brother was extremely proud that he could do something for me that might save my life.

MDA promptly filed for insurance clearance on the allogeneic bone marrow transplant, and just as promptly, the insurance company denied the expense.

CHAPTER 30

The Next Big Plan

T he MD Anderson team had ideas about how to convince my insurance company this was not just a trial, that allogeneic bone marrow transplants had been done successfully for a very long time, and the fact that they wanted to do one on a breast cancer patient should not make a difference. They would appeal the case and continue to appeal, I was assured. MDA did not intend to give up on me.

Neither did my friends. Judy Francis and Billie Pierce visited me at Rotary House that fall. I'd been keeping everybody posted by phone, so they knew about the bone marrow transplant. Now, I had to tell them about the insurance company's refusal to pay.

"What we'll do is have a fundraiser," they decided.

Back in Aspen, with zest, determination, and no holds barred, they took it upon themselves to raise the money, and what better way than to throw an amazing fundraising "Event"? They scheduled it for January 14, 1999. The local newspaper got behind it, donating space to spread the word: *Come to this event to help raise money for Victoria Johnson who needs a Bone Marrow Transplant.*

Thank God for friends. Even though I had the best insurance, if it failed to come through, and if I decided to have the transplant, I'd need a lot of money.

A Home in the Shadow of MDA

For three months following the purchase of my townhome, I was in my element. I pushed myself through the tough chemo days, to get to those precious ten to twelve days of functionality. Then I picked out the tile, the carpet, the paint colors, appliances, cabinet color, wood floor finish. My house-design project gave my mind, body, and spirit the best medicine ever, an opportunity to be creatively engaged in work I loved: decorating, designing. I'd loved that kind of creative work since building my first home in Marietta, Georgia, and now it captured my every waking moment and energized me. As I brought together all the collections from my various lives and created a home for myself that was exclusively "me," I no longer felt so absorbed by the day-to-day torture of my disease.

After putting his money and energy into buying the house, I believe Bob felt better about moving on with his life. When I think about it now, knowing him better, I'm not sure we would have gone the distance even without cancer.I did make it two years in my townhome, and well into three, when Bob broached the topic of selling the house as per our agreement. Death was still out there in the future, and I'd no desire to move away from a place that was ideal for me, so we had a period of contention between us. Fortunately, I was able to renegotiate, get him out of the deal but keep my townhome, and a couple of years later, out of the blue, Bob called. His son-in-law had been diagnosed with cancer. Bob wanted him to be treated at MD Anderson, and naturally, I said I'd help with whatever he needed.

It felt good to be needed. I was glad to be able to help someone besides myself, and especially Bob, who'd done so much. His son-in-law was treated, cured, and I understand he's still doing fine.

As Bob and I re-established our friendship, I told him about my commitment to apply my "good days" to living life as thoroughly as was possible.

"You know, I still have the condo in Palm Beach," he said. "You're welcome to use it in the off season."

His offer cheered me on many levels. It was a tangible sign that we were still good friends, and spending time on the beach was a part of my history I'd come to believe I could never reclaim. Having that possibility out there lifted my spirits tremendously.

Face to Face with Reality

With the knowledge that I had a bone marrow donor but no insurance, MDA continued to go forward with the plan for an allogeneic transplant. Meanwhile, I continued taking chemotherapy to banish the existing cancer. The beginning of January marked my sixth cycle, with two more to endure, and by late January Dr. Gajewski's transplant team was pushing me for a decision.

And as usual, I needed more information. Before doing a transplant procedure, the team wanted me to be as close to "cancer remission" as possible, yet after the initial jolt, my cancer had failed to continue responding satisfactorily to FAC. Allogeneic bone marrow transplantation was considered a "feasible procedure for patients with poor-risk metastatic breast cancer." In words no doctor would say, this was considered "last chance" treatment.

I would be hospitalized and high-dose chemotherapy induced. This is called ablative, or myeloablative, treatment, which would bring me as close to base line as possible, destroying diseased bone marrow to make room for the new marrow. The marrow infusion would be done intravenously, would not require an operating room, and I would be monitored during the procedure for side effects. In a successful transplant, the new marrow would migrate into my larger bones and begin producing normal blood cells.

During the initial recovery, which was expected to take two to three months, I'd be highly susceptible to infection and would be isolated. "Extraordinary" precautions to prevent infection would include prohibiting visitors, plants, flowers, fresh fruits, or vegetables from being in the room. After this initial recovery period, full recovery would require a year or longer.

I asked Dr. Gajewski if I could watch a bone marrow transplant procedure in progress. When he said no, I asked to tour the unit where I would be treated during recovery. This was clearly an unusual request, and he tried to discourage me but finally agreed to arrange it. I could bring one person to escort me, he said, and a nurse would guide us through the facility for observation.

The tour took place near the end of my eighth and last treatment cycle. That final cycle was so difficult that I had to go in a wheelchair, and I took my mom. We went to a part of the hospital I hadn't seen before, emerging from the elevator to find a single desk in front of a huge enclosed area. While we waited for our guide, a woman came off the elevator with a set of plastic golf clubs. Having obviously been here before, she shoved the clubs through an opening in the wall that looked like an elaborate doggie door. I asked what the toy clubs were for.

"My husband's doing so well that he's getting bored," she said, "but he still hasn't recovered his strength, so I thought the lightweight plastic golf clubs would give him something to do. I put them through the window to be sterilized."

The woman's enthusiasm about her husband's progress was the only bright moment in the situation we were about to encounter. Our guide arrived, handed us each a cap, gown, mask, shoe covers, and gloves to wear, and asked if either of us was carrying a purse or anything else, which we weren't. I'd read the instructions before we came, so I knew we couldn't take anything inside. The guide led us behind the wall, which opened into a glass-enclosed rotunda. Beyond the glass were the recovery units, each large enough for a hospital bed, the patient, and when necessary, a doctor. Beyond the bed, another glass wall enclosed the area where doctors and nurses wore complete protection suits. To tend the patients, yet keep them fully isolated against infection, the staff thrust their arms into flexible sleeves and gloves mounted in the glass.

Folding chairs, one outside each room, with a small desk attachment offered seating for a visiting family member. A blackboard mounted behind them provided a place to write messages, "You can do it!" or "We love you!" or "You look so good today!" A patient could read the message from inside the glass enclosure. Behind the visitor chair was just enough room for Mom and me to pass.

I'd never seen people so sick and so reactive to the environment that they lived in a bubble and were treated from outside with mechanical hands. In one room, I saw a man whose white skin had turned reddish brown because he'd contracted graft-versus-host disease, which I knew could be life-threatening and was only one of many potential complications. In other rooms, I saw patients who looked scarcely alive as they waited to find out whether their bodies would accept the new bone marrow. I watched a visitor hold a photo of two children up to the glass and tap lightly to get a patient's attention. When there was no response, the visitor just sat and watched. What these patients and their loved ones had to endure day after day was mind-boggling.

We moved slowly around, and I saw a few patients who were actually awake and slightly sitting up. Then we came to the man whose wife we'd met. He was using his walker and making slow swinging motions with a plastic golf club, apparently a big step in his progress. His wife said he'd been there two months and would soon be transferred to a less isolated facility, where he'd spend another three months.

"He's going to make it," she said, her voice and face filled with hope.

I reminded myself that it was possible I'd come on a day when there were a lot of new transplants, and I was seeing them at their worst. Dr. Gajewski and his team had prepared me for what to expect and assured me it wasn't as bad as it looked, but I was still shocked, which is why patients are discouraged from going there.

Seeing the reality face to face like that crushed any optimism I held for the procedure. Visitors going up to the glass, tapping on it, trying to get their loved one's attention, just hoping and waiting for the smallest response. It reminded me of new parents staring into a room filled with newborn babies, tapping and hoping their baby will look their way. I thought, *You come into this world bald, naked, and discolored, not the prettiest thing in the world, and maybe you'll be put in an incubator, but at least your parents know you'll improve. In the transplant incubator, you're naked, bald, discolored, and might go out of this world that way.*

Was I ready for that bubble room, with people tapping to see if I was alive?

A New Direction

On January 14th, my Aspen friends pulled off an unbelievable fundraiser after only two months of organizing. In the "Hell" days of my chemotherapy, I experienced the festivities by speaker phone, but I could tell that Club Chelsea was crowded and people were having a great time. Sandy, Billie, Judy Francis, Judy Alexander, and all my other friends kept me on line throughout the actual auction and part of the evening. When I tried to give a speech over the phone, the microphones didn't work quite right, so Judy Francis read my speech to the crowd. Sadly, the third host, Christine Gershel, had lost her mother to cancer two days earlier and couldn't be there.

My friends raised over $120,000 in one night, creating a catalyst for similar events in Aspen. After that night, whenever one of our own was diagnosed with cancer, no matter how much insurance they had or didn't have — after all, insurance never covers enough when you're fighting a long, hard battle — the locals get together and throw a fundraiser. For me it proved that there are good times to be had no matter what, and that my friends were truly incredible to be so supportive and giving.

Observing the patients in the Transplant Unit, however, and reading about the various problems that can occur with an allo-geneic transplant made me realize that before I accepted this as my final option, I wanted to thoroughly investigate every other possibility. Lying in my bed during those last few months of 1998, I'd seen frequent news reports of a new drug, Herceptin, which was showing incredible results for breast cancer patients in early and Stage 3 trials. Due to this remarkable success, the Federal Drug Administration was planning to fast-track Herceptin to get it approved.

My understanding was that approximately twenty-five percent of breast cancer patients express a gene called Her-2/Neu. These patients were found to have an extraordinarily aggressive cancer and to die earlier than breast cancer patients without the gene. After years of research, Dr. Dennis Slamon, who was now the di-rector of the Revlon/UCLA Women's Cancer Research Program, was instrumental in developing and testing Herceptin. The new gene-based treatment was touted as "revolutionary" because it tar-geted cancer cells specifically without damaging normal tissue. Though successful only in women who were Her-2/Neu positive, for them it was a miracle drug.

Following the news of Herceptin closely, and knowing my doctors wanted me to decide on the transplant immediately after the end of my last FAC cycle, I asked to be tested for the Her-2/ Neu gene. Dr. Theriault agreed. The test was positive.

Little was known about the long-term effects of Herceptin, since it had only become available in the fall of 1998, and no one thought it would be effective taken alone. It was a drug to add to other chemotherapy regimens. Eager to know more, I read the book, *Her-2: The Making of Herceptin, a Revolutionary Treatment for Breast Cancer,* which answered most of my questions about how the drug had performed in breast cancer patients during the trials. But I wanted to know how it would perform in *me.*

Since no one could answer that, I decided the best place to find out was at UCLA, where the drug was developed and tested. One fact from the book that stood out for me was the role Ron Perelman, owner of Revlon, had played. Since 1989, Revlon had contributed over $13 million dollars to UCLA's research in women's cancers, and Dennis Slamon had spent much of that money on studies of Her-2/Neu. The book quoted a representative as saying, "The science that ultimately led to the development of the drug would not have happened when it did without the support of Revlon."

In the '70s, '80s, and '90s, Ron Perelman and I had tried to date at least once a decade. Our decade dating never worked out, but I called him now for a very different reason. I didn't know if he would remember me or take my call, but there's never harm in asking. I'd say to any patient: whoever you know, no matter how high or low in the process, don't be reluctant to reach out. You never know who will help or how far that help will take you.

"Ron," I said, "it's Victoria Johnson."

"Are you coming to New York?"

"No, I wish I were. Ron, I have advanced breast cancer. I'm at MD Anderson, I'm Her-2 positive, and I want to meet Dennis Slamon. My only other option is a bone marrow transplant, and I'm not entirely comfortable with that. I'm convinced Dr. Slamon is the only person who can give me the story about what this new drug, Herceptin, may or may not do for me. Can you get me in to see him?"

CHAPTER 31

One in a Million

Home with Herceptin

With late spring came my new regimen, Herceptin and Taxotere. Smiling as I received the drugs on my first day, I held the book *Her-2*. Sister Alice sat beside me, praying that this was the miracle drug we hoped for.

When I'd met with Slamon's team, he reviewed my test results for Her-2. Then because I'd tested so high, which in this case was a good thing, he performed his own test, and I still tested high. His words had sent me floating out of his office on a cloud.

"Victoria, if Herceptin's going to work for anybody, it will work for you."

I had a good feeling about Herceptin. Even though it was new and different from the standard, I felt strongly it was the one for me. With Dennis Slamon and MDA working together, supporting me in my decision, and holding on to the option of a bone marrow transplant if this didn't work, how could I ask for a better scenario?

The new drugs didn't take me down so drastically, so I was feeling better longer and happy to not dwell on my disease every day. I had no problem driving to the hospital for treatment. When you feel better, you think the cancer must be getting better. Your mind plays these tricks, and that's okay.

Feeling stronger, I also was able to do more. I'd gotten my townhouse up and running. With spring turning into summer, I wanted to do something outdoors. One huge hardwood tree shaded my backyard patio, which I wanted to fill with color. At

Teas Nursery, one of the best in Houston at that time, I filled my cart with flowers, buying only annuals, because I wanted instant blooms. I wasn't concerned with whether the plants would bloom again in years to come. The future was for later. This was my year.

My treatment cycle was now weekly, rather than every three weeks, so my "good days" were unpredictable, but I usually had two to four per week, and I'd spend those days outside in the garden as much as I could. I took precautions with my catheter, covering it not only with a sterile bandage but also with plastic, exactly as I was instructed to do when taking a bath. I also wore a long-sleeved shirt and a mask anytime I was gardening. Once a week the catheter and the entire area around it had to be sterilized and the bandage replaced. I'd learned to do it myself but usually went to the hospital, knowing they could do a better job. If it should come loose in between, I did it myself, but that was rare, and it never occurred at all during my gardening.

Being outdoors a few hours each day despite the heat, planting, mulching, watering, was unbelievably great therapy for me. I didn't know a thing about Texas gardening, and that didn't matter. I loved hibiscus, which I discovered need more sun than my shady yard could provide, but I bought hibiscus anyway and enjoyed the blossoms as long as they lasted.

And So It Goes …

In late May, a few weeks into my gardening passion, my catheter started itching and burning under the bandage. I removed the bandage, saw that it was inflamed and went to the ER.

"You have a catheter infection," the nurse said, not seeming particularly concerned.

Apparently, it wasn't uncommon, because it's an exposed tube going into your chest. She cleaned and changed the tube and covered it again with a bandage. She also took a sample for culturing

— MDA takes samples of everything, because you never know. Then I received IV antibiotics for a few hours, plus more antibiotics to take for the next two weeks. The area was painful, but not terribly so. I had a slight fever, which was odd because I rarely get fever.

A week later, late in the day, someone phoned from the hospital and asked me to return to the ER.

"We need to take another test sample from your catheter," she said.

Again, since MDA tests everything in so many different ways, I didn't think much about it. I took my purse and drove there, totally unprepared for more than having some fluid taken out. I never went to MDA that they weren't taking fluids out or putting them in. Before I knew what was happening, I was in a hospital bed with an IV pole being rolled in, three nurses, and a couple of doctors, and wondering: *What's going on here?*

A physician introduced himself as Dr. Demitrios Kontoyannis, from the Infectious Disease department.

"It appears you have an infection called Nocardia," he told me. "It's a rare bacterial infection affecting the lungs, brain, or skin, and occurs especially in people with compromised immune systems from AIDS or bone marrow transplants, or in your case, chemotherapy. What's most unusual in your case is that the Nocardia invaded your catheter. It's almost always inhaled."

He conveyed to me the seriousness of this particular infection, but only after I pressed him for details did I learn the worst. Apparently, even with appropriate therapy, the mortality rate for Nocardia is high, as much as fifty percent when found in the lungs, and if it's in the brain, mortality exceeds eighty percent.

But This Is Good

After admitting me to the hospital, Dr. Kontoyannis wanted to treat me with penicillin and sulfa drugs, which Nocardia responds to best, but I'm allergic to those two drugs, so he prescribed the two "next-best" antibiotics for forty-eight hours to see how I would respond. If they didn't work, I'd be placed in ICU and risk the allergic effects of penicillin and sulfa drugs.

He tested my lungs and brain, because that's where Nocardia quickly starts eating away. And yes, the Nocardia was already in my lungs, but an MRI of the brain showed it to be clear.

Because Taxotere, a chemotherapy, weakens the immune system and lowers blood counts, it had to be discontinued while I was being treated for the infection. Herceptin, however, being a gene therapy, wouldn't adversely affect the immune system, so Herceptin alone became my new cancer fighter, which was a bit scary because it was also the drug most unknown.

After a few days in the hospital, the IV team came around daily to teach me how to manage the infusions at home. I learned that I was leaving the hospital with the IV, and that I'd be on the antibiotic treatments for at least two to three months, every six hours, twenty-four hours a day. This was mid June; I wouldn't finish until August. With further study, I also realized that anybody who contracts an infection as serious as Nocardia would likely have died of a bone marrow transplant.

After I was diagnosed with this rare and deadly infection, all discussion of a transplant ended. So as bad as it was, and *if* we could cure it, having contracted the Nocardia when I did had saved me from probable death had I gone forward with a transplant as prescribed.

CHAPTER 32

Comeback Girl

Approaching my first anniversary of dealing with a terminal diagnosis, I felt as well as one could expect and in good spirits. I'd fought a ferocious year and was still alive.

My weekly Herceptin infusions didn't hit me as drastically with flu-like symptoms of weakness, vomiting, and diarrhea as when Taxotere was included in the regimen. Heart damage remained our chief concern, for which my doctors planned to test frequently. For the first time since treatment started, I wasn't experiencing the worst side effects of chemotherapy.

Fighting Nocardia, however, proved to be an entirely different experience. The doctors had removed my chest catheter immediately after diagnosis and had inserted one in my left arm to administer antibiotics four times daily, as well as the weekly Herceptin treatments. The continuous cocktail of antibiotics kept me feeling well most of the time, but managing the infusion schedule soon rendered me anxious and exhausted. I'd sleep fitfully waiting for an unknown nurse to enter my home at midnight and wake me for the IV, which took ninety minutes, then I'd scarcely get to sleep again when she'd wake me a six a.m. for the morning IV.

At first I couldn't accept it, a different nurse coming every night when I was most vulnerable. I told the nursing agency that, no matter what it took, I had to have the same person each time. Once they were able to work that out, the same nurses came most nights, plus one relief nurse, and I felt less anxious. She'd leave, though, and it seemed I'd just finish dressing for the day and eating breakfast when noon arrived and I had to handle the infusion myself. Setting it up, waiting for the IV to finish, then cleaning up took an hour and a half each time. Nervous that I might do something wrong, that I might make a lethal mistake, I found the ordeal exhausting.

As July approached, dealing with four Nocardia infusions a day and going to the hospital weekly for Herceptin became my new routine. It wasn't life as I'd known it in the past, but it was life. It was what I had to do to survive.

The Drama of Houston

As with chemotherapy, I learned to adjust to the illness and fatigue of managing my disease to arrive at those precious windows of time, after the noon infusion finished, around one-thirty or so, until about five-thirty, when I was FREE! If I felt well enough, I could spend three-and-a-half hours enjoying my favorite activities before I had to be home for the next infusion.

Rose-Incarnation had blossomed during the months I was moving in and decorating my townhome. I renamed the business "Caution to the Wind," since I now designed ornate pillows, throws, and other soft furnishings for the home, in addition to gift baskets. As much as I loved designing and creating, I also loved shopping for the fabrics. The mental and emotional therapy were, in themselves, invaluable, and my little business also turned a profit.

One Saturday after I removed my twelve o'clock infusion, I felt ready to be out of the house. No one was visiting at the time, so I was on my own. Driving my beloved Jeep Cherokee, which had accompanied me from California, in 1993, to Colorado, and now to Texas, I headed toward my favorite place, the fabric store, stopping for gas at a station just past the medical center. The tank was on the driver's side. When I finished pumping and turned around to hang the nozzle back in its holder — my car drove off.

Astonished, I stood with my mouth open, watching it.

"That guy just stole your car!" said a man pumping gas behind me.

The service station attendant ran out. "That man took your car?!"

So I wasn't imagining it. This really was happening.

During this shocking standstill, as my Jeep turned into the street, the thief looked back at me with huge bulging eyes, obviously high on drugs. As he sped out of sight, more people ran out of the store and up behind me.

"Lucky you have your purse," the attendant said.

Still in a daze, I glanced down to see my purse hanging over my shoulder, my wallet inside.

"You need to call the police," someone suggested.

That's when I realized my cell phone was in the car. I went inside the station and phoned, the service attendant waiting nearby for me to finish.

"Sorry you lost your car, ma'am," he said. "But you still have to pay me for the gas."

Outside again, on that blistering hot afternoon, I explained to the female police officer what had happened.

"You left your keys in the car?" she said.

"Well, yes, I was right beside it pumping gas."

Looking at my Colorado driver's license, she asked, "Do you realize this is Houston? A couple feet closer and this would've been a carjacking."

"I've lived in New York and LA," I said. "I'm accustomed to big cities. This thief came out of nowhere."

"Actually, he was probably hanging out at that bus stop." She pointed to the covered bench not ten feet away. "He watched for the best opportunity and took it. Do you have someone you can call to pick you up?"

"No."

"You'll need to make a list of everything that was inside. For us, in case we get the car back, but also for your insurance company."

Uh-oh! "My insurance papers were in the car. They have my home address on them. And my house keys, with my gate code on the key ring!"

"You're kidding me." The officer stopped writing and started toward her squad car. "We need to get to your house. He could be stealing more than your Jeep."

When I reached for the passenger door, she said, "You'll have to sit in the back."

It was like climbing into a furnace. "How do I open the windows?"

"Can't. Sorry, and I can't move the partition, either, and there's no air conditioning back there."

I heard her call for backup. By the time we drove the mile to my home, another police car with two officers had arrived. My neighbors, peering out their windows, must have wondered what was happening. In the early days of living there, they'd seen me arrive home from the hospital in a Texas Medical Center Police shuttle when I was too sick to drive, but this was different. I was in the back of a squad car, like a criminal.

The officers went up to my door, guns drawn, and somehow opened it without bashing it in. I watched from the doorway as they went through the rooms downstairs, just as you see on TV, each taking one room at a time, saying "Clear!" then moving on to the next room and out the back door. After they secured the downstairs, they moved slowly to my upstairs bedroom. They checked out the entire upper floor then motioned for me to come up, and I quickly saw why.

My first concern when they went upstairs had been, *Oh no, I had no time to straighten up before I left. My bedroom's a mess, my bed is unmade. "* Before I could apologize for my unmade bed, I realized that's not what they were staring at.

I suspect they didn't quite know what to make of this scene. Was it the makings of a drug lab? On a table by the bed lay numerous bags of IV fluids, large syringes full of saline flushes, needles to puncture the catheter tube, bandages, cotton, alcohol, and beside them, the IV pole.

Seeing the look on their faces, I said, "You do know I have cancer?"

They didn't reply, but I saw relief on their faces. They wanted to know if anything had been disturbed or taken. Fortunately, it appeared the car thief had not been in the house.

My neighbors across the street, Mead and Diane, who'd become close friends during my six months in the new house, took me to rent a car. Two days later, a police officer called to say they'd found my Jeep and to give me the address where I could pick it up.

"This is a bad part of town," he added, "but if you don't come, we'll have to tow it to the police compound. You can pick it up there."

"Did you catch the man who stole it?"

"No, we chased him, but he jumped out and got away. Your car was in a high-speed chase."

"Is it damaged?"

"It's drivable. You'll need to have it checked out."

I had to pay $190 to get my stolen car from the police compound. It went from there to the body shop for repairs, which tapped my insurance for several thousand dollars. The repair shop turned it around fairly quickly, but for the next couple of weeks, I was too frightened to drive anywhere besides the hospital.

Real or Artifactual

Refusing to let this incident rob me of what was most precious — the short amount of time I had left in this world — I settled into a pleasant routine of working on my business between antibiotic infusions at home and weekly visits to MDA, for Herceptin and to see my infectious- disease physician. Every three weeks I also had a chest X-ray, to make sure the Nocardia was responding to treatment.

In mid-August, Dr. Kontoyiannis began tapering me off the antibiotics. My chest was clear. I'd beaten the fifty-percent odds and come back from the dreaded Nocardia. To assure that my brain was also still clear of the infection, he ordered a CT scan.

On August 23, I received the most amazing news from Dr. Theriault. My breasts, liver, bones, and other organs showed the first indications of improvement. Even without Taxotere, *the Herceptin was working!*

No one had expected this. The two breast tumors definitely were not growing and might even be a fraction of a centimeter smaller. From that original horrifying diagnosis nearly a year earlier, I'd come back strong, thanks to my "miracle" drug, and was ready to continue the fight.

Because the brain CT done a few days earlier showed "a very subtle asymmetry in the right cerebellum, which might be artifactual," a follow-up imaging with MRI was recommended.

I'd seen that word "artifactual" before and knew that it meant the findings might be false.

"What do you think it is?" I asked Dr. Theriault.

"There's no way to tell until the MRI gives us a better reading."

Doctors don't like to tell you what they think, only what they know, which is understandable, but I pressed anyway.

"You promised to always be honest with me," I said. "What are the possibilities?"

Reluctantly, he nodded. "It could be scar tissue from Nocardia that wasn't seen in the brain initially and has responded to treatment. Or it could be Nocardia. Or it could be a brain tumor. But let's not get ahead of ourselves. The MRI will tell us more."

He ordered an MRI of the brain to be done that same afternoon.

Brain Surgery

When Dr. Theriault called scarcely a day after he'd given me the best news since my diagnosis, it was not to tell me the results of my brain MRI but to say he was sending me to a different physician.

"Dr. McCutcheon is a neurosurgeon," he said. "He'll be better at interpreting the scans and determining what this is."

Reddish hair, fair skin, and around my age, if not younger, Dr. McCutcheon did not look like my vision of a neurosurgeon. He looked like he could be my brother.

But he was soft spoken and had all the qualities you'd want in a person about to deliver the most devastating news imaginable. If I could wrap myself around the fact that I might actually overcome this new development, buy some time, and ignore the dismal facts I'd learned during that week, this man might convince me it was possible. His kind, positive, self-assured demeanor immediately instilled confidence.

"You have three separate and peripherally located metastases in the right cerebellum," he explained from what he'd seen on the MRI scan.

"Three?" The other words meant little to me compared to that number. My research had informed me that one tumor was serious, multiple tumors were ominous. "Why weren't these seen on earlier brain scans?"

He shook his head, apparently as baffled as Dr. Theriault and I about the sudden appearance of these tumors. I believe neither of my doctors wanted to remind me that I had incurable Stage 4 Cancer and this was merely another step in the progress of my disease.

"They're small," he said, "the largest less than one-and-a-half centimeters, with no migrating cells, although we won't know for certain until we get inside. I believe it's quite possible these tumors can be removed."

Dr. McCutcheon explained the risks I'd already read about, of which the worst, of course, was brain damage, paralysis, and death. The risk of seizures terrified me, too, but I understood that I would be given an anticonvulsant to diminish that risk, along with corticosteroids to prevent brain swelling. Dr. Kontoyiannis would be on hand to culture for Nocardia. The tumors were in close proximity and could be removed with one incision of four to five inches. A small part of my skull would be removed and later stapled back in place.

The hope would be that the tumors were solid, because migrating cells could not be surgically removed. I asked the usual question: "What happens if I don't do the surgery?"

And received the usual answer: "They'll become larger, spread, and you'll start having seizures, or falling, losing brain functions such as vision and speech. You'll be hospitalized."

When I pressed him for how long I could expect to live, he wouldn't commit, but based on the growth rate thus far and the literature I'd read, I figured about twelve weeks.

"They're located in an accessible area, Victoria, so I feel comfortable doing this surgery, and I believe you have a good chance for recovery."

I came to terms with it that day in his office. After all, what choice did I have? Like the bone marrow transplant, if this didn't work there was no coming back. But I agreed to the procedure and was scheduled for September 8, 1999 to have a craniotomy.

CHAPTER 33

A 4-0 Silk Stitch

MDA is an impressive hospital. The staff assigned a representative, I learned later, who took my family to a nice area to wait during my six a.m. surgery. Mom had flown in. Sister Alice, of course, was there, too. The representative brought them coffee, asked if anyone needed anything and frequently updated them on the procedure. Knowing how well my family and friends were treated, I felt once again fortunate to be at a facility that provided the best care possible not only for me but for them.

With no qualms about inserting herself into any hospital situation, Sister Alice walked alongside as a nurse wheeled me to pre-op, talking to me at first, then, as I was pre-medicated, reading the Meditation on Health: *There is a Divine Power within me that permeates my entire being, that makes and keeps me whole.*

As the initial sedation meds took effect, I could still hear her voice: *Restfully and peacefully I repose... and let go of nerves. I yield myself fully to the healing of Christ. His peace and love pervade my whole being. All tension is relieved... There is a Divine Power ....*

The doctor called for me to be taken into surgery. Sister Alice walked alongside the gurney to the operating room, where the surgical staff waited, and when we arrived at the door, she said a prayer. Then they nodded for the attendant to bring me in. When the anesthesiologist said to count backwards, I turned to see Sister Alice smiling, making the sign of the cross.

That's the last I remember until I awoke in the ICU.

The surgery lasted about four hours, Mom told me, and just

as you'd see on TV, my handsome doctor went to the waiting area afterward to talk to her and to my friends.

"The surgery went fine. We removed three tumors, and I feel quite positive about the results. Victoria did well, and she's in the ICU now, where you can see her anytime you like, but it might be a while before she wakes up."

Of course, I didn't know this until later, since I was still out. When I did finally come around, I felt groggy and confused to see people in the room. I didn't recognize anyone.

Almost instantly, I started vomiting. Nurses swarmed into action, moved everybody out and somehow stopped the vomiting, which was important because I shouldn't be moving. Morphine, apparently, was the cause, so they had to change my drugs.

The next time I awoke, I was a little clearer. I knew I was in ICU. I saw a nurse watching me. My bandaged head felt twice its normal size. The operation site felt bizarre, invaded, changed, like when you have a cut that requires stitches and you can feel them tugging with every movement. The pain was horrendous, even though I was on pain meds and steroids.

Before I could go home, they wanted me to walk. I was amazed that I was scheduled to be in the hospital for only five days. The material I'd read must have been outdated, because it said brain surgery patients should expect to be hospitalized for weeks. I soon learned the reasons you're released so soon; not because you're ready to go but because insurance covers only five days unless there are complications, and because when you're susceptible to infection, the safest place to be is almost anywhere but a hospital.

A physical therapist came each day and made me move a little more.

"Can you put your foot on the floor if we hold you?" he said, a day or two after surgery. "I don't know." I could sit up, but I didn't know how to move my leg, so I panicked, thinking I was paralyzed.

"Don't worry," he said. "It takes time."

Gently, he swung my legs around off the side of the bed, then he and a nurse held me while I tried to remember how to walk. If I hadn't been so medicated, I would have been so frightened despite their reassurance.

I also had difficulty talking. When someone asked a question, even though I knew the answer, I didn't know how to say the word I was thinking. An odd sensation, but after I made it happen once, the process of talking came back quickly.

Walking didn't happen quite so fast. The therapist strapped me into a harness with a dozen different hand holds, which two people held so firmly that if I stumbled, I knew I wouldn't fall. With daily practice, trying to move my legs, I finally shuffled one foot forward, then the next. Within another day or so I was walking on my own, but always with a gait belt, which was less cumbersome than the harness, and with the therapist holding the strap, ready to catch me if I fell. The day I went home, I left with the gait belt and orders that someone supervise and support me at all times, that I never get out of bed by myself.

The first day home was the worst. Each day, I increased the number of minutes I walked around the room and sat up in a chair. After ten days, I decided it was time to walk outside. I'd been cooped up indoors as long as I could stand, not venturing farther than around the downstairs part of my house or my backyard patio. Mom cinched the gait belt around me, grasped it firmly, and we went outside.

Five townhomes separate mine from the first parking area and green space. As Mom and I inched our way down the sidewalk in that early evening, my neighbor John came outside. John and Dawn lived three houses down, Mead and Diane lived directly across from me, and both couples had been following my progress since the day I moved in.

"I can't believe you're outside walking two weeks after brain surgery," John said.

He called Mead, and before long I had a fan club gathered round, applauding every step. "You can do it! You can do it!"

Proudly, I Did Do It

It took me thirty minutes to walk four houses down and back. But I did it.

That was the day I said to Mom, "I don't know what the results of the surgery will be, whether the surgeon was able to remove all the brain mets," which I'd learned was short for brain metastases, "but thank God I lived through it." I never told anyone that deep down I'd believed Dr. McCutcheon might have to come out from surgery and tell Mom I didn't make it. My brain had been exposed, invaded by surgical tools, and sewn back together with silk thread, as I might stitch a seam in one of the pillows I made for Caution to the Wind. Surgical staples held my skull together. Yet here I was, walking, talking, and, because of the massive doses of steroids, I had more energy than ever.

Brain Radiation

Three weeks later, I met with Neurology Oncologist Dr. Eric Strom about the radiation treatments that would, we hoped, eliminate any radical cells that had migrated from the tumors. He felt I was a "good candidate for whole brain radiotherapy" and scheduled me for simulation.

My friend, Kathy, the patient at MDA at that time who was often one step ahead of me in what I would be experiencing, was already scheduled for brain radiation. I wanted to know in advance exactly what to expect, so Sister Alice pulled some of her angel strings and arranged for me to watch Kathy go through her simulation. Even though there's no actual radiation taking place, the technicians usually won't allow anyone inside the room. Kathy graciously agreed, so I was in, and it was a dramatically informative experience.

I'd tell any patient: Anytime you have an opportunity to learn from another patient or take advantage of a moment, don't be afraid to say to the doctor, "I want to see what you're going to do to me." If that means pulling strings to get special dispensation, so be it. Learn what you need to learn. If you prefer not to know, as many patients do, then that's all right, too. Do what most relieves your anxiety.

During simulation, technicians plan the radiation therapy exactly as it will be enacted during actual radiation, when there's no room for mistakes. A special mesh head mask was formed and bolted to the table to hold my head precisely in place. Specific radiation angles and doses were entered into the computerized machine. Although I'd done well with numerous brain MRIs, something about lying there with my head locked down while the machine moved around to various angles triggered my claustrophobia, as it does for many patients, I'm told. So before I had my first radiation treatment in early October, I took anti-anxiety drugs. During the radiation, I felt a strobe-like sensation inside my head, but no pain, and after the first visit I no longer needed the drugs.

The pain came the next day. Having previously tapered off the steroids that prevented swelling after my brain was assaulted by surgery, I'd opted not to take more steroids during the radiation.

"What will the steroids do for me?" I'd asked Dr. Strom.

"Primarily, they prevent headaches."

"Does everyone experience headaches after radiation?" Without the positive effects of steroids, I probably wouldn't have come back so fast from the surgery. They did keep the swelling down, and I had no edema that had to be drained, no stroke-like symptoms, so the steroids had done a good job, but I always preferred to take as little medication as possible.

"Every case is different," Dr. Strom admitted. "It's entirely up to you if you'd like to try it without them."

I expected any effects from the radiation would increase over time, not hit me immediately. But the next night, I had the worst headache of my entire life. I felt as if my skull would split and my brain would come bursting out. I also had chills, fever, vomiting, and mental confusion.

I called the ER and spoke to the attending physician, who said if I could control the pain with medication I had on hand, it should be safe to wait until morning to see Dr. Strom. Early the next day, I went in and begged him to do whatever it took to stop the headaches. He gave me an IV of Decadron, a corticosteroid, prior to my next daily treatment, and a prescription to take continuously. Having radiation therapy five days a week for three weeks, fifteen treatments in all, was at first an ordeal, but like all the other therapies, it quickly became routine.

It All Falls Down

Before the radiation therapy, Dr. Strom had said I shouldn't have too much hair loss. I'd been without hair, for the most part, long enough that this wasn't high on my list of concerns. At the time, my hair was still quite short from the surgery, with about a third of it shaved, a sort of abstract Mohawk.

But one morning fairly early in the treatment, I was sitting outside on my steps watching the squirrel that came to visit me daily, and I reached up to scratch my itchy scalp. A handful of hair came out. I touched it again, and another handful. Then another. Every hair, gone. I'd never lost it that dramatically, even during my FAC therapy. When I called Dr. Strom and told him what happened, he seemed taken aback.

"Come in," he said. "I want to see it.'

Which, of course, I did.

"It's most unusual for it to come out like that," he said. "But since it has, it probably will never grow back."

"Is it possible the dosage was wrong?"

He hesitated. "No, I don't think so, but we'll double check."

He recalculated everything, and nothing was amiss. For that moment in time, I believe we both felt I might have been over-radiated, which would have been disastrous.

By comparison, being forever bald was no big deal.

A Time of Miracles

With my brain tumors ablated by surgery and radiation, and while I was still zipping around on steroids, I decided to go home to Aspen. Dr. Theriault arranged for me to take Herceptin at the Aspen Valley Hospital, which, unbeknownst to me, had a chemo-therapy room now.

My visit the previous Christmas was spent down valley with my family. I hadn't been well enough to spend any time with my friends. This fall would be my opportunity to say thank you in person to Sandy Iglehart, Judy Francis, Christine Gershel, Billie Pierce, and to everyone who had so compassionately phoned, vis-ited, and sent cards and gifts, helping me through this difficult time. Then they had invested even more of their time, money, and energy in that amazing fundraiser.

Victoria Rose

I stayed in Aspen about ten days, enjoying this brief freedom from the tedium of my disease. I felt blessed to be alive, appreci-ating the good days and not expecting them to last.The blessings stretched, however, into a splendid fall and holiday season, with no significant setbacks, only the typical side effects from chemotherapy and the residual effects of radiation, which were entirely manageable. Amazingly, my cancer was still considered stable. Life was worth living again. From November 1999 until several months into the New Year, I continued to feel good.

It amazed me to look back at everything I'd gone through, often with little hope of seeing another sunrise, and to review all that had worked against me. In hindsight, I realized that the decisions I'd second-guessed were the best decisions I could have made. My doctors and I agreed that if I'd gone ahead with a bone marrow transplant, I most likely wouldn't have made it. The Nocardia proved it. But even more miraculous, if I'd not contracted Nocardia, the metastatic breast cancer tumors in my brain probably wouldn't have been discovered while they were still small and operable. Or before too many random cells had escaped for radiation to be effective. So my "worst case" scenario turned out to be a miracle.

Making it through the brain surgery and radiation with no significant ill effects was yet another miracle. I still had no hair and believed Dr. Strom might be right about it never growing back, but that was a small price to pay for this period of well-being.

March of 2000 brought another incredible occurrence: my niece and namesake, Victoria Rose Waldrip, was born, and I was in the room with my sister to witness the birth. Carla, brave soul that she was, had chosen to have at her bedside her significant other, Vinny Galbato, her son Jesse, who was about ten at the time, our mom, and me. Even my father got caught up in the mix but ended up asleep on the sofa.

With no children of my own, I was delighted to be a part of this experience. Mom, having birthed three kids, was rather laid back about it. Vinnie was capturing the whole thing on video. Jesse was so cool. I was the one standing beside the bed urging Carla to "breathe, breathe," playing the role of baby coach and expert, without knowing a thing about what I was doing. A nurse handed the baby first to Carla, then Carla passed her to Mom. She was all of three minutes old, rosy pink and pretty as a rosebud, when I took her and went to sit beside Jesse. Carla had already chosen to name her Victoria, after her "dying" sister.

"Rose," Jesse said. "She's Victoria Rose."

And that was it. We sat together holding sweet Victoria Rose while Vinnie kept the camera rolling. To this day, that's one of my most cherished memories and videos.

A Whisper of Remission

Except for an ongoing problem of fatigue, for which I was referred to a Fatigue Clinic, and pressure pain behind my nose and eyes, plus occasional electric-like pains in the scalp, I continued to feel great. These difficulties were attributed to post radiation by my new physician in the Neurology Clinic, Dr. Arthur Forman. Weeks passed, then months. My checkups showed no recurrence of cancer from the neck down. My MRI's showed no changes in my brain. By June 2000, when my ultrasound of the left breast and axilla showed "no evidence of disease," and a reassessment of the liver showed "no evidence of metastasis" as well, I began to hear whisperings of the word "remission."

Was such a thing possible, that within two years a person with Stage 4 metastatic cancer to every organ, including the brain, could hear the word "remission"? Dr. Theriault, who was not one to get overly excited or to show emotion, was doing a great deal of smiling that day. I was feeling especially proud in that third week of June 2000, when I sensed rather than heard those whispers of "remission." No one would want to jinx it by saying the word out loud.

The comeback sensation of buoyancy and light when you

thwart disease is amazing and ephemeral, like holding on to a cloud. It felt so good to feel good. Yet at any moment I might lose it, so I kept looking for ways to live joyously, making choices that incorporated treatment and survival along with time to *live* the life I'd gained.

Then, on June 27, the whispers of remission I'd been secretly clinging to wisped away into nothing as my physicians solemnly delivered the same reversal I'd experienced ten months earlier. My excellent assessment and prognosis was followed by the discovery of a new brain tumor.

CHAPTER 34

St. Mary-of-the-Woods

There was a certain freedom to being bald. I'm no longer asked, "Is that your natural hair color?" Or worse, "Is that your real hair?"

The new brain metastases were discovered about the time my hair finally started growing in again after it all fell out post-radiation. Since the tumor was small, we had a great deal of discussion about whether to remove it or wait and see how it developed.

One More Month

When the next scan showed no additional tumor but measurable growth of all three, Dr. McCutcheon and I agreed it was time for surgery. Because they were located in different areas, two on the right side, between the previous incision and the midline, and one tumor on the left side, he would remove the duo in one surgical procedure, wait six weeks for me to recover, then remove the third tumor.

"That's one option," he said.

"There's another option?"

He hesitated quite a long time before saying, "I could do a double craniotomy."

"I know what that sounds like, but what does it mean?"

"I would perform the surgery on one side, close, then while you're still under, I would operate on the other side."

"Is it more dangerous to do two surgeries in the same day?"

"No more dangerous than doing one."

What would be the difference, I wondered, other than having pain on both sides at once? Recovering from brain surgery obviously takes longer than *having* brain surgery. With the first option, I'd need twelve weeks of recovery, with the second only six. During that time, I'd remain on Herceptin, but if any other cancer developed, I wouldn't be able to address it.

While I tried to think ahead in the most objective and positive way, it seemed unfathomable to me that I could survive two more surgeries, that my gifted surgeon could open my brain on one side, and as I explained it flippantly to a friend, step out for some air, a cup of coffee, a chat, then regroup, come back in, turn me over and start cutting on the other side. While this process seemed unique to me, I knew that if he hadn't done it before Dr. McCutcheon wouldn't know it could work and wouldn't have suggested it.

On another level, I was now expected to recover from a total of six brain tumors in little more than a year. How could I not be damaged? How could I truly expect to be normal again? I began wondering what it might be like to survive the surgery but with damage forever to my vision, speech, or worse.

Going to the Brain and Spine Clinic over the past year, I'd seen a different world than in the chemotherapy area. Before and after surgery, patients there are somewhat ambulatory; otherwise, they'd be hospitalized or arriving for treatment in an ambulance. So they've survived. But I'd seen the effects of what cancer and brain surgery had done, and truly disturbing cases were not uncommon. Many patients were paralyzed to some degree, but for one man I recall, the cancer had taken not only a portion of his brain, it had also migrated into his neck, face, and jaw. Being pushed in a wheelchair, he appeared to be completely paralyzed on his right side. He could move his left arm a little. His head hung toward one shoulder, his speech was incomprehensible, and his skin grafts were healing hideously.

Was this going to be me? Could I risk such a dreadful result?

Yet what choice did I have? This was now two and half years

after my original diagnosis, which had been shocking at the time but not nearly as bad as what I later had to overcome. When Stage 4 Cancer couldn't get any worse, because it had gone to my liver, it now had attacked my brain six times, and I was about to be opened up twice in one day.

So I bit the bullet and told Dr. McCutcheon, "I'm going to be the most amazing cancer patient you've ever seen. I'm going to get through this and any other horror the beast throws at me. I'm going to make history with MDA."

Proactive

On December 11, I had the surgery, and by mid-January 2001 I was back up and running again. I don't remember much about the recovery, except that in many ways it was easier than the first time, without as much confusion or difficulty in speaking or moving.

And thank God my hair decided to grow back, because the scars were enough to frighten small children. There was little of my scalp that didn't have a bump, knot, or crevice. Like a mismatched jigsaw puzzle, where pieces that don't quite fit are pushed into place anyway, and have healed that way, with scar tissue in between. Without hair, my head looked like a cracked eggshell.

Dr. Theriault, Dr. McCutcheon, and I decided to become proactive in our approach to future brain metastases. In addition to the Herceptin, which continued to keep my cancer at bay from the neck down, Dr. Theriault suggested a class of chemotherapy called Navelbine, which safely attacks any residual cancer cells before they can multiply and grow into tumors. I'm not sure what constitutes a lifetime dosage of brain radiation, but I was told I'd reached my maximum, so we were limited in what we could do.

My seasoned friend Kathy called Navelbine the "death drug." Her brain mets had been scattered and were thus inoperable, so her doctors could prescribe only radiation and this new class of chemotherapy.

"Navelbine's the last-chance drug everybody gets just before they die," Kathy said. "My friend, who'd just come off of Navelbine when I started taking it, told me, 'Kathy, you know what taking this drug means,' and I assured her I knew. I'm sorry you have to take it, Victoria."

Kathy's friend did die, but not before I started taking Navelbine, and sadly, Kathy died, as well, a few years later. Yet Dr. Theriault had faith in it, as did Dr. Arthur Forman, a neurology oncologist educated in all chemotherapies and their side effects.

Dr. Forman wore suspenders and a bowtie. A miniature rose adorned his lapel, plucked daily from his personal garden. What I liked best was that he didn't mind saying what he *thought* as well as what he knew. The first time I had a spinal tap, now renamed "lumbar puncture" to make it sound less formidable, which happened each time a new tumor was discovered to make sure it wasn't also in the spine, Dr. Forman handled the procedure and made it as painless as it could possibly be. I felt lucky to be assigned to him, even if he did side with Dr. Theriault on the subject of Navelbine.

Navelbine's a serious drug, however, insofar as it's a vesicant, which is a chemical that causes extensive tissue damage and blistering if it escapes from the vein. The nurse had to be specially trained. The IV had to be injected into a good vein with no chance of collapsing, and the nurse couldn't leave or look away from the injection for a second. I had to remain absolutely still. Fortunately, it took only seven minutes for the IV drip to finish, so we both sat, our eyes locked on the injection site, and waited. Then we could breathe.

I continued with the Navelbine for six doses, which took me into April. Nothing changed, except that it made me ill, and I was tired of being ill. I chose to discontinue it. My doctors agreed that six doses was a good stopping point. It was not intended to be a forever drug.

Confession

From the day we met, Sister Alice never mentioned church to me, but the more I grew to love her, the more I wanted to know about her religion. At least once a week, we had dinner together, and during one of our dinner discussions I asked if I could go with her to Mass.

"Oh, hon, of course you can. When would you like to go?"

That's all it took. The following Sunday, I happily and with reverent fascination accompanied her to Mass.

Houston boasts over a hundred Catholic churches. The church Sister Alice chose to attend was a small white house in a nearby residential section — the Rice University & Texas Medical Center Catholic Student Center. With my first visit, I understood why she loved it. Like Sister Alice herself, this little church is warm and energetic.

Mass is held in the converted living room-dining room, which has a beautiful altar but is filled with chairs instead of pews. The congregation includes university professors, medical professionals, and neighborhood residents who prefer the smaller setting, but the informal atmosphere attracted mostly college students. No getting down on your knees, since there was no hassock. Musicians from Rice University came every Sunday to play for us, and one girl could not play her guitar with shoes on. On Sunday mornings, the church provided bagels and muffins, then after Mass, we'd eat lunch together, cooked by a volunteer who'd signed up to shop for, cook, and serve the hundred or so congregants who stayed. The idea behind the lunches was primarily to make sure the students had one good home-cooked meal each week. I volunteered for my turn, of course. Sunday Mass provided an enriching environment for me.

Sister Kitty was church director at the time. Father Mark, the chaplain, was young enough to interact and communicate well with the students. An ordinary guy loved by everyone, it's good that he was a great priest, because he could have broken a lot of hearts.

What I liked most about the Catholic service was the ritual. I liked being able to participate and was inspired by the level of attention the congregation gave to what was happening. Father Mark never had to yell to keep his audience engaged, because we felt very much a part of the communion. Most of my life had been void of structure—not to say that's bad, it had always been good for me, but the discipline and structure of a group with thousands of years of stability gave me a comfort I'd never found in other churches.

Regardless of what one feels about the bad stories we hear too much of concerning priests, those stories are about individuals, not the religion. I can completely disassociate from that, because I don't go to Mass to judge or be judged.

After I'd recovered enough from the second brain surgery, I told Sister Alice that I would like to convert to Catholicism. She explained about the class I'd have to take, the Rite of Christian Initiative of Adults, and that I would need a sponsor.

"I'll be your sponsor," she said, as if adding a new responsibility to her already heavy schedule was no problem at all.

Sponsoring me meant attending every class with me. Our studies were intense, because the school year condensed them into sixteen weeks.

Scheduled to be confirmed on Holy Saturday of Easter weekend, I gave no thought at first to my past and how the church might view it, but I was truly serious and proud to be converting, and as my confirmation date approached, I began to feel obligated to make Father Mark aware of my years with *Penthouse*. I was new to Catholicism and although I wasn't looking for forgiveness, since I felt no sin in working with the magazine, I did want to be completely open and honest. So I called him and made an appointment to talk.

His upstairs office held his big desk, a standing bookshelf, and a visitor chair, where I sat.

"I want to tell you about my past," I said, "because I wouldn't feel right being confirmed if you didn't know. If it makes a difference, I certainly understand."

"I'm sure it won't make a difference in God's eyes or mine, but go ahead."

"When I was young, I was a model and an actress. There was one very controversial job I held where I received a lot of criticism. I can't say that I made a mistake. I don't honestly feel it was wrong, or that if I had it to do over again I wouldn't. I'm not here to say I did a bad thing. I just want to tell you."

He was listening intently.

"In 1976, I was Pet of the Month for *Penthouse* magazine, and in 1977, I was the *Penthouse* Pet of the Year. I continued to work for the magazine for about ten years."

"Oh," he said. "*O-kay.*"

He rose from his chair, fanning the air with his hand. "Whew, it's hot in here."

Obviously stalling, perhaps doing some extra praying, he walked to the wall, fiddled with the air conditioning, then paced behind his desk as if in deep thought. From his expression, I knew he must be reconsidering the decision to confirm me on Sunday, and how to let me down gently.

"Well!" he said, still pensive but as if he'd reached a decision, "I'll bet my brother's got that issue of *Penthouse*."

That was such a tension breaker, as if I'd just given him an interesting bit of news. Yet I knew it was a shock. He'd expected anything but that.

In that small church, I assume confessions were rather benign. I'd dropped a bombshell, and Father Mark handled it with such grace. For a minute or so, he didn't speak, he paced. Then he went to the bookshelf, which was filled with hefty volumes, and removed a Bible. Either it was marked or he knew the place he wanted quite well, because he turned right to it and started reading to me.

"From John, eight. *Then the scribes and Pharisees brought to Him a woman caught in adultery. And when they had set her in the midst, they said to Him, 'Teacher, this woman was caught in adultery, in the very act. Now Moses, in the law, commanded us that such should be stoned. But what do You say?'*" Father Mark paused before continuing. "*'He raised Himself up and said to them, 'He who is without sin among you, let him throw a stone at her first.'*" Another pause, then, "*And Jesus was left alone, and the woman standing in the midst. When Jesus had raised Himself up and saw no one but the woman, He said to her, 'Woman, where are those accusers of yours? Has no one condemned you?' She said, 'No one, Lord.' And Jesus said to her, 'Neither do I condemn you; go and sin no more.'*"

After he finished reading, we had no further discussion.

Standing, I said, "Thank you, Father Mark."

He nodded. "You will be a very good Catholic."

A Fine Run

After telling Father Mark, I felt compelled to tell Sister Alice. In many ways I was more concerned about divulging this information to her. I suppose I didn't want to disappoint her. I called her that afternoon and arranged to meet her at Rotary House. I waited for her at a table in the bar area, where we each ordered a snack.

"Are you excited about being confirmed on Sunday?"

"I actually met with Father Mark today," I said. Then I described our conversation, painting a picture for her of his reaction, from, "Whew, it's hot in here!" to reading to me from John 8.

Sister Alice laughed so hard I thought she might fall out of the chair. She couldn't contain herself.

"I can just see him!" She slapped the table with effusive delight. "Hon, do you realize what you've just done?"

"No."

"You've already been to confession, and you're not even Catholic yet."

I don't know how much she knew about *Penthouse*, but she'd taught teenagers in Chicago schools for many years, so I know she was aware of the workings and temptations of the outside world. At any rate, this didn't faze her, and she got the best laugh from it. As we talked, she mentioned going back to her home chapter at St. Mary-of-the-Woods Convent in Terre Haute, Indiana, which she did every couple of months. I decided to ask another favor.

"Do you think I might visit there sometime?"

"Of course you can. Now, hon, I go there for retreat in the summer, so that's not the best time to take a visitor, but the fall is nice. Would you like to go then?"

"I really would."

Having that trip to look forward to in the fall encouraged me through the hot Houston summer of 2001. I was actually feeling quite well, considering all that had happened since my diagnosis in the summer of 1998, and I was intent on squeezing every delicious moment of living out of these "good" days, never knowing what new difficulties might lurk ahead.

Fall arrived, and with it my eagerly awaited visit to St. Mary-of-the-Woods. This was early October 2001, just after the tragedy of September 11, and people asked me if I wasn't afraid to fly.

"Are you kidding me?" I told them. "I'm flying with Sister Alice. She's as close to God as anyone could ever be. If anything happens, there's a good chance that, by association, I'll go where she goes." That usually got a good laugh.

The Sisters of Providence Convent is on the same grounds as St. Mary's College, and the grounds are spectacular, with public tours conducted frequently. Sister Alice made special arrangements for me to stay in Owens Hall, where she stays, not in the visitor house. Her room and mine were exactly the same, with a twin bed, one table and lamp, a small bureau, and a simple cross on the wall above it, nothing else. There was a communal bath down the hall, with dormitory-type showers. The Sisters of Providence numbered around four hundred that year, but only forty or so would be in residence at any one time. Like Sister Alice, they were assigned to provide services to many different parishes and ministries.

The Sisters not only take a vow of poverty in their lifestyle and possessions, but also in the way they nourish their bodies. We each made our own breakfast of toast and jam, coffee or tea, in the kitchen of this little house. Our main meal was served around two o'clock in the dining room, good, healthy food, well prepared, which everybody ate together. During the day, the nuns had duties to perform between prayer times. The convent provides a hospice for older nuns and a medical clinic. It's also a sustainable vegetable farm and — to my surprise — alpaca ranch. In the early evening, a light meal of fruit, cheese, bread, and crackers was laid out. There was a social room at Owens Hall, where the nuns could watch the news. Their work took them out into the world, so they stayed well informed.

None of my friends believed that a convent would ever allow me in or that a nun would be my best friend, or that I would go there and stay in a place that had no amenities whatsoever, but sleeping in that humble room, eating the same simple foods as the nuns ate, going to bed at dark and rising early with them was an indescribable pleasure.

Knowing the nuns had schedules to keep, I generally tried to stay out of the way, even though Sister Alice said I should do whatever I wanted. One morning after my shower, I was having breakfast, and a Sister I hadn't met was there eating at the same time. She welcomed me and told me about her work. It seemed she traveled daily to the Federal Correctional Complex in Terre Haute and ministered to the prisoners. One of them was Timothy McVeigh, the Oklahoma City bomber. She was assigned to him while he was on death row, and she had witnessed his recent execution.

I've thought of that moment often and always wished to know more, but at the time, I wasn't quite sure what to ask. Even a nun must have to cope with tremendous emotional turmoil at such a time, witnessing the death of a man who caused so many deaths.

Walking the grounds daily, I filmed the nuns as they sheared the alpacas or harvested the fields. Some of the older nuns wore habits, a picturesque sight as they walked to and from the convent. Sister Alice and I took a long stroll every afternoon. Then we'd visit Carter Hall, the nursing facility, where I accompanied her as she checked on the nuns being cared for. Just as she did at MDA, she'd stop in to say hello or to bring a moment of cheer or prayer to someone feeling low. I felt honored to be included.

The convent's architecture and artifacts were spectacular, and Sister Alice showed me everything. I went with her to prayers in the various chapels, including Blessed Sacrament chapel, with its lavish Italian décor, and the St. Anne Shell Chapel, in which the ornate interior was created completely of shells carried from the nearby Wabash River.

During our weekend, the Susan G. Komen Race for the Cure took place on the grounds, their pink tent visible at the college about a quarter mile away. Seeing a thousand pink-clad women running by, I felt drawn to walk down to the tent for the closing ceremony.

I couldn't help remembering that long ago first meeting in Aspen with Sandy Goldman Israel and hundreds of women, each trying to find the pea in a simulated breast. Win or lose, the Komen contestants must have enjoyed a fine run that October day on the beautiful grounds of St. Mary's College and St. Mary-of-the-Woods Convent.

And win or lose, I was feeling pretty good about outrunning cancer by two years past my projected "drop-dead" date.

CHAPTER 35

A Year in the Fast Lane

What happens when you outlive the statistics? For me it was a mixed blessing. I couldn't help feeling a bit like Wonder Woman. To survive three open brain surgeries and six tumors without significant brain damage was a feat in itself. To live through the deadly infection Nocardia while still in the throes of cancer was amazing.

Shocking to everyone, including Dr. Slamon at UCLA, was that Herceptin alone had decreased my cancer from the neck down. A gene therapy, Herceptin was approved to be given with chemotherapy. No one expected it would work by itself, and no one trusted my improvement to continue.

Yet they weren't quite sure what to do next. With no protocols to guide us, my treatment remained in a "wait and see" mode for most of 2002.

We like to use the word remission because it makes patients feel good. It reassures their family and friends. I think it helps other patients more than it helps me. Dr. Theriault wanted to call my condition "complete remission on Herceptin therapy," and I'm sure it was deemed great progress in the cancer world, but I wasn't ready to use the word remission, because to me it actually means: You don't have cancer today.

All it takes is one random cell to start it all over again.

If you're talking about ten or twenty years after treatment, then perhaps you just no longer have cancer. Remission is a state of mind, a good word, but one that has never applied to my particular case. In February 2002, however, still in treatment for Stage 4 metastatic breast cancer, I was doing extremely well to have come so far. I was stable. My scans showed no active cancer. Life couldn't get much better.

Turning 50

As women, I think we all have some fear of growing older, whether it's losing our external beauty, sex appeal, youth, or the approach of the dreaded menopausal years. In my world, aging was forbidden. Growing old gracefully was not an option. We would forever remain thirty-nine.

In Aspen, when a new astrologer or numerologist gave readings at a party, you'd have to write down your name and birth date. I'm sure I wasn't the only woman to shave off a few years and receive a reading that didn't apply. I also recall my girlfriends and I, in our early forties, discussing what to do about telling our real age when we had to go to the doctor. One of my friends suggested, "I guess it depends on how sick you are."

One day, the year my nephew Jesse turned five and highly inquisitive, he wanted to know how old I was.

"I'm thirty-nine," I said.

Ever so innocently, he asked, "When will you be forty?"

"Never."

His eyes grew round with disbelief.

"God is not going to make you turn forty?"

"Oh, no," I said. "God would never do that to someone like me."

Jesse bounded down the stairs shouting to my sister, "Mommy, Mommy! God is never going to make Aunt Victoria turn forty!"

Even from the distance I could hear the sarcasm in my sister's response.

"Oh, yeah, and Aunt Victoria is also delusional."

Needless to say, I'd already turned forty and forty-three, but turning fifty was never supposed to happen. After my diagnosis, I expected never to have to worry about growing old gracefully, so turning fifty on March 1, 2002, marked one of the happiest days of my life.

Twelve o'Clock Position

In June, when I went in for my regular ultrasound and mammogram, all the stability was over. For the first time, Herceptin had let me down. Dr. Theriault found a new tumor in my breast in the same place as the original cancer. In July, I saw Dr. Singletary, who'd been scheduled to do a mastectomy before liver metastasis took that option off the table. Now she suggested a mastectomy as again the preferred treatment choice. It would give me the best chance of getting rid of the cancer, she said, although there was no guarantee that taking the breast off would keep the disease from coming back.

Suddenly, I felt as if I'd gone full circle. Four years earlier, I'd come to terms with having a mastectomy, but then that treatment option was considered no longer viable, and I came to terms with the fact that my cancer was too advanced for a mastectomy to make a difference. Now, I'd gone through so much, come so far. Herceptin had come to my rescue, and I was beginning to reclaim my existence, adapting to living in Houston, enjoying my work and, as much as possible, my daily existence. After trying so hard to establish my new life with cancer, considering a mastectomy made me feel as if I were losing all I'd gained. It felt like giving up.

I expressed my reluctance to Dr. Singletary. Knowing that my cancer had not behaved in a way that cancers usually do, that I'd already lived through more than most breast cancer patients, that the new cancer was still quite small, and that I wanted to preserve my body image as long as possible, she gave me a second opinion.

A segmental mastectomy, which is more than a lumpectomy,

much less than mastectomy, would remove the tumor and a small amount of surrounding tissue. Once inside, she might see more cancer than what was apparent on the ultrasound. If it had migrated into the surrounding area, the segmental might become a mastectomy. Dr. Singletary preferred that I sign off on the possibility of a mastectomy before going into surgery.

Another option Dr. Theriault presented was to treat the cancer again with traditional chemotherapy. This was a tough decision for all of us. We assumed from the images that I was now cancer free everywhere except the breast. The disease had started in the breast, metastasized to other organs, and now was in the breast again. Before deciding, I met with Dr. Howard Langstein, a plastic surgeon who felt he could manipulate some tissue from my clavicle are down into my breast at the twelve o'clock position and get a nice result, which would avoid having reconstructive surgery.

After much thought, and based on my history, I decided on the segmental mastectomy, followed by the tissue procedure Dr. Langstein had explained, and thirty treatments of breast radiation. I chose knowing it might not be the best solution, but it was the solution that felt right to me. I also signed off on having a full mastectomy, if necessary.

CHAPTER 36

Beauty and the Beast

As soon as I signed permission for removing my breast, should it come to that, a skeptical part of my brain began dwelling on mammary trivia. Did you know that breast augmentation is such a popular procedure that over 350,000 are done every year in America? Reverend Debra Jarvis wrote in her book, *It's Not About the Hair,* that after losing a breast to cancer she started looking at other women's breasts, wondering which were real, reconstructed, or imported. Sally Struthers, who's best known for her part as Gloria on *All In The Family*, once said, "If a man is pictured chopping off a woman's breast, it only gets an R rating, but if, God forbid, a man is pictured kissing a woman's breast, it gets an X rating." Some guy on a blog philosophized that "it's not about your bra size, it's about your heart size." Clearly, he doesn't wear a bra.

On July 16, 2002, almost four years to the date since an Aspen doctor had said he could "operate on Thursday and remove my breast," Dr. Singletary performed my segmental mastectomy. She wasn't completely sure she'd achieved clean margins. If not, the cancer would grow back eventually. I read between the lines of everyone's opinion, however, that even if she had achieved clean margins, a recurrence in the breast or elsewhere was merely a matter of time.

Would taking the breast off have been better? I don't know, but by the end of July I was "healing nicely" and happy with the result. My left breast was slightly higher than my right breast. Dr. Langstein said that my left breast would drop after the swelling was down and the tissue completely settled. I was actually impressed that two tumors, no matter how small, could be taken out of my ample but not overly large breast and the small amount of tissue around my skinny collar bone could replace it.

Riding It Out

In early August, Dr. Theriault confirmed the high probability that disease would recur in the left breast because of the presence of ductal carcinoma in situ, or DCIS. With DCIS, the cancer cells are confined to milk ducts in the breast and have not spread into the fatty breast tissue or to any other part of the body. In other words, this is the most treatable type of discovery, a good thing, in my opinion.

He discussed chemotherapy again, including Navelbine, but I still wasn't impressed with the data, or lack of data. Even though there seemed to be some evidence that Navelbine and Herceptin worked synergistically, neither of us believed that adding Navelbine to Herceptin at this point would be substantially beneficial. My interpretation was that once again the doctors were stymied. They didn't know for certain that chemotherapy would work. From this I decided to go forward with the radiation.

I also intended to get as much living done as possible before my cancer came back. I flew to Georgia for a visit with my parents, then to Aspen, where I celebrated the success of this most recent surgery with all my friends. Once again, my doctors and I had bitch-slapped the beast into submission. Life was good.

In September, I met with radiologist Dr. Marsha McNeese. When radiation commenced in October, the plan was to treat the left breast, including a "boost," which I assumed meant an extra burst of radiation, to the tumor bed. But still, every visit to Dr. Theriault included a discussion about adding a chemotherapy drug to Herceptin, usually Navelbine. I was still hesitant, because Herceptin seemed to be working, at least from the neck down. Yes, the breast cancer had returned, but would it have come back much earlier if not for Herceptin? No one could say.

In the fall, I flew to LA to see Dr. Slamon again, my first time back since that initial visit. As much faith as he had in Herceptin, and my success, and the positive research that continued to pour in, he too recommended adding a chemotherapy to it. He suggested Taxotere and Carboplatin. Research also indicated that Herceptin, which had been in use now for four years, could be taken every three weeks instead of weekly, with the same expected results. This was excellent news for cancer patients, especially those who don't live as close as I do to a treatment center. As much as I liked the thought of having treatments less often, I needed time to consider it and for the three-week cycle to prove itself.

Knowledge is a great thing, but sometimes there's simply no data to draw on. While there was no clear indication that the gene therapy, Herceptin, had completely stopped working, there also was no certainty that it wouldn't stop working in the future. Naturally, I wondered how long this could last, but I had faith in Herceptin, and it didn't take me down like traditional chemotherapy, which could steal all the life out of living. I'd done that, survived it, and I could go there again if necessary, but meanwhile, I focused on enjoying life in 2002.

My ultrasound showed no new cancer as I approached the holidays, and I had at least six weeks before another scan. Deciding to spend Christmas in Georgia, I put off dealing with decisions until the New Year.

Glow

A sad discovery I made during 2002 and 2003 was that all my cancer acquaintances were dying. Patients on the same appointment schedule often run into each other, and in the early days of what is usually a brief and sporadic but heartfelt relationship, we'd strike up conversations, compare notes, exchange emails. Everyone wants to talk in the beginning. I realized I'd seen many new patients come and go. They'd disappear and I'd learn they didn't make it. That's hard to deal with on a continual basis. I can't imagine how hard it must be for the doctors, to try so hard to save every patient yet see so many patients die, regardless. The MDA doctors I've met truly care about their patients.

Often, the patients who vanished seemed to have a less serious cancer than Stage 4, like mine, yet here I was going along doing crazy things to improve my lifestyle. I began to wonder *why me?* Why was I making it when others didn't?

Even sadder was to lose my close friends. Diane, my friend and neighbor from across the street, died of complications from diabetes. Terry, my upstairs neighbor in Aspen, died from melanoma. I continued receiving the *Aspen Times*, and too often I read about another person I knew, diagnosed after I was diagnosed yet dying while I still lived.

Go For It

In early 2003, it became apparent to me that my breasts were neither the same size nor symmetrical. Breast radiation had destroyed the tissue and the nice work Dr. Langstein had done. An insignificant issue in the scope of cancer, but I was otherwise doing well, with no recurrence. I wanted my life back. So I told Dr. Langstein I wanted breast implants.

He looked at me as if I'd lost my mind. He must have wanted to say, *Are you crazy? Girl, you have Stage 4 breast cancer. What are you thinking?* But he said it much more tactfully. "Victoria, I'm not sure you fully realize the extent of what you're considering."

"I know they're not going to save my life or do anything medically for me," I said. "I don't want huge breasts. I just want them to look their best for my fifty-one years. I know I'm very lucky, but they don't look good anymore. Make them even and symmetrical."

His surprise and alarm gave way to a discreet smile.

"I could do that," he said. "I could do a beautiful job. But I don't recommend it, Victoria."

"How long have you known me? And consulted with my other doctors? You were there when I accepted having the least amount done with hope of having an excellent result, and it worked. But now it doesn't work anymore. If I look good, I'm going to feel better, have less stress about getting dressed, shopping for clothes or buying a bra. I don't know how long I've got, but if I get one year, looking great and feeling great, it will be more than I have now."

"It would not be an easy surgery. Having those little tumors removed was minor in comparison, yet that was not easy."

"Nothing has been easy since the day I was diagnosed," I argued.

There's an unspoken philosophy at MDA that whatever makes you feel better or feel better about yourself is a good thing. Dr. Langstein said if I wanted the surgery, he'd do it.

CHAPTER 37

Precious Years

In those early months, every scan taken during my checkups seemed to show a little something that needed further imaging. Then it would turn out to be insignificant. This happened frequently enough that I sensed I should pay attention. Maybe it was nothing now, but was it only a matter of time before *nothing* turned to something?

My February examination revealed that I'd healed nicely from the recent breast surgery, however, and had "No Complaints" about the breast augmentation. I was over the immediate effects of radiation, had no new brain tumors, no serious treatments to drag me down in the past several months, and I was now taking Herceptin every three weeks instead of weekly.

I posed to Dr. Theriault that I imagined it would be harder for an individual in their twenties or thirties — even fifties — to face a terminal prognosis than for someone who'd lived a full life to their seventies or eighties. He said, "No, it's actually the opposite. It's harder for people who've lived longer to handle the prospect of dying."

After rethinking it, I began to understand why. The longer we live, the more we know about life, the more connections we have to cherish, and the more we have on our list of things to do before we die. It's natural to want to hang onto those final precious years — or days.

To that effect, sensing that these insignificant findings on my scans might develop into something I'd have to deal with later, I decided to make the best of my time until that happened. Whatever I wanted to do with the rest of my life, big things, little things, I'd better do them now, while I had energy and was feeling relatively well.

A note on my constantly updated "Cancer Advice List" reads: Give your friends and family members as much attention as possible — compliments, shared memories, great moments. Let them know what they've contributed to your life. Not only does it keep you distracted from the miseries of your disease, it tells them their life meant something, that they made a difference in this world, left a mark that was noticed.

So that's exactly what I did. I hit the road traveling as often as possible, seeing all the people I cared about.

The Other Bob

I decided I would make every attempt to see Bob Guccione. At a time in my life when I was searching for direction, Bob had opened doors to a future I'd never imagined. Whether or not it was the most sensible choice, my years with *Penthouse* provided not only an exhilarating journey but also a portal through which I entered other adventures, experiencing life in all its best and worst variations.

Having heard about the difficulties Bob was having, the financial collapse and sale of *Penthouse*, the loss of his personal wealth, and his losing Kathy to cancer a year before my diagnosis, I felt the time had come to retie our connection. After Kathy's death, I'd written Bob a long condolence letter. She was his companion and closest friend long before they married. He depended so much on Kathy; I couldn't imagine him managing his life without her. Worst of all, Bob now had cancer, too.

After I was diagnosed, I'd sent Bob the first letter I wrote to all my friends. He'd responded with a phone call. His voice at that time was much raspier than I remembered. I didn't know the extent of his cancer, but I'd heard that a lump was removed from his throat. I learned later that he'd taken radiation treatments yet had chosen not to have chemotherapy. Bob believed in alternative medicines, as did Kathy, and his conspiracy-alert viewpoint of life, which many people share, extended to the Food and Drug Administration. Knowing what I'd gone through and imagining what Bob must have gone through after being diagnosed, I think we were both concerned about seeing each other. How had life and disease distorted the images we held in our minds?

I told Jane, still his executive assistant, about the dates I'd be in New York and where I'd be staying. Quickly, I received a call back.

"Bob wants to know if you'd like to stay at the house."

Those words were so familiar that a wave of nostalgia gathered me up and replaced my trepidation with longing for days past. I was also interested to meet April, his current companion.

"Really?" I was delighted, even while a whispered admonition raced through my mind: *You can never go home again.*

"I must warn you that Bob cannot speak well, which is why he rarely sees anyone anymore. I can understand him, April and the staff can, those closest to him. And he probably won't come to dinner, but we still have a small staff, and they'll make dinner for you every night. Bob wants you to know that he'd like you to be here."

In that stirring moment, I lost all the caution with which I'd approached Jane about this meeting. Bob and I had shared many glorious years. Whatever had transpired for each of us since our last encounter could not erase those years. As I packed and prepared for the trip, anxiously awaiting the day, my mind wandered through a decade of happy, engrossing memories.

The Shadow of a House

Met by the five Rhodesian Ridgebacks pounding down the stairway, I might have been walking into 1976, except that neither

Guy nor Dell, Bob's long-time assistants, was waiting in the big downstairs entry. Guy had died and Dell had moved on.

The home office was still located in the same place. Jane was there, as she'd always been. She said they'd made up my old room on the fifth floor for me, just above Bob's suite, where I'd always stayed when I visited. Everything felt familiar, yet not quite the same.

The grandeur and energy and excitement were gone. The constantly ringing phones of the past were quiet. The staff was a skeleton of what it had once been. The few enormous antiques that remained seemed dwarfed by the vastness of the house. And his beautiful art collection had vanished, leaving only shadows on walls once graced by Picassos, Soutines, and Chagalls. The paintings that did remain seemed oddly familiar, and I realized they were Bob's own work. He'd never displayed them before that I could recall. They were vibrant and sensual, yet not at all sexual, and were reflective of his favorite modern Expressionists.

I recalled a TV interview we'd filmed that had taken place in front of one of his favorite pieces, a Degas, I think, when Bob instructed me to pull my hair up in a certain way. Only later did I realize, seeing the interview on television, that he'd positioned me just so, replicating the image in the painting, in which a woman was putting her hair up. That moment was so representative of his style of creating photography and art, a blend of the two mediums. Such a simple technique, yet it created a lovely, imaginative interview unlike the bland, almost barren settings we usually see.

The thing that actually saddened me as I strolled through the somewhat tattered house that had formerly stood so grand and had accommodated so many gatherings of famous personalities was the absence of Bob's personal aura. No matter how powerful or celebrated his guests, Bob's persona had reigned. His individuality had permeated the structure and furnishings, invigorated the staff, and infused the atmosphere with mysterious sensuality. A house is a house, but seeing someone you've loved lose so much of himself is heartwrenching.

Jane had told me I probably wouldn't see Bob at dinner, that he'd probably visit with me privately, but April phoned my room shortly after my arrival and said she'd join me for dinner. I was glad to have the opportunity to meet the woman who was now such an important part of Bob's life. Then Jane called upstairs as I was dressing to go down.

"Good news," she said. "Bob wants to join you, after all. He won't eat, he can't, but he'll be there."

As we all get older, if we love each other, we don't really see the years. Bob looked like Bob, a little worn around the edges, but so was I.

April, petite, blonde, and attractive, sat in Kathy's old place at the table, and I in mine. Bob wasn't shy or embarrassed about trying to talk. He could speak in a very soft tone, with difficulty, but I could understand him for the most part, and when I couldn't, April was great at popping in with "He said…" and then we'd continue our conversation.

He must have strength of steel, I thought, to sit watching us gorge ourselves on his famous homemade spaghetti and other incredible foods that he no longer could enjoy. With a feeding tube, he took in only liquid nourishment. Considering the lung and throat cancer he was fighting, to look as good as he did and still have the muscle tone he had in 2004 was amazing.

As it turned out, Bob came down for dinner every night I was there. One Sunday afternoon, I was in my room and he called to say that a couple I knew, not family but close enough to be family, were coming over, and he'd like me to come and join them. I thought this was great, not only because I looked forward to dinner with old friends but because it indicated to me that Bob was, like me, determined to live the life remaining to him.

Throughout those few days, Bob and I did a lot of talking. I told him about my cancer. He'd ask questions, provoke memories. On the last night at dinner, I said, "Do you mind if I take photos?"

He didn't, so I snapped a few, then Jane took some of all of us together. I was about to take the camera again when she said, "Let me take one of you and Bob together."

Only after I'd returned home and developed the prints did I see how easily Bob and I had resumed our former closeness. And in that final photograph, we'd unconsciously assumed the same pose as the one he took of us for my Pet of the Year photo layout almost three decades earlier.

Familiar Friends

Heartened and exhilarated by my visit with Bob and everyone in the Guccione household, I reconnected with my friend Jeff Zelmanski while I was in New York. It was like we'd never parted. Over lunch, we chatted about the magazine, where it was now compared with the glitzy, glamorous *Penthouse* we'd known and loved. No one except Dottie Meyer, who was Pet of the Year right after me, and a few other executives we knew were still employed there and making the transition from old management to new.

The next day, Dottie and I had lunch, and after catching up on old times, I finally worked up the courage to ask a question I'd harbored over the years. When the moment seemed right, the question popped out.

"Did you know that while I was at the magazine, Bob and I were in a very close relationship for many years?" I'd never told anyone. I don't know why I felt the need to reveal it now, except that I had cancer and was feeling the nostalgia of visiting with Bob, and the loss of a treasured and unforgettable time in my life. I just needed to talk to someone who'd been with me at the magazine and had shared a similar experience.

"Well, of course I did. Everybody did, at least everybody in Bob's world that mattered. We all thought you'd replace Kathy."

I was shocked. I'd thought we were so discreet. That's when I realized I'd never taken the relationship seriously enough to consider spending my life with Bob. It felt great to know now that had we decided to go further with our relationship back then, I'd have had support.

Things have a way of working out as they're meant to, I believe. This trip certainly did.

Thank You for a Lifetime

The future is so unpredictable. Only a few years after I took this trip, on October 20, 2010, Bob Guccione passed away. It hit me harder than I expected. Even though the end was inevitable, what a shock to see it on the evening news. By then, he and April had moved to Plano, Texas, where she had family and could better care for him during those final days. He was so close, just a short flight, and I'd hoped to see him one more time.

A multidimensional and multitalented individual, Bob was always bigger than life. The press never quite understood "all" of him. I don't believe anyone did. I know that he contributed to the woman I became. That same day, I posted a message: *For Bob Guccione ... When I walked into your townhouse on that afternoon in June 1976, and you came down that massive staircase, I knew you would change my life forever. And you did. I am grateful for every moment. You were my friend and mentor. I will miss you deeply. My heart is with you and your family. Thank you for a lifetime of opportunities, experiences, and memories. Today is a sad day for those of us who really knew and loved you. My heart goes out to the Guccione family.*

His daughter, Nina Guccione, responded: *You know he loved you so much!*

Bob's cancer didn't change who he was. It could not extinguish his spirit, his essence. On our last day together, he was still a man of vision who could look at you and make you instantly trust in him. Our relationship was encapsulated in an impenetrable place in our hearts. When Bob and I were together, no one else existed. He made me a part of his family, made me an international cover girl, and cooked me pasta. He will be forever in my heart.

A Cancer Moment

In August, feeling refreshed and cheerful from my months off, I went in for all my usual scans. My suspicion of the "nothings" turning to "something" proved prophetic, as the scans showed a new mass in my left breast.

Despite my early prescience, disappointment hit as hard as it had six years earlier, possibly because I was coming from the magnificent highs of seeing all my friends to this harsh reality, like crash landing from a sky dive.

There was a fine line, Dr. Therault told me, between attacking the new cancer aggressively and trying to knock it out or going at it less forcefully with a drug that's less harsh but will provide a better quality of life. It wasn't as if I hadn't heard this all before, but now we were farther along by six years. I'd lived through the worst chemotherapies, yet the cancer had not gone away. It simply skulked back there in the shadows waiting for the most devastating moment to pounce.

After all considerations, I decided to take Xeloda, which is the pill form of the chemotherapy Capecitabine, to get the cancer under control again and buy some time. I also continued to take Herceptin, even though it had stopped working. My faith in it held, and I hoped it would kick in again.

This chemotherapy didn't take me down to the ground, as FAC had done, but it was unrelenting. There were no "good" days, when I felt well enough to participate in favorite pastimes. I suffered some sort of chemo-related misery daily.

Before the segmental mastectomy in 2002, I'd agreed that if the cancer came back, Dr. Singletary would do the mastectomy. Some women would have said, "Just take off both breasts, in case it comes into the other," and I completely understand that way of thinking, but it had not been mine, and in many ways, I was much more prepared for it now than I'd ever been.

Because of the metastases, my doctors had also believed, although they didn't say it quite so callously as I am, that I would never have the opportunity for a mastectomy because my cancer would never be under control enough. Death was a more likely prognosis.

But now, I'd survived several years, multiple brain surgeries, the segmental mastectomy, and through it all I'd been able to maintain my body image. What a great fight. After picking myself off the floor and out of my instant emotional collapse, I considered this new diagnosis in two ways: 1) I'd lived long enough, and my cancer had become stable enough, to have the mastectomy, and I'd lived six years longer than I expected without losing my body image; and, 2) because of the way my cancer had originally presented, and because of my progress over six years, taking the breast off completely now, with no tissue for it to migrate to, might actually take the cancer.

Although I wasn't happy about doing the mastectomy, I'd enjoyed my cancer "moment" during the early months of 2004, feeling great and looking more like my pre-cancer self than anyone could imagine as I flew from coast to coast visiting family and friends. I believe that's why my doctors' terrible news didn't devastate me as much as it might have. At this point in battling the beast, losing my breast offered the greatest possibility of a cure. It was finally and definitely the right thing to do.

CHAPTER 38

Latissimus Dorsi

Thanks to *Penthouse* and my ten daring years with the magazine's explicit exposure and frank scrutiny of my body — which side is better, which breast is better, where should we aim the light—it became second nature to talk about how to make my body look best for the camera, just as you'd angle a product in the best direction. Those years gave me the boldness and confidence to discuss at length the process of mastectomy and breast reconstruction, but as prepared as I thought I was to accept this, is any woman ever prepared at that moment?

A Risky Decision

The way I understood the problem was this: The amount of tissue Dr. Singletary would be removing from the breast area would leave none to work with. Many times, surgeons do a procedure called skin-sparing surgery, but that wasn't my case. Everything had to be removed.

Usually, transplant tissue is harvested from the abdomen. If Dr. Langstein made an incision at the lower part of my abdomen to extract transplant tissue, because of my short waist and too-flat stomach, by the time he pulled the skin down again and sutured it, I'd end up with my belly button peeking out of my pubic hair.

After an MRI, Dr. McCutcheon found "no sign of residual or recurrent tumor" in my brain and cleared me for surgery. Dr. Theriault found a new lesion, but it was confined in the breast, with no metastases. With so many warnings, this was a bold decision to make, but I felt they were missing the point. Nothing we did was going to change the fact that I had Stage 4 breast cancer. With or without the reconstruction surgery, the disease was likely to come back eventually, and the treatment would be the same. And either way, I had extensive recovery time ahead. My thought, as before, was: whether I have three more months to live or three more years, I want to preserve my quality of life and self-image as much as possible. I clearly was aware that my reconstructed breast would never mirror my real breast, but it would provide volume and I would at least be able to wear most of my usual clothing.

Dr. Singletary scheduled me for a "left breast modified radical mastectomy." Following our lengthy discussion about the risks to me, and to the entire surgical team, Dr. Langstein agreed to do the reconstruction at the same time.

Mom flew to Houston for the surgery. I didn't want anyone else around this time, and I didn't tell her the extent of the risk involved. If I explained what Dr. Langstein had told me, Mom would say, "You always make good decisions, Victoria." Then she'd worry.

Before the surgery, Dr. Langstein had to mark the areas of my body that would be incised. He took photographs of my entire torso and abdomen, to guide him in creating a breast on my left side that would match the one on my right, and to get the correct alignment and symmetry. Then using red and blue markers he created an extensive array of lines and arrows on my breasts and body in a code that he and Dr. Singletary understood, MDA's version of body makeup. I lay quietly, knowing he was concentrating on making each mark just so. When he carefully took a second set of photos, I couldn't help wondering just how these would be used in the operating room. A big overhead monitor would no doubt display my nude breasts, still the center of attention, as they'd always been.

Both doctors performed their parts with excellence, and after enduring a painful five days, I was released on February 27 with drains coming out of my side from the breast area, drains coming out of my back, and a bag attached to my waist to catch the fluid. One of my more descriptive family members, who visited a week or so later when I was able to laugh about it, said I looked like a portable Kool-Aid dispenser. But that first day out, I saw no humor in my situation. My hospital stay had been miserable, and now that I was at home, I felt and smelled like road kill. So I bandaged myself in plastic and duct tape, as I'd been instructed, and sat on my shower floor, letting the spray gently pummel me until the hospital stench was finally gone and all the hot water had run out.

Mom stayed to help me with wound care. Difficult and painful, the cleaning had to be done precisely. She knew how serious it was, and there was no way I could do it myself. I should have brought in a nurse, but I didn't realize that at the time.

Our instructions were to clean the drainage ports by starting at the wound and wiping with a sterilized pad outward in a circular motion. Mom and I, in the close quarters of my bathroom, were both new at this. Sore all over, I held my arm back so she could work.

Then she made a mistake, and I lost my temper.

"Mom, I just told you, you can't do that!"

She was trying so hard, but she kept making mistakes. In the end, I had to do it myself. I realized something was not right, and for the first time saw my mother's decline. She'd been so stoic and helpful during these many years of my disease. The change in her was startling.

Looking back now, I realize that if cancer can have an upside, it was the chance to spend these years with my mom, sharing quality time as mother-daughter, adults and equals, so different from times we shared when I was young. That's why I kept bringing her out so often. I could have called on friends to fly in or hired nurses, but it was always nice to have my mom there. As it turned out, this was her last trip to Texas to help me, although I still brought her out to visit. Even that soon become too arduous.

The Good Stuff

Despite being a physically difficult year of painful ordeals, 2005 in many ways was a year of triumph. The culmination of two spectacular events contributed to that perception.

Several months earlier, CNN had filmed a presentation at MDA, interviewing dozens of individuals, from Dr. Mendohlson and other faculty to nurses, clergy, staff, caregivers, volunteers, and patients, including me. Each patient received the same three questions to answer, and, of course, our answers varied broadly. When *Taming the Beast: Inside the War on Cancer*, hosted by Dr. Sanjay Gupta, premiered in August 2005, I was happy to see their "first-hand stories of cancer patients beating the odds" included two portions of my interview, and a maxim that has become my personal tag line: "It's time to use the good china!"

China, to me, meant special occasions. What better time to use the good china than now, when I might be living my last special occasions? From that day on, it became my tag line, and I was thrilled to see that Dr. Singletary and CNN had chosen to use that quote.

A Big Grown-Up Decision

This year of extremely difficult treatment and two major surgeries accomplished what my doctors and I had hoped but caused more pain and associated side effects than I'd ever had. It also left me with important new challenges. For me to go forward in my life mentally, physically, emotionally, even sexually, I had to figure out how to come to terms with personal relationships. With the important people in my life, I chose to deal honestly and completely. Imperfections that would have mattered in earlier years no longer held the same level of significance.

One of my most devastating childhood experiences occurred in first grade. Because I was out sick with a cold for five days, I missed the announcement for Picture Day. On Monday, my first day back, all the other kids were dressed their best, and the teachers lined us up to take turns in front of the camera. My dress looked fine but was not the one I would have chosen if I'd known a photographer was coming. When my picture arrived, not only was I not wearing my favorite dress, I looked sad and confused, because I hadn't known what was going on, and worst of all, my bangs were jagged. Mom had missed a piece when she cut them. My curly ponytail didn't show at all in the straight-on headshot, drawing even more attention to the imperfect bangs. First year of school, my first official school picture for everyone to see, and I wasn't perfect.

My parents bought the whole package, so the photo pops up periodically to haunt me. In my view, I wasn't even pretty. I never got over the devastating feelings I associate with that photograph, and perhaps needing to be perfect drove me to many of my lifelong decisions.

After my mastectomy, perfection was no longer possible. My breasts had in some way ruled my life since my teen years, when at sweet sixteen I won the Miss Perfect Figure contest at Lake Spivey, but life had changed all that. I was now wearing my latissimus dorsi — my lat muscle — in my chest instead of my back. How strange it felt. I decided that whatever intimacy I might or might not have in the future would not be based on how my body looked.

Not long after I was diagnosed and started on chemotherapy,

a friend came to me and, in her slow, Deep South accent, said, "I have someone I want you to meet. He's got a lot of money, Victoria, and he can help you get through this. But you can't tell him you have cancer; it might scare him away."

"Ohh-kay ... so what should I say? That I have a severe case of alopecia or that I choose to be bald to make a bold statement?"

"Oh, wear a wig, silly."

"So ... we're making love," I said, picturing it and honestly trying not to laugh. "I throw my head back in passion, my hair falls to the pillow, slides off and drops to the floor. Don't you think it might kill the moment?"

Botoxed forehead perfectly smooth, her lips pursed in confusion.

"I guess you'll have to tape it on," she said. "You know, like a toupee?"

"I can do that. But since I'm on chemo for the next eight months, there's a good chance I'll throw up on him. What should I say? Bulimia?"

"You'll think of something. You always do."

The truth is, the men I chose to be in my life never said or did anything to suggest they noticed that my chemo-surgery-radiation-battered body was less than perfect. But when you've done your utmost to achieve perfection your entire life, it's hard to stop. Before any intimacy, I had to be comfortable enough to know that revealing my slightly lopsided breasts wouldn't make a difference. And if a relationship didn't work out, that wouldn't destroy me, because the people who truly mattered were already in my life, and there were many considerations more important now than just sex.

This was a big grownup decision for me, yet one that did not come with as much angst as I would have imagined several years earlier. I felt fortunate for having a long adjustment period — of living with cancer and still having my breasts — to come to this decision. Regardless of how my relationships might change, not the people but the dynamics, my new relationship with myself was going to take priority. The word "pretty" was going to be redefined in my life.

CHAPTER 39

Heart to Heart

S unday is my day to dance with God. I speak to as few people as possible, don't take phone calls or answer email or the doorbell.

Instead, I do the many silly, crazy, goofy, completely unnecessary things that create a day of festivity. I turn on the Christian Country Rock station, turn it up as loud as it goes — until the neighbors start complaining — then dance, prance, sing, pretend I'm the dancer-singer I envisioned on stage so long ago, rocking and rolling with my band, shaking the cancer and lymphedema right out of my body as I swing around in a rockin' two-step.

The glory of it is that 2005 drew to a close and I was still singing and dancing with God in my seventh year of cancer. Life was good.

Another Day, Another Test

I'd learned over the years that many of the warnings my physicians issued were CYA (cover your ass) discussions. They hadn't wanted to do the reconstruction because I might get an infection, or if the cancer came back, it would be difficult to treat. Having no statistics for where I was now in fighting my disease, they always advised proceeding with caution.

"You're doing the best of any patient I know with your circumstances," Dr. Theriault boasted when I went in for my January appointment. "Jump on the table and let me give you a quick checkup."

This time, he found a lump high above my left breast. An ultrasound confirmed "evidence of recurrent disease with a subpectoral lymph node." The mastectomy had not achieved what we'd hoped.

By now, the cancer had returned often enough that it came as no huge shock, but it was overwhelmingly disappointing for me and my team. The good news: my brain was still cancer free. Having been off all treatment for a few months, I felt great and didn't want to return to the daily misery that came with the harsh chemicals, so after a heart scan came back clear, I asked to go back on Herceptin as a single-agent therapy, hoping it would work. Dr. Theriault agreed to try it for a short while, so after an initial loading dose, I resumed Herceptin treatment every three weeks. Within three months, the disease in my subpectoral lymph node had decreased in size and showed no metabolic activity. My miracle drug was performing its magic once again.

Yes, I have osteoporosis and there's talk of needing granny glasses with bifocal lenses — the changes you expect with aging occur faster when you have cancer and seven years of cancer therapy — but I continued to dance with God as 2006 progressed from spring to summer.

Calendar Guys

Every day is an adventure. How will I feel? Until I'm up and around, I simply don't know. Once I have that first cup of coffee, I can usually tell.

If my bad days start crowding together, I'll bargain with myself. "One more day you can wait it out, but if you wake up feeling like this tomorrow, you go to the hospital," or, "By three p.m., you're either better and going to the grocery store or you're going to the ER."

On a day in October, after battling an upper respiratory infection for nearly a week, I walked into the kitchen feeling slightly lightheaded. Fortunately, this was my cleaning lady's one-day-a-week to be there. She came in while I was making coffee.

"Are you okay?" she asked.

"I think so. Just a little nauseous."

I went to the bathroom and she went upstairs. When I opened the bathroom door to come out, she was coming downstairs again, and the last thing I remember is the horror in her face as she looked at me.

She broke my fall. I learned later that I was headed right for the corner of the table.

In and out of consciousness, I heard her screaming into the phone in Spanish, and the next thing I knew I was on the sofa, propped up on pillows, surrounded by policemen and firemen in uniform, all looking down at me.

"I know you," I said groggily. "You're the calendar guys."

"Can you tell us your name?" someone asked.

I must have answered correctly, because they continued asking questions — did I know my address, where I was, my birthday... They lifted me from sofa to stretcher and rolled me out to a waiting ambulance. All the while, I kept thinking what a handsome bunch of young men they were, and all we needed was a photographer to create an instant calendar.

Outside, my whole neighborhood had come to watch, and I soon realized why. Besides the ambulance, there were two huge fire trucks and a police car — for one woman who fainted. I wondered what my housekeeper had said in Spanish to bring out such an impressive, not to mention sexy, battalion of rescuers. It must have been a slow day for emergencies.

During an overnight stay at the hospital, with extensive tests, the doctors analyzed my blackout as a vasovagal syncope episode, which basically means fainting. Because of the high possibility of heart problems associated with Herceptin, they scheduled a follow-up test, which I passed with flying colors.

The New Miracle

Shortly after this episode, a friend emailed me with news about a therapy just approved by the FDA, a drug called Tykerb, which seemed tailor-made for my situation.

This triumphant news softened the less than gleeful information I received the following day when I went in for my regularly scheduled ultrasound. The minute the wand touched my breast, I knew, and the reaction of the technician's eyes confirmed it: A new spot, in the same place as the last one.

Outside, a tropical storm raged. I navigated Houston's flooded streets back to my townhome and went straight to the bedroom. My housekeeper had put the mail on my bedside table, and lying on top was my weekly *Aspen Times*, with the headline, "This Business of Dying." I was so depressed I wouldn't even drink water so I didn't have to get out of bed to pee.

The next day, I went to see Dr. Theriault carrying a copy of the report on Tykerb. The discovery seemed like another miracle. Tykerb was said to be "effective for women whose disease has progressed on previous therapies." The drugs named were the same drugs I'd taken, including Herceptin. Dr. Theriault started me right away on a combination of Tykerb and Xeloda.

Unfortunately, I didn't tolerate the drugs well. They caused severe diarrhea, extreme cramping, weakness, nausea, mouth sores, and complete inability to function. I often felt I was going to pass out. Determined to make it work, I researched Tykerb and the concept of layering, and learned that Tykerb could be given in a lesser dose than I was taking.

Naturally, I presented Dr. Theriault with this information. I reminded him that everyone thought Herceptin wouldn't work without the inclusion of a traditional chemotherapy, but it had worked for me as a single agent. Because of the toxic side effects, I knew I couldn't take the Tykerb-Xeloda cocktail at the current dosage for twenty-one days, as prescribed.

Dr. Singletary assessed whether the lesion might be treated with radiation and determined it could have necrotic effects on any previously radiated areas, necrotic meaning "dead tissue." Radiation, therefore, was not a viable alternative.

Dr. Theriault agreed to lower the Tykerb-Xeloda dosage, and somehow I managed to continue the cycles until July, when I gave myself a break from chemotherapy to speak for another event.

I Will Survive!

At the MD Anderson annual symposium in Aspen, which that year was titled, "The End of Cancer As We Know It," I was asked to speak on the same panel as Dr. John Mendelsohn and four other notable doctors in the field of cancer treatment. I couldn't help feeling intimidated and a little frightened.

Yet as each brilliant speech followed another, my confidence plummeted. Further intimidation came as I was introduced by Dr. Mendelsohn. Not only one of the most influential men in cancer history — credited with discovering Erbitux, a new and effective form of treatment for several types of cancer — he was also president of a world-renowned hospital as well as the most powerful, well known and well liked man at MD Anderson.

When my turn came to follow these illustrious physicians at the lectern, the only thing I could think to say at first was, "What an honor it is to stand on this platform where the MD Anderson doctors have stood just before me, a hospital that has done so much for cancer and for me, and speak on their behalf to my beloved friends in Aspen who have encouraged and supported me through all these years ... Thank you from the bottom of my heart."

Between "What an honor" and "Thank you," I managed to speak for twenty-seven minutes. Having given this whole period of disease and treatment a great deal of thought, I delivered a heartfelt presentation. I told my story and also talked about being a patient at MD Anderson, mentioning the hospital's many "amenities."

Then I said, "A question I've been asked many times in many ways is, 'How have you survived so long when others haven't?' People think I have some sort of secret, but I don't. What I do have is a great hospital and great doctors, good intuition regarding research, the ability to absorb all my research, which I thought I could never do — yet I believe everyone in this audience can also do given the same set of circumstances. I had the grace of God and plain good luck. I also had a 'balls-to-the-wall' attitude. My closing to you is, 'We are strong, we are spirited, and we will--"

On my last word, I pointed to the sound man, and the room blasted with Gloria Gaynor's "I Will Survive." The audience joined in singing, shouting, laughing, and the presentation ended on another very special uplifting, heart-touching moment.

CHAPTER 40

Three More Months

I've had three months to live for so many years now. The period between tests or scans ranges from six weeks to three months — or when things are really looking up, six months — depending on where I am in my ongoing cancer treatment at any given time. When I hear the news that a PET scan or MRI of the brain is clear and stable, I know I have three months to live.

Not three months to die, but three months to *really* live, to enjoy life without a cloud of the unknown looming. I can put cancer aside for three more months.

It took me a long time to do that, to resist being constantly consumed with every new emerging piece of news, every bit of information I could decipher from my never-ending medical records. Eventually, I stopped trying to absorb and comprehend medical data so that I knew more than my doctors (ha). I still stay on top of new treatments and trials, but I've developed a level of trust with my doctors.

Now, I'm seeking balance. I'm living life to the best quality I can muster.

On returning to Houston from Aspen, I enjoyed a few days of basking in the glow of my success as a speaker and contemplating how I might repurpose that energy into written form. I tend to do best using an outline and speaking more or less extemporaneously for brief periods, or writing short pieces sparked by an emotional provocation. With my energy at a peak, from my exhilarating visit to Aspen as well as my two weeks free of chemo-torture, I looked forward to moving past my upcoming hospital appointments and making great headway on my book.

A Good Patient

Looking back, I see 2007 as a difficult year, a Tykerb year with, thankfully, a few bright spots woven in. My cancer seemed to weave recurring patterns in the carpet of my life, coming back to reweave the same spot over and over.

I talked with Dr. Theriault at length about my reluctance to continue Tykerb-Xeloda therapy after completing the cycle on July 15th. My most recent labs revealed that my blood cell count was okay, and an ultrasound showed only three tiny nodes remaining in the clavicular area.

"Your disease is substantially improved," he said during our forty-five-minute discussion. "Why would you stop taking the treatment now, just when it's working?"

"I have no life when I'm on those drugs. I exist between bouts of nausea despite the Zofran, diarrhea despite Imodium. I have chemo-related hot flashes and night sweats. I need to take back my life, if only for a while."

"What does that mean? A week? Two weeks?"

I shrugged, which is not my usual response, but I really couldn't answer his question. I realize now that I was procrastinating, buying time to enjoy living.

"You have two options," Dr. Theriault said after thinking about it for a moment. "You can continue on Tykerb-Xeloda, complete the median period of four-and-a-half months, and see if we can reach full remission, then continue on Tykerb alone, which is not likely to maintain a remission — or you can stop, wait, and watch."

His expression told me this was the wrong choice, but I said, "I'm going to take that gamble."

Dr. Theriault smiled slightly and nodded, although I knew he was disappointed with my decision. I wasn't behaving like a good patient, but he respected my reasoning. I was just so damned tired of fighting.

"What are you going to do with this hiatus?" he asked.

"I plan to travel, but I'll come home for my medical appointments. While I'm away, I'll have the mental and physical respite I need to make the next decision."

"You know, Victoria, a two-month break is okay. But if the disease progresses, we'll have to try something."

Progression

Scans and tests tend to be clustered to make the most of my time and my doctors' time in reviewing them, so early August presented me with two very long, hot days at MDA. The first day included an MRI of the brain, which was always the case for my appointments with Dr. McCutcheon. The next day when I was scheduled to see him, every one of my scans ran late.

I quickly saw that I'd never make our two-thirty appointment and instructed each of the various departments to call his office and tell them I was still in bone scan or heart scan, to keep them posted. Around five-thirty, I finished but still hadn't seen Dr. McCutcheon, and his staff usually starts leaving by five p.m.

Taking a bottle of water, I walked out on the patio and sat down to call his nurse.

"I missed our appointment," I said. "Is he even still there?"

"Yes, he's still here."

"It's so late. I'm exhausted, and I don't want him to wait any longer. Let's just call it a day. I know he'll call if there's anything we need to talk about on the MRI."

"Are you sure you don't want to come in? I know he'll be glad to see you."

My brain scans had been showing up clean for seven years, so he had recently lengthened the interval between appointments to six months. I always enjoyed my esoteric chats with Dr. McCutcheon when we didn't have important medical issues to discuss, but that day I just wanted to go home.

"We've been doing this for so long now," I said. "And I'm sure he's had a long day, as well. We don't have anything to talk about except whether the scan was clean or not. If it wasn't, I know he'll call me."

She agreed to pass along the information. We disconnected, and I started gathering my things, when my cell phone rang. The caller ID told me it was Dr. McCutcheon.

I took a deep breath and sat down again before answering.

"Hello," I said, as brightly as I could muster. "So… I guess there's a problem."

"Yes," he said, "I'm afraid there is."

"Is it operable?"

He hesitated. "Come on up and let's talk."

CHAPTER 41

God in the Bathtub

No one sees the vacancies left by six brain tumors. Or the mental damage. I'm good at hiding the scars, both physically and mentally. But at some point, I still have to deal with both.

The rollercoaster of my disease has taken me from despair to triumph and back to despair so many times that I'm wondering just how long this ride can last. Something inside keeps carrying me along, no matter how many times my wheels fall off or how many screws are missing.

I'm very good at covering up my limitations, putting my best face forward. It's what I've done all my life, and I've always lived life on the edge.

Right now, I'm teetering. I've come to the realization that if I don't die of cancer, there's a real possibility I'll die from the treatment of cancer.

The grave news of August 7th surprised and distressed all of my doctors, but most emphatically my brain surgeon, Dr. McCutcheon. None of us expected that after seven years I would develop a new "cerebellar metastatic lesion" — a new brain tumor.

Retirement

Dr. Theriault told me once that all my medical treatment data, including scans and my numerous complaints, will be saved for research. Pathology will save a sample of every biopsy. So even after "ashes to ashes, dust to dust," my body will remain part of the investigative process, providing information for years to come. Until then, I am a single research engine, discovering daily what works and what doesn't.

One of the first patients to be treated with Herceptin soon after its release, I'd helped prove it was a true miracle for breast cancer patients who express the Her-2 gene. And following my gut instinct, I'd shown that, despite the doubts of Dr. Theriault, and of Dr. Slamon's team at UCLA where the drug was developed, Herceptin could work as a single-agent drug. I'm always questioning the purpose of my cancer, and in one small way I see this as fulfilling that purpose. I'd taken many other cancer drugs with various results, and now I'd tested the new "miracle," Tykerb. In my estimation, Tykerb had failed me abysmally. Not only was it too harsh for my long-term use, but now I had a brain tumor. I felt it had allowed the cancer to get out of control.

Now, the cancer was eating away again at both my chest and my brain, and there was no miracle drug to save me. What was left for me to try? My doctors presented me with options, but they had no data to guide us. I was facing what could be my last tough decision.

Two Weeks in Hell

Dr. McCutcheon scheduled me for something called stereotactic radiosurgery. Basically, it's a single, high dose of radiation focused and delivered to a specific area of the brain. The effects are dramatic enough in the target area to be considered surgical. The radiation doesn't remove the tumor, it distorts the DNA of the tumor cells, so that they can no longer reproduce or retain fluids, and they disperse gradually.

That part sounds simple. After all, I'd had brain radiation before and, in fact, was told I'd reached my lifetime maximum, but this beam would not affect the previously radiated area.

To avoid zapping a portion of healthy brain tissue with their surgical beam, my head again had to be rendered completely immobile and the computer had to be programmed precisely. This time, however, it wouldn't be a head mask holding me in place. Instead, they would secure a steel frame to my skull with Allen-head screws then screw the frame to a table for the radiosurgical procedure.

From the day Dr. McCutcheon and I discussed it until the date of the actual surgery, I had about two weeks to think and to retract my decision. Two weeks of hell.

I agonized daily, one day ready to go ahead, the next day worrying. What if the calculations are wrong? Damage to the ocular region could mean blindness. Damage to the brain stem could mean paralysis or death. I'd been lucky for nine years. There comes a time when everyone's luck runs out — and maybe I'd be too damaged to even know what had gone wrong or to understand who or where I was. My aging parents were no longer able to help, other than supporting me emotionally. I'd been the one-in-a-million exception often enough to know that medicine has plenty of accidental or unanticipated occurrences. Where would I go if this surgery was the one in a million that failed?

On August 22nd, Dr. McCutcheon admitted me for the twelve-hour procedure, attached the frame, and the stereotactic radiosurgery went forward on schedule.

Life Goes On

My neurological checkup in November showed that the surgery was successful. But after the holidays, an ultrasound showed the lesion in my chest had increased in size. The new miracle, Tykerb, and its dastardly sidekick Xeloda, had failed. Dr. Theriault and I engaged in a serious discussion about what to do.

"We've tried everything else," he said, and he laid out two different chemotherapy treatments, both extremely harsh. "These are the best options at this time."

"I've been off Herceptin for nine months. Is there any chance it would work again?"

"No, I really don't think that's possible." His compassionate eyes told me this answer was as hard for him to give as it was for me to hear.

Unwilling to forsake my quality of life for what I knew awaited me with either treatment Dr. Theriault proposed, I decided to fly to LA and seek a second opinion. The severity of my situation had escalated since my last meeting with Dr. Slamon, and during that same time his team had been continuing to collect results from other patients. I hoped he could provide a more encouraging proposal. His team gave their full collective attention to my case, but no one thought Herceptin would work for me again at this stage in my treatment. They gave me the same two options Dr. Theriault had proposed.

After my February ultrasound showed the cancer was still growing, Dr. Theriault asked for my treatment decision.

"I don't think I can do it again," I said. "Maybe it's time to let nature run its course."

"Are you sure that's the choice you want to make at this point?"

"Maybe not, but give me another thirty days." My birthday was coming up. If it was to be my last, I wanted it to be a good one.

Although I knew my cancer was thriving like a fertilized garden in the spring without the arsenal of chemicals to hold it back, my body felt stronger each day as it healed from the side effects. I decided to tell no one yet of the current circumstances or the tough choices that lay ahead, or about my thoughts of surrendering to the inevitable.

Instead, I set about enjoying my days while also starting to tidy up my affairs, taking care of the many small things that need to be handled while I still felt well enough. This is a common practice with cancer patients every time you go in for surgery or take on a serious new treatment. In the past, while my attitude was to prepare for the worst and hope for the best, my positive outlook usually pushed aside this tendency to set things in order "just in case." But this time, it felt like the thing to do. For the logical, practical, cancer-trained side of my brain, the inevitable seemed apparent, even as my intuitive, illogical, gut-feeling side of my brain whispered, "It's not my time yet."

So often in the past — beginning with turning down the bone marrow transplant and opting for Herceptin, choosing the segmental as opposed to the mastectomy — my intuition had proved valid. When I didn't have any historical data to rely on and just followed my gut instinct — I'd rather do this than that — my choices had all been good. They had been right for me.

But now I wasn't sure. Was it really intuition or just procrastination?

Persistent Procrastination

Before my thirty-day hiatus came to an end, I had another ultrasound. Although the technicians will never discuss your results, Dr. Fonage, the radiologist who usually handled it and had been following my progress from the beginning, looked at my scan that day and said, "Victoria, are you going to take treatment?"

When I didn't answer right away, he added, "Because if you are, you have to do it now."

Dr. Theriault said pretty much the same thing when I saw him later that day. I knew in my heart that my plan was not to take the drugs, but I didn't want to say it outright.

"My thirty days aren't up yet," I said, still procrastinating.

On Good Friday, March 21, 2008, after wrestling with the decision all day, I gave into a complete meltdown and found myself screaming at God in the bathtub.

"Are you telling me to give in? That it's time to stop fighting?"

No, I didn't hear God's voice. But I continued raging anyway.

"No! I will not! Not yet, I will not quit! And I will not give up my right to go naturally!"

At my next appointment, when all my scans confirmed I was stable everywhere except for the cancer in my breast area, Dr. Theriault pressed me for a treatment decision.

"I'd like to try Herceptin again," I said reluctantly, knowing how strongly he believed it wouldn't work. I knew he was right. He said it wouldn't work, Dr. Slamon said it wouldn't work, and my own intellect told me it wouldn't, but I'd decided not to do the toxic chemotherapies that made me too weak and sick to function, so what other choice did I have? "I don't expect Herceptin to perform as it has in the past, but maybe it will just slow the cancer down a little."

"You're right," he said, "I don't think it will work for you this time, but it can't hurt to try."

So in April of 2008, after a biopsy to make sure the carcinoma was still Her-2 positive, I received a new loading dose and went back to taking Herceptin every three weeks. By June, we could see no growth in my disease, and when it still had not increased in size by August, Dr. Theriault and I accepted the good news: Herceptin once again was working its miracle.

My disease had stabilized. Dr. Theriault smiled his biggest smile.

"I think this could be a medical history moment we just made," I said. "There's no better time than this to break out the good china."

That historical moment has stretched and stretched and stretched — thanks to Herceptin, my disease is still stable three years later.

CHAPTER 42

A Stellar Year

L ooking back, I don't know where I got the energy to work so hard on this book and still participate in more events than at any time since I was diagnosed. My medical appointments were, if anything, more frequent than in other years as I tried to stay on top of the continual issues of living with cancer and aging with cancer.

Amazingly and against all odds, Herceptin was still working for me. Living every day was easier with Herceptin. I still had my usual scans and checkups, but the relief from surgeries, radiation, and other major cancer treatments gave me the opportunity to participate in everything I was asked to do for cancer research programs.

My writing consultant was a hard taskmaster. During our first year, we completed the entire career section, which could have stood on its own at more than 450 manuscript pages and over 100,000 words. Yes, she told me we needed to cut it, we still had to write the cancer section, but I wasn't ready yet to let go of the stories I knew people would most want to hear. So I kept writing, and she helped me shape the pages into a story, and every week we met to revise and continue.

That feeling of wanting to participate in cancer outreach persisted, though, and in mid- January, I phoned Michael Frick, associate vice president of development at MD Anderson Cancer Center, and invited him to lunch. Michael was well acquainted with my friends in Aspen, Frances Ginsberg, who was on the institution's Board of Visitors, and Sandy Iglehart. Early in my treatment, Michael had called to introduce himself and check on how

I was doing, but I was in chemo at the time, and I forgot to call him back. A few months later he called again. This time we talked, started a friendship, and have continued to stay in touch over the years. I'd worked with him to help get the first Aspen symposium started. But when I phoned in January, Michael and I hadn't talked in a while.

At lunch, I said, "Michael, why do you think MD Anderson doesn't take advantage of my story more than they do? I've spoken for them a couple of times, but I'm willing to do more, and I'm good at it."

In February, Michael phoned.

"I have something in mind," he said, and explained that MDA was planning an event to launch a major fundraising campaign to raise a billion dollars in 2010. "Eight cancer patients will be profiled. Would you like to be one of them?"

Of course I would.

Along with the other seven patients, I met with the MDA staff for preparation and a dress rehearsal. Our speeches were brief, based on our personal stories but written by professional writers, and we were instructed to follow them precisely.

The evening event arrived and was more emotionally and visually spectacular, I believe, than any I've ever attended. Former Miss America Phyllis George emceed the program, which presented a number of exceptional performances, including a bagpipe rendition of "Amazing Grace" that filled many eyes with tears. The doctors who spoke brought the event to a personal level by telling about someone close who had died of cancer or someone in the audience who had survived or was still battling cancer. As the evening drew to the final performance, which was our speeches, the room went completely dark and the audience was asked to hold their applause until all eight patients had spoken. A solemn note was struck by the orchestra that started softly then rose to signify the beginning of something great to come, and a spotlight shone on the first speaker, Jason.

He was selected to be first because he seemed to have the most speaking experience, and he did an excellent job. Behind him a large screen displayed the MDA slogan, "Making Cancer History." Jason's final words were the same as all the other patients, except me, "MD Anderson made my cancer history." On the final word, he waved his hand at the screen and a big red line struck through the word "cancer." It was dramatic, and the audience gasped softly, then solemnly awaited the next speaker.

The spotlight moved around the circle to me. We had already decided that I couldn't say "… made my cancer history," because I'm still in treatment, so I was to say "…is making my cancer history."

When the spotlight found me in front of the standing microphone, I started my speech. The audience was still in darkness, so I couldn't see anything, but I heard a rumble of voices and noises that hadn't happened during Jason's presentation. I couldn't tell what was going on.

About two lines into my speech, I heard someone from the audience shout, "We can't hear you!"

Then a man from the sound crew touched my elbow and softly but insistently called my name.

"Victoria! Try this hand mike."

I said, "You mean I've got to start over?"

The mike came on just as I said that, and I had to laugh at myself. Trying not to appear flustered, I said to the audience, "I want to thank you for that rehearsal," which got a big laugh and broke the tension.

I started over with my story, and from that point on, the night wasn't so somber. Some of the patients had never spoken before, and even though I had, I was quite nervous myself. My ad-lib,

I was told later, made the other patients more comfortable. The remainder of the evening went smoothly and ended on a much lighter note, even with the patients' stories tugging at heartstrings.

Shelby Hodge, a longtime Houston columnist, wrote an online review that specified the survivors as the highpoint of the evening, and in a letter addressed to "All," Tom Johnson, president of CNN, said, "If I knew a superlative that would be stronger than "magnificent," I would use it… Having the ballroom encircled by those cancer survivors, with each giving their story, made me want to empty my bank account for more cancer research and treatment."

After the event, I received an email from Sandi Stromberg, Program Manager, External Publications for MDA, asking to use a quote from my story in the spring issue of the hospital's magazine *Conquest*. My quote did appear in the spring issue, I was mentioned in the spring issue of a sister publication, *Promise*, then the summer issue of *Conquest* published a piece of my story along with my tagline, "It's time to use the good china!" Most valued, however, was a personal note I received on February 18, 2010, from Dr. John Mendelsohn, a true visionary, and his wife, Ann:

Dear Victoria, Many thanks for your part in "Making Cancer History." Your efforts this evening are truly inspirational and much appreciated. Regards, your friends at MD Anderson.

From Mighty Acorns

An Emerson quote that I've grown to love is one that I now try to live by: *It is one of the beautiful compensations of life that no man can sincerely try to help another without helping himself.* My big MDA evening would be a mighty hard act to follow, but it fed my desire to play my part in bringing the need for more cancer research to the hearts and minds of Americans. I couldn't cure cancer or even donate money, but I realized I could speak fluently and often.

A few weeks later, I received another call from Michael Frick.

"This is short notice, Victoria, but I thought of you because there's someone in town I'd like you to meet. Can you come to the Marriott Hotel lobby tomorrow afternoon? I want you to tell your story to a man in our direct marketing company. We'll only have about twenty minutes, because he has meetings lined up all day."

Thus I met Richard Murdock, and we instantly connected. Perhaps I sensed that he was a cancer survivor even before he told me, because I had good feelings about him.

"Richard's company handles most of the direct mail marketing for MD Anderson," Michael explained, "and has done so for nineteen years, an unusually long run for a marketer."

"I guess we must be doing something right." Richard laughed.

I told my story, as Michael had asked. Richard asked questions and more questions. Michael started looking at his watch, but Richard continued our conversation for an hour, while Michael went into another room to meet with whoever was next on their schedule.

"I'm not the one who makes the final decisions on fundraising letters," Richard said, "and we don't always use patients' stories, but we do from time to time. I hope we can use yours. It's a powerful story."

In the summer, Debra Campbell phoned from another part of MDA's development department to tell me they would like to use my story in their fundraising letter for the fall. They sent the text Richard had written for the campaign letter and asked for my approval. When my copy of the final printed letter arrived, my tagline appeared not only on the letter but in huge type on the front of the envelope. And the letter was signed by Dr. Mendelsohn.

Michael told me later that they used the letter twice, to two separate groups of potential and previous donors. I had great hopes that my little acorn of encouragement would grow into a strong, green money tree for MDA. In an email, Richard Murdock wrote, *"... the renewal mailing (to existing donors) that told your story did very well, surpassing last year's Winter Renewal results. So you can feel pretty good about that!"*

CHAPTER 43

It's Time to Use the Good China

Today is Wednesday, and I have treatment. My schedule got shuffled around. I found myself back in the Main Building, where I started thirteen years ago, crawling on the floor with FAC chemotherapy. You don't forget moments like that. A volunteer came by and asked if I would like something to drink.

"Hot chocolate," I said.

She handed me the hot water and packet. I reached for them one at a time, explaining that I could only use one hand.

"I'm trying to warm my arm for the IV injection," I added.

"Wow, you must have done this for a long time to know that."

Her remark made me stop and realize how many tricks I've learned. To ensure hitting the vein in my one usable arm (which avoids stirring up the lymphedema in my left arm), I always drink lots of warm liquids and arrive well hydrated. Once in the treatment room, I ask for a warm blanket to wrap my arm. If I'm cold, which is usual when sitting in a cold stainless-steel room while cold liquids drip into my veins, I'll ask for two blankets. Best to layer clothing summer and winter, because my personal temperature never seems to match what everyone else is feeling. I'm a pro at this.

Today the nurse will ask, as always, if I have any new changes, and I want to say, "No," but when she pulls up my sleeve to put in the IV, she'll see the rash. I'll have to explain my newly diagnosed problem, Reactionary Urticaria. I dread this moment. There's a chance the reaction is caused by too many years and doses of Herceptin. My body has become reactive to everything. But if I confess this, she'll withhold the medication until she calls

Dr. Theriault. He'll respond with an adamant, "Give her the drug," and will be slightly annoyed that the nurse questioned his orders. We look at it this way: rash versus cancer, which is more serious? Cancer wins hands down.

In one way, the hospital reminds me of the modeling business, sitting around waiting rooms with lots of "hurry up and wait." For unexpected delays, which happen so frequently they shouldn't be unexpected, I take healthy snacks like bananas, fruit-and-nut bars, protein shakes. I've also learned to schedule my treatments, when possible, between 11:00 a.m. and 2:00 p.m., when room service is available. It's not the Four Seasons, but the tuna salad isn't bad. If I miss lunch and I tell them my blood sugar is too low, they'll bring me juice and crackers. I've learned to "milk it."

MD Anderson's décor in calming shades of blue and green is meant to be soothing. Flowers and landscapes feature prominently in the paintings. Fish are everywhere, swimming continuously in their colorful aquariums, quite beautiful and mesmerizing to watch, which I'm sure is the intention. Puzzles scattered on waiting-room tables offer aimless distraction while I wait; or if really desperate, I could knit polyester yarn into silly little squares. I prefer bringing something interesting to work on or to read. At present, it's the rewrites for this book.

Sitting here today, I thought about the many simple things I've learned that I wish I'd known thirteen years ago. Although this isn't a how-to book, because everybody's cancer experience is different, I will share a few suggestions in this final chapter. My most important advice, however, is this: PAY ATTENTION.

Anyone can make a mistake. Everyone's human. Listen when any medical person is talking. When you don't understand, ask questions. When you receive treatment, know your medical ID number, know your medicines, and double-check your dosage. Check the IV bag to make sure it's correct and you're getting the medication intended for you. Accidents occur at even the best hospitals and with the best personnel in the world. Stay as alert as possible.

Also if possible, take someone with you to doctors' appointments and treatments, to help you absorb the information, especially in the beginning. Two minds are better than one, four eyes better than two. Focused on your diagnosis, you may not be fully engaged, and you'll appreciate that extra pair of ears later, when trying to recall your doctor's advice. After so long, I usually go alone now, but I'm thankful to have had loyal friends and family and Sister Alice in those early days.

I feel fortunate that I've been able to repay just a little of Sister Alice's loving grace by helping other people struggling with cancer for themselves or their families. Social networking has provided a new world in which I'm able to connect individually with patients I know. For as long as possible, I will continue to tell my story at cancer symposiums and events, when asked, and my goal is that this book will also provide hope and guidance.

Hopes and Dreams Can Evolve

Cancer expert Dr. Bernie Seigel, in *Love, Laughter and Medicine*, said, "Refusal to hope is nothing more than a decision to die." It's not easy to stay positive every minute of every day, especially through the unrelenting side effects of ongoing treatment. But if you do not hope, or if you have the mindset that you're dying no matter what you do, you send that message to every cell and fiber in your body. Your mind and body receive that message clearly and react to it.

The longer I live with cancer, the more issues I deal with daily. There's not a part of my body that hasn't been affected in varying degrees. Memory loss from brain surgery, vision and hearing impairment, sinus and allergy issues, lymphedema, osteoporosis, stomach and kidney problems, neuropathy, premature aging, thinning hair, skin changes, loss of muscle tone — yes, nose to toes — and particularly distressing for a woman, the loss of body image.

At this point, however, I'm living fairly well with cancer and its side effects. I'm even considering an accidental death insurance policy. After my diagnosis in July 1998, dying from cancer was a given, so why concern myself with term-life or accident policies? Today things are different. I'm active, I'm traveling, I drive on Houston's congested roads. An accidental death policy doesn't seem unrealistic. In my bizarre way of thinking, this is a good and truly positive outlook.

When I was diagnosed at forty-eight, I already had lived quite a life, which helped me accept it a little easier, I think. Yet like anyone else, I had hopes and dreams for my life to come, and they created the driving desire I needed to fight from my core — with perseverance I didn't know existed. I had to find hope.

But hope is not a thing you can pick up at Macy's. I learned to create hope through prayer, laughter, working, acceptance of each day's adjustments, and a willingness to change my lifestyle as necessary. I decided early on that I would not give up, that I would fight like a great warrior while making every day I had left the best it could be.

Hope is to have expectations. For me, expectations offer a sense of progress, of moving forward, of something new always waiting just over the horizon. When you have no expectations you've nothing to look forward to.

Design your own hope. No one really knows how long terminal is. Expect to recover, to outlive your prognosis. Expect that your friendships and close relationships will thrive and evolve. None of us can predict the future, but hopes and dreams can evolve, too.

There's No Such Thing

My road ahead is uncertain, and I'll always be trying to stay one step ahead of the cancer. I accept nothing as fact, knowing every day brings newness, and will continue trying to make the best of it. I've survived this far by incorporating everything I could learn and do to live at my best each day, medically, emotionally, and spiritually. If my body can't take any more treatment, I'll tell my doctors I need a week off. At other times the doctors may want to be conservative, but I feel strong and push for aggressive treatment. All this gives me a sense of control, although I know my treatment and the results I can expect are ultimately in the hands of God and my doctors at MDA. That, too, gives me comfort, because I trust in God and I trust my doctors.

Everyone at MD Anderson has done their part in preserving my life. Why I have this disease and others don't, why I've lived so long with it while others haven't — these are not things I dwell on. I believe God has a purpose for all of us, whether or not we understand that purpose.

Tonight, I had dinner at the Rotary House, in the same dining room where I sat with Mom thirteen years ago. I stood in the same ladies' room that I stood in thirteen years ago, when I was adjusting my scarves, tams, and headgear to cover my bald head. Now, I brush what's left of my famous red mane, a sad mess of what it once was, and know that I'm lucky to have any hair at all. As I looked in the mirror tonight, I got a flashback of seeing my face there so long ago and knowing it was the face of a dying Victoria Lynn Johnson. Now, it's the face of an aging Victoria Lynn Johnson. A little worse for wear, but I'm still surviving, praying I can buy just a little more time. The goal I had thirteen years ago I still have today. Whoever said "thirteen is an unlucky number"?

I'll turn sixty in March. Sixty is much cooler than being fifty-nine, stuck in middle-age mediocrity, a place I hate. Age is a privilege. Every day over my original prognosis of eighteen months is a good thing. Sixty says to me, "You've done it."

Everything has changed at Rotary House, yet nothing has changed. Although the restaurant has expanded its outer limits, my table was in the same place by the open railing looking down into the lobby. The staff is still trying to entertain very worried families and very sick patients with very lively music. Pajamas, robes, and surgical bandages are still acceptable dinner attire. The staff moves quickly. Patients in wheelchairs and with IV poles still move slowly, and there are more of them.

As my friends Caroline and Sidney Kimmel have said so well, cancer is a war. We're all fighting it, each in our own way. If I died tomorrow, my battle with cancer would be considered one of the most successful of this era, and in life or after death, I believe some good will come from my journey. My desire to make a difference in this war will be accomplished.

I once told Dr. McCutcheon that I planned to make history with MD Anderson. Two weeks ago, he confirmed that I'm his longest living and most successful cancer patient on Herceptin. With thirteen years of Stage 4 Cancer behind me, still in treatment, still kicking death to the curb, and who knows how much time ahead, I'm a living example of what cancer research and treatment have accomplished. We now have the science to live longer with all types and stages of cancer, but we need science to also create a better quality of life, to catch up with the demand. The future was not always so positive, but today it can be for many who are touched by this dreadful disease.

Many of the people you've read about in this book have died of cancer: Bob Guccione, Kathy Keeton, Shirlee Beriro, Kathy and Zee Mouse at MDA, Lord James Hanson, and Andreas, of course. But many others in this book have fought cancer and survived: Pat Hill, the talented staff photographer at *Penthouse*, Brett Hudson,

Robáire Pascal, Patrick Terrail, David Koch, Sandy Goldman Israel,; and I'm sure there are others I don't know about. I refer to them all as Cancer All Stars, because they took charge of their disease in whatever way they felt was right for them. Determined to outlive their prognosis, they didn't let the disease take control.

Before I started to write this book, the past was a place I seldom visited. I'm a person who looks forward, takes risks into the future, never one for regrets, a strong believer in studying my prospects and creating my own future. I'd been a pretty daughter, a model, a centerfold, an actress, a sister, a wife, an aunt, and a good friend. Now, I was a patient.

Cancer taught me to participate in my life in ways I never had before. I look at Stage 4 Cancer right in the eye every morning, and I learn to live with it, to make accommodations for it.

If you're reading this book, chances are you or someone in your family is under attack by the deadly beast. If it's you, and if you take one thing from this book, make it this: Participate in your own wellbeing. Remember, there's no such thing as a proper cancer patient. You can get angry at cancer, and if that makes you fight it, that's okay, but after a while you're going to have to stand up to it face to face. Don't lie on the sofa feeling sorry for yourself. When others see you fighting to make your life better, they'll chip in and fight right along with you.

Ten thousand deaths a week from cancer are ten thousand too many. And every day of life, with or without cancer, is too precious to leave sitting on the shelf next to the good china.

THE END

EPILOGUE

It has been seven years since this book was finished and it is still lacking the final chapter. That has now been written, as of April 16th 2019, when that raging beast, cancer, claimed the life of Victoria Lynn Johnson. She passed away at her home, in hospice care, just a few weeks after her beloved Pomeranian Rosie Belle, died. Both of them survived twenty years together fighting this disease. One could say she won the battles with cancer for twenty years but eventually lost the war.

She persevered and lived her life to its fullest, attacking each new medical crisis with the courage and intelligence she learned to hone after many years as a cancer survivor. In her quest to "live a normal life with cancer," she leased a new SUV the color of her hair (reddish bronze). I was with her those last few months as she fought with every ounce of her being until she lost the use of her left arm, a victim of the cancer spreading to the left brachial plexus. She tried pinpoint radiation to the area after it was deemed too dangerous to remove the tumor by surgery. It didn't slow the tumor down or decrease the severe pain in the area as she lost the use of her arm completely from shoulder to fingertips. I installed a knob on the steering wheel of her car so she could drive using her right hand. After a year and a half, the car only had 3000 miles on it. The car helped her feel she was still in control. She was reluctant to give it up even when she couldn't walk anymore. I watched her daily put the left arm in a sling that rubbed her neck raw and then wrapped around her waist as support for the sling with its clasps of Velcro to hold everything in place. This apparatus allowed her to get through the day doing the things that she felt meant living her life on her terms rather than as a cancer victim.

She had hired a wonderful secretary and assistant named Kerri Norwood to help her with the daily tasks she insisted upon doing, such as driving her to the MD Anderson appointments and other places she forced herself to travel to, as well as using the computer for corresponding to friends and relatives, and of course helping her to dress and bathe. I will always be thankful for the care and friendship Kerri provided for her.

Her indomitable spirit allowed her to continue treatment every three weeks until MDA told her the cancer had spread to the brain and spinal cord. Her oncologist, Dr. Barcenus, (Dr. Theriault had retired) told her there was no more treatment that could be done. Answering her question as to long she could expect to live, he answered, "Six months," and suggested she go to hospice (MDA has to authorize hospice, and it lasts for six months.)

She replied, "What if I live longer than six months?"

He answered, "Then I would authorize another six months." She refused and continued at home on her own.

In a very short time, it became evident that she could not live alone without assistance. She was falling and on one occasion had to be transported to the hospital emergency room. I had previously had a chairlift installed for her because she could no longer walk up and down the stairs in her home. There were no bedrooms on the first floor, and she was still caring for her dog, Rosie Belle, who had to be carried up and down the stairs. In September of 2018, I employed Elie Aguilar and Flora Rodrigues, two wonderful caregivers, to alternate caring for her during the day. Victoria still insisted she wanted to be alone from 11:00 p.m. until she woke the next day. I was still visiting her 2-4 times a week for dinner and conversation, and I could tell her concentration was waning after dinner. Many times, she could eat only a few bites and then was ready for bed.

Our last dinner outing was on Christmas Eve, 2018, with another couple. I had to support her from the car to the table in the restaurant, cut up her food, and after dinner, support her as she shuffled back to the car. She could barely stand alone. How she pulled herself together even with Kerri's help, I will never know. Her will was immense. Her outfit was stunning, and she looked beautiful.

That was the last time Victoria left her house. The time for the caregivers was increased to 24/7 and within a very short time she went into in home hospice. Even from the hospital bed provided by hospice she continued to put on her makeup and present herself in her finest color- matching pajamas, never allowing herself to appear "sick." Until the end, she would try to get out of bed unassisted to walk to the bathroom, but she soon lost the use of her legs and could not support herself no mattered how hard she tried.

Finally, this gallant, beautiful woman slipped away from us at 5:00 a.m. on April 16th, 2019, still exquisite in her final repose. She was laid to rest on a sloping hillside in Atlanta, Georgia, on a sunny, cool April afternoon, surrounded by her remaining family and friends. As one would expect who knew her, she had planned her own funeral and it went off without a hitch, complete with the white dove release and bagpipes playing "Amazing Grace." Even the deep russet clay of Georgia beneath which she is buried matches her hair.

She would be pleased.

I would be remiss if I did not mention those in her life that helped her immensely during her battle with cancer. After Bob Bradley and Victoria decided it was in his best interest to sever their relationship (much to his chagrin) another great friend from Aspen, Mr. Jerry Holsher, allowed her to stay in the house that she and Bob had purchased until the day she died and for some time after. So, to Jerry, I offer my grateful thanks and appreciation for your generosity. Throughout all this ordeal her good friend, Caroline Kimmel, along with her husband Sidney, offered unwavering support further defining the meaning of true friendship. It continued even after Victoria's death so all bills could be covered. Thank you, Caroline and Sidney; friends like you are very rare. To all of Victoria's friends in Aspen who rallied around her, at Sandy Iglehart's request, when she was diagnosed to organize that amazing fundraiser, thank you all so much. To Roy Waddy, the chef who cooked for us for three years to provide her with wholesome, natural foods, thank you so much. To her friend and lawyer, Bruce Buckley, for all your help—thank you so much. And to her friend and next-door neighbor, in the truest sense of the words, Kathy Zweig, thank you for traveling to Atlanta to attend the funeral and offering your support in any way that was needed.

Proverbs 31:25 defines a "Woman of Valor" in this way: "She is clothed in Strength and Dignity. And laughs without fear of the future."

This is an apt description of Victoria Lynn Johnson.

RIP

W Kenneth Horwitz

CPSIA information can be obtained
at www.ICGtesting.com
Printed in the USA
LVHW010042201120
672133LV00017B/350